DID YOU KNOW THAT . . .

- A raw potato in salty soup makes it less salty
- When frying or sautéing, you should always heat the pan before adding oil or butter to eliminate sticking
- One dozen medium oranges equals four cups of juice
- To keep cookies soft, you should place a slice of bread in your cookie jar
- Adding lemon juice instead of salt to the water will make pasta less starchy

The Kitchen Klutz

■ Colleen Johnson ■

St. Martin's Paperbacks

THE KITCHEN KLUTZ

ISBN: 0-312-95787-4

Printed in the United States of America

St. Martin's Paperbacks trade paperback edition / May 1996

10 9 8 7 6 5 4 3 2 1

*This book is dedicated to Lenora Johnson, my mother,
for so graciously sharing her abundant knowledge and love
of the kitchen with me.*

ACKNOWLEDGMENTS

My sincerest thanks to the following for helping make this book possible—their support is immeasurable:

Lenora Johnson, my extraordinary mom and supreme cook, without whom this book would be nonexistent;

Sam Johnson, my wise father, for encouraging and guiding me in writing this book;

Heather Jackson, my enthusiastic editor, for her brilliant and constructive editing;

Alison Picard, my literary agent, for believing in the book;

Heather Johnson, my twin sister who's an outstanding pediatrician but desperately needs this book;

Chase Cole, for his continual behind-the-scenes support and being the guinea pig for my cooking;

Beth Poe, for being a true friend;

And all of the creative, talented people at St. Martin's Press who helped put this book in your hands.

TABLE OF CONTENTS

FOREWORD

It seems as though whenever I attempted to cook, I always ended up calling Mom for help, and, of course, she always had the answers. A few times, though, when I was preparing dinner for guests, I wasn't able to reach her— which left me frantic in my cooking endeavors!

Upon informing Mom that I was helpless when she wasn't home for my telephone calls, she told me to start writing down her answers and tips so that I would always have her help. Thus, the idea for this book was formed.

The following pages cover basic guidelines and helpful tips for when you are buying, storing, measuring, cooking, and serving food. I have included information learned from years of kitchen experience . . . almost anything you might need to know in the kitchen when Mom can't be reached!

I sincerely hope this book proves as useful to you in the kitchen as my Mom has always been to me. One word of advice: Even though you now have this cooking companion, don't forget to call Mom occasionally for help; there's still no substitute.

Colleen Johnson

P.S. If you have any tips or helpful advice for the kitchen, I would love to hear from you. My address is: Colleen Johnson, P.O. Box 158385, Nashville, TN 37215-8385.

RULES FOR THE KITCHEN KLUTZ

Don't be afraid of the kitchen. Remember, anyone can cook! Once you become familiar with your kitchen, you will enjoy using it and realize it's a fun place to be. One of the most satisfying aspects about cooking is that you can create a finished dish that can be enjoyed not only by you but by others as well. Sharing your cooking with family and friends can be most gratifying.

By following a few basic rules, anyone can go from being a kitchen klutz to an accomplished cook:

1. Always preheat your oven.
2. Always use a timer.
3. Remember to use a lid on your pot, skillet, or Dutch oven when cooking tough foods such as broccoli, carrots, pot roast, and inexpensive cuts of meat. Using a lid retains moisture, which tenderizes tough foods.
4. When following a recipe, always read the recipe through at least once before beginning. Take out the ingredients you will need and place them on your counter. Measure exactly and use the specified amount. In addition, if a recipe calls for a greased and floured pan, do this first and make sure to use the correct pan size.
5. If using glass cookware to bake, lower the oven temperature 25°F.
6. The more you use your kitchen, the better cook you will become.
7. Be creative. Remember there is no right or wrong when it comes to taste.
8. Enjoy the kitchen. It's there to help you enhance food.
9. When in a bind, refer to *The Kitchen Klutz* for answers to your questions.

And, most important of all, *be confident*—it can make all the difference between being a kitchen klutz and a kitchen wonder.

□ □ □ □ □ □

BASICS FOR THE KITCHEN

There are numerous items available to help you in the kitchen. While many are useful, not all are essential. All you really need in a kitchen are a few pots and pans; a measuring cup and measuring spoons; a couple of mixing bowls; some basic utensils, such as spoons, spatulas, and knives; and a couple of potholders and you are ready to begin your cooking adventure.

The more you cook, the more you will want to purchase additional kitchen equipment that is time-saving and makes cooking easier. Kitchen items may be purchased at hardware, cookware, department, grocery, and discount stores, garage sales, and are available in a wide range of prices. And, remember, your kitchen equipment and utensils will give you many years of use.

Following is a list of basic kitchen equipment, utensils, and pots and pans that are helpful and that you will eventually want to purchase for use in your own kitchen.

BASIC KITCHEN EQUIPMENT

Apron
Baking pans
Bottle and jar opener
Can opener
Colander
Cookie/baking sheets
Dish towels or cloths
Electric mixer
Fire extinguisher
Food processor
Flour sifter
Funnel
Grater
Kitchen tongs

Kitchen scissors
Knives
Ladles
Loaf pan
Long-handled fork and
  spoon
Measuring cups
Measuring spoons
Mixing bowls
Muffin pan
Pastry board
Pie pan
Potholders
Pots and pans

Rolling pin
Skillet
Slotted spoon
Spatulas
Strainer
Teapot/kettle
Timer
Vegetable scrub
  brush
Vegetable peeler
Wire baking rack
Wire whisks
Wooden spoon
The Kitchen Klutz

There are many staples used regularly in the kitchen. Most of these have a long shelf life if stored correctly. If you are stocking your pantry, here's a list of basics to acquire and keep on hand.

BASIC NONPERISHABLE STAPLES TO KEEP IN YOUR PANTRY

Baking powder
Baking soda—also keep a box in the refrigerator to absorb odors
Beans—various dried and canned
Bouillon—canned, cubes, granules
Canned fish—tuna, crab, salmon
Cocoa
Chocolate
Coffee—ground, instant, whole bean
Condiments—ketchup, mustard, mayonnaise
Crackers
Extracts—vanilla, almond
Flour—all-purpose
Fruit—canned
Garlic—minced or chopped in jar
Gelatin—unflavored, flavored
Herbs—various dried
Honey
Jams, jellies, preserves
Juices—canned
Milk—evaporated, sweetened condensed, shelf-stable
Mixes—cake, cookies, frosting
Mushrooms—in cans or jars, dried
Nuts—pecans, almonds, walnuts

Oatmeal—regular and quick-cook
Oils—olive, vegetable
Onions—dried, canned
Pasta—various dried sizes and shapes
Raisins
Parmesan cheese—jar or cannister
Peanut butter
Pepper
Pickles
Red or green pepper sauce
Rice—long-grain, Arborio, wild, blends
Sherry—drinking
Salt—regular and kosher coarse
Soups—canned, dried mixes
Soy sauce
Spices
Sugar—granulated, confectioners', brown
Syrups—molasses, maple, corn
Tea—regular and herbal
Tomatoes—canned, paste, sauce, whole, diced
Vegetables—canned
Vegetable shortening
Vinegar—white, cider, wine
Worcestershire sauce
Yeast

Following is a list of perishable cooking items that are used regularly in the kitchen.

BASIC PERISHABLE COOKING ITEMS TO KEEP ON HAND

Item	Place of Storage
Butter or margarine	Refrigerator
Cheese—processed, cream, grated	Refrigerator
Eggs or egg substitute	Refrigerator
Fruit—frozen	Freezer
Lemons	Refrigerator
Limes	Refrigerator
Juice—fresh varieties	Refrigerator
Juice—frozen varieties	Freezer
Milk	Refrigerator
Onions	Pantry
Potatoes	Pantry
Sour cream and/or plain yogurt	Refrigerator
Vegetables—frozen	Freezer

3

Herbs and spices are essential in cooking, especially when trying to season without the use of fat. Following is a list of herbs and spices that are commonly used:

HERBS AND SPICES TO KEEP ON HAND

Herbs	Spices
Basil	Allspice
Bay leaves	Caraway seeds
Coriander	Cayenne pepper
Dill	Chili powder
Marjoram	Cinnamon—ground
Oregano	Clove
Parsley	Créole/Cajun spice mix
Rosemary	Cumin
Sage	Curry powder
Tarragon	Nutmeg
Thyme	Paprika

MEASURING IN THE KITCHEN

Knowing how to measure correctly is essential to being a good cook. Measuring according to recipe directions can make the difference between success and failure. Not all food items are measured in the same manner. Measuring cups to measure liquids come in either clear plastic or glass, in 1- or 2-cup sizes, so that they can be held at eye level to check the amount without spilling any of the ingredients. Dry measuring cups, which are usually nesting and come in $1/4$ -, $1/3$ -, $1/2$ -, and 1-cup sizes, are used for measuring dry ingredients and shortening and are designed to be leveled off with a knife or spatula. When measuring less than $1/4$ cup, use measuring spoons. The following are general instructions for measuring the basics:

Baking powder, cornstarch, cream of tartar, salt, soda, spices: Stir and then fill the measuring spoon. Level the spoon with a knife or spatula.

Flour: If presifted, use a spoon to place flour into a measuring cup. Do not pack or shake the flour. Level the cup with a knife. If not presifted, sift the flour first and then fill the cup. Be careful not to press or pack together.

Shortening: Shortening should be at room temperature before measuring. Pack firmly into the measuring cup (a metal cup works best) and level off with a knife or spatula.

Liquids: Use a liquid measuring cup with a spout, to prevent spilling. Pour the liquid into the measuring cup and read the measuring line at eye level. Liquid measuring cups have a space between the cup line and the top of the cup, so you do not want to fill the measuring cup completely to the top, just to the measuring line.

Grated or shredded cheese, nuts, dried fruit, coconut: Pack lightly into a measuring cup until level with the top of the cup.

Bread crumbs: Spoon dried bread crumbs lightly into a measuring cup and level off. Do not pack the crumbs or shake the cup. When measuring soft bread crumbs, pack them lightly into the measuring cup and press them gently before leveling off.

Syrup, molasses, or honey: Grease the measuring cup first and fill it slowly, since syrup, molasses, and honey overflow easily. Be sure to scrape the cup thoroughly when adding the ingredient to your recipe.

Butter or margarine:
$^1/_2$ stick = $^1/_8$ pound = $^1/_4$ cup = 4 tablespoons
1 stick = $^1/_4$ pound = $^1/_2$ cup = 8 tablespoons
2 sticks = $^1/_2$ pound = 1 cup
4 sticks = 1 pound = 2 cups

Eggs:
1 extra large egg = $^1/_4$ cup
1 large egg = $^1/_5$ cup
1 medium egg = $^1/_8$ cup

Sugar:
Brown—pack firmly into measuring cup, unless otherwise specified.
Powdered—Do not pack. Level with a knife.

SUGAR MEASUREMENTS

1 lb. brown sugar = 2 cups, firmly packed
1 lb. granulated sugar = 2 cups
1 lb. liquid syrup = 1$^1/_2$ cups
1 lb. confectioners' sugar = 2$^1/_2$ cups unsifted or 3$^1/_4$ cups sifted

Remember: Dry measurements should be level, not heaping.
Level dry measurements off with the flat side of a knife or spatula.

ABBREVIATIONS

c. = cup
doz. = dozen
gal. = gallon
lb. = pound
lge. = large
oz. = ounce
pkg. = package
pt. = pint
qt. = quart
sm. = small
tsp. = teaspoon
Tbsp. = tablespoon

COMMON KITCHEN MEASUREMENTS

EQUIVALENT WEIGHTS AND MEASURES

1 dash = less than 1/8 teaspoon
1 tablespoon = 3 teaspoons
2 tablespoons = 1 ounce
4 tablespoons = 1/4 cup
5 tablespoons + 1 teaspoon = 1/3 cup
8 tablespoons = 1/2 cup
16 tablespoons = 1 cup
1 ounce = 6 teaspoons or 2 tablespoons
4 ounces = 1/2 cup
8 ounces = 1 cup or 1/2 pint
16 ounces = 1 pound or 2 cups or 1 pint
2/3 cup = 1/2 cup + 2 2/3 tablespoons
5/8 cup = 1/2 cup + 2 tablespoons
7/8 cup = 3/4 cup + 2 tablespoons
1 cup = 1/2 pint or 8 ounces
2 cups = 1 pint or 1 pound or 16 ounces
4 cups = 1 quart or 32 fluid ounces
16 cups = 1 gallon
1/2 pint = 1 cup or 8 fluid ounces
1 pint = 1 pound or 2 cups or 16 fluid ounces
1 quart = 2 pints or 4 cups or 1/4 gallon or 64 fluid ounces
1 gallon = 16 cups or 8 pints or 4 quarts or 128 fluid ounces

ONE POUND =

2 cups liquid
2 cups granulated sugar
2 1/2 cups packed brown sugar
2 cups butter (4 sticks)
3 cups raisins
3 large onions
3 medium potatoes
4 cups shelled pecans
4 small tomatoes
4 cups grated cheese
4 cups cocoa
5 cups shredded coconut

Using the correct pan size is important because the size of the pan affects the cooking. If you use too small a pan, your recipe may overflow or not cook thoroughly. On the other hand, if you use too large a pan, your food will overcook and dry out. In addition, some recipes give you the pan size to use but not the number of servings. The following chart will help you determine which pan size to use as well as the number of servings.

BAKING PANS AND CASSEROLE DISH MEASUREMENTS

Type of Dish	No. of Servings	Volume
Loaf pan		
9 × 5 × 3"	8–10 servings	6 cups
Pie Pan		
9" diameter	6–8 servings	4 cups
10" diameter	8–10 servings	6 cups
Rectangular		
13 × 9 × 2"	10–12 servings	15 cups
Ring Mold		
8¹/₂ × 2¹/₄"	8–10 servings	4¹/₂ cups
Round		
two 8 × 1¹/₂" layers	10–12 servings	4 cups, each pan
two 9 × 1¹/₂" layers	12–14 servings	6 cups, each pan
Square		
8 × 8 × 2"	8–10 servings	8 cups
9 × 9 × 2"	10–12 servings	10 cups
Tube or Bundt		
7¹/₃ × 3"	10–12 servings	6 cups
9 × 3¹/₂"	14–18 servings	9 cups

The following chart will help you when purchasing canned items. For example, if a recipe calls for 2 cups, buy a 16 ounce can.

CAN SIZES CHART

Size of Can	Number of Cup Servings
8 ounces	1 cup
12 ounces	1¹/₂ cups
No. 300 (14–16 ounces)	1³/₄ cups
No. 303 (16–17 ounces)	2 cups
No. 2 (20 ounces)	2¹/₂ cups
No. 2¹/₂ (29 ounces)	3¹/₂ cups
No. 3 (46 ounces)	5³/₄ cups
No. 10 (6¹/₂–7 pounds)	12–13 cups

STORING

Proper food storage is essential for food safety and for maximizing the flavor of foods. In general, food should be stored in one of three places in the kitchen: the refrigerator, freezer, or cabinets/pantry. Where you store a food item depends on the type of item and whether it has been opened or not. In addition, some items, such as mayonnaise, dry milk, evaporated milk, and condensed milk, may be stored in the pantry before opening and must be refrigerated after opening. If you are in doubt, it's safer to store food items in the refrigerator. You may also check the label on certain items for storage instructions.

Do not leave any food that is stored in the refrigerator or any cooked food at room temperature for more than 2 hours. In addition, remember to reseal potato chips, pretzels, cookies, crackers, cereals, and other box or plastic bag foods after opening them. A clothespin or bag clip works great and helps seal in the freshness.

When Storing . . .

In the Refrigerator

Keep your refrigerator temperature at 35-40°F. This means your refrigerator should be *cold*. Try not to keep your refrigerator too full because the cold air needs to circulate around the food items to cool them adequately. The crisper in the refrigerator is a good place for all vegetables and salad greens because it is a confined compartment and therefore has a higher humidity. Humidity prevents water loss, which causes wilting. When storing items in the refrigerator, use plastic bags to retain moisture and keep foods from absorbing additional odors. Keeping an open box of baking soda in your refrigerator also helps absorb food odors. Remember to allow hot foods to cool up to 1 hour before placing them in the refrigerator, except for foods containing seafood, meat, eggs, poultry, and milk. Always refrigerate these products as soon as possible since they are the most perishable. If your electricity goes off, your refrigerator should remain cool for 4 to 6 hours, depending on how hot the kitchen is and how often the refrigerator door is opened. If possible, do not open the refrigerator door while the electricity is off. When power is restored, discard any foods that have a bad odor or that are warm to the touch.

In the Freezer

Keep your freezer at 0°F. When preparing foods to be stored in the freezer, always press the air out, wrap the food tightly, and use only heavy-duty/freezer foil, plastic bags, or moisture-proof containers in order to keep ice crystals from forming on the food, and to retain flavor. Keep purchased frozen foods in their original packaging, except for meat. You may keep purchased frozen meat in your freezer up to 2 weeks in the store wrapper. Almost all foods may be frozen to lengthen their shelf life except the following:

- processed cheese
- hard-cooked eggs; uncooked eggs in their shells
- salad greens
- raw tomatoes
- any food containing alcohol

These foods should be stored in the refrigerator. Never refreeze beef, chicken, turkey, fish, shellfish, or any other prepared casseroles or dishes. Once these foods are thawed and cooked, they must be eaten, stored in the refrigerator up to two days, or discarded.

Many freezers need to be manually defrosted. If you do not have a self-defrosting freezer, you will need to defrost it manually when 1/2 inch of frost accumulates. Wait and defrost when there isn't a lot of food in the freezer. Remove everything from the freezer and place the food you remove in coolers with ice or wrap it in blankets or towels. Unplug the freezer. Place large pots or pans containing hot water inside to help speed the defrosting process. Leave the door open. You will probably want to place bath or beach towels on the floor to soak up any water that spills. You may use a putty scraper or metal spatula to scrape some of the ice off but do not use an ice pick because you might puncture the freezer or coils. Dump the pans of hot water out frequently because ice chunks will fall into the pans and cool the hot water. After dumping out the water, refill the pans with hot water and place them back inside. The whole process should take 45 to 60 minutes. The late spring is the best time to defrost your freezer, before you place the summer's fresh vegetables and fruit in your freezer for winter storage. Once the freezer is defrosted, wipe it out with a solution of baking soda and water and dry thoroughly.

If your electricity goes off, your freezer should keep frozen foods for 24 to 36 hours. Do not open the freezer door. When the power comes back on, you will need to dispose of any frozen foods that have melted or feel warm. In addition, any foods with a bad odor should be discarded.

COOKING TEMPERATURES

Recipes often say to cook at a "low temperature" or in a "very hot oven." The following chart will help you determine what temperature to set your oven on.

OVEN TEMPERATURE CHART

Degrees Fahrenheit	Degrees Celsius	Oven Temperature
250	121	Very low
300	149	Low
325	163	Moderately low
350	177	Moderate
375	190	Moderately hot
400	204	Hot
450–500	232–260	Very hot

9

TIPS FOR THE KITCHEN KLUTZ

To Bake: Preheat your oven to the temperature stated in the recipe. Place whatever you are cooking in a pan. Place it in the oven, either covered or uncovered. Set the timer. When meat is baked uncovered, it's called **roasting**. Unless specified in your recipe, place the pot on the oven rack in the middle of the oven.

To Boil: Place liquid in a pot or pan on the stove. Turn the stove on high heat. The goal is to heat the water until it bubbles—which means it has reached a temperature of 212°F. Usually when you add food to boiling liquid, it stops boiling momentarily. Once it returns to a boil, lower the heat and let the liquid continue to boil. With most recipes, begin timing when the liquid returns to a boil after the food has been added.

To Broil: Preheat your oven on the "Broil" setting. Place whatever you are cooking in a pan and place it in the oven on the top rack. Set the timer. The broiler is the top heat element in the oven. To broil successfully, you need to place your pan toward the top of the oven. Many recipes will tell you exactly how far the food should be placed from the broiler. When a recipe states "3 inches from the broiler" it means the surface of the food should be 3" from the broiler. If possible, use a broiling pan which is a special pan that has two parts—the food is placed on the top part which has slits through which the juices can drain into the bottom part. You may also place food on a wire rack and place this in a pan for the same effect.

To Deep Fry: Place enough shortening or vegetable oil to cover the food in a deep pan (there should be 3" of space between the oil and the top of the skillet) Turn the stove on low to medium heat and gradually heat the oil. When the oil reaches the desired temperature, slowly add the food. Do not add too much food at a time. There should be room around the food for it to cook evenly. Once food is fried, drain it on paper towels. If you need to keep it warm, place it in a preheated 300°F. oven. Remove any loose food in the pan with a metal slotted spoon before adding additional food to fry. Do not let a pan sit on the stove over heat very long without food—it can catch on fire. If grease catches on fire, douse it with baking soda, sugar, flour, or a chemical-based fire extinguisher. *Do not use water on a grease fire.*

To Sauté: Place 2–3 Tbsp. of oil in a skillet on the stove. You may use any type of oil, butter, or margarine. Turn the stove on medium heat. Let the oil heat 15–30 seconds. Add whatever you are cooking to the skillet. Lower the heat and let the food cook, turning occasionally, until it is soft or light brown.

To Simmer: Place liquid in a pot on the stove on medium heat. When the liquid is hot or begins to boil, turn the heat down to low heat so the mixture barely bubbles. The goal is to cook the food at just below or at boiling point.

—Lower the oven temperature by 25°F when using **glass cookware**.

—If you **burn a pot or pan**, fill it with 1" of water and 1 Tbsp. of baking soda. Bring water to a boil, remove from the heat, let it sit for a few minutes and then scrub the pot.

—Cover a pot of boiling water to quicken **boiling** time.

—To keep a **bowl** from slipping on a work surface, place it on a wet folded towel.

—To keep a mixture from **boiling over**, rub the rim of the pan with butter first.

—To **open jars** easily, set them upside down in hot water first. You may also use a manual can opener (also called a church key) and use the pointed end to pry under the lid between the jar and the lid. Do this several times around the jar until you hear the vacuum seal break. The jar will then open with ease.

—To separate two **glasses stuck** together, fill the inside glass with cold water and place the outer glass in warm water.

—To prevent burning the bottom of a **double boiler**, place a jar lid in the bottom pot. The lid will begin to rattle when the water has boiled away, and you will know to add more water. Remember, the water in the bottom pan should never touch the bottom of the top pan.

—For a homemade **funnel**, use the corner of an envelope and cut off part of the tip.

—To remove **grease** that has spilled on the floor, sprinkle baking soda on the spill and scrub with hot water.

—To cut down on **odors in the refrigerator**, leave a box of opened baking soda inside.

—If you need to **mix by hand**, count 150 strokes per minute of electric beating time.

—To make **cleaning the kitchen** easier:

—Clean as you cook. While your food is cooking, rinse the preparation utensils and dishes and place them in the dishwasher or the sink to soak.

—Line your burner drip pans on the stove with aluminum foil and change the foil whenever it gets dirty.

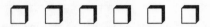

BEVERAGES

Beverages are easy for the kitchen klutz to prepare with the guidelines and tips in this chapter. The most difficult part is deciding which beverage to serve since there are countless choices. Numerous varieties of coffee as well as tea are available, and fruit drinks are now mixed in so many different combinations that you will need to take additional time when deciding what to buy. Be sure to read the labels of fruit juices to check the amount of juice contained as well as other added ingredients, and notice the sodium content since many sugar-free drinks have increased amounts of sodium. If you drink wine, beer, or liquor, you are probably already aware of the many brands and kinds available—it's all a matter of personal taste. Just make sure the beverage does not overpower the food and vice versa. Ice-cream drinks are fun to make because you can use any syrup or sauce as well as any flavor of ice cream to create your own concoction. It's fun to experiment and surprise your guests or family with a new flavored drink, and even if you're a kitchen klutz you will receive compliments and cheers.

BEER

Beer should be stored in a cool place in an upright position or in the refrigerator. Unpasteurized draft beer should be refrigerated immediately and drunk within 1 to 2 weeks. Once you have chilled beer, keep it cold or refrigerated until serving.

Keep your beer mugs in the freezer so they will be frosty and cold when you are ready to use them. To prevent a lot of foam when pouring, hold the glass at an angle and pour down the side of the glass. Straighten the glass to an upright position just before the glass is full to add a "head" to the glass.

Light-bodied beer should be served between 45° and 50°F. Darker, more full-bodied beer will have the best taste when served between 50° and 60°F. When choosing which type of beer to serve with food, a good rule to remember is the more spicy and seasoned the food, the fuller-bodied the beer. **Remember: Always serve something to eat when people are drinking alcohol.**

CHAMPAGNE (SPARKLING WINE)

To be called "champagne" officially, the sparkling wine must be produced in the Champagne region of France. Most refer to any sparkling wine as champagne, regardless of its origin. Champagne is classified as one of the following: **Brut** is the driest and highest grade; **Vintage** is very dry; **Sec** or **Dry** is slightly sweet; **Extra Sec** or **Extra Dry** is moderately sweet; **Demi-sec** is sweet; **Doux** is very sweet; and **Blanc de blanc & Year** means only the white Chardonnay grape is used, and the champagne is ultra dry, extra fine, and from grapes of the same year.

Champagne should be stored on its side to keep the cork moist and airtight and in an area that maintains the same temperature, preferably at 55°–60°F., but no higher than 75°F.

One bottle of champagne contains six 4-ounce servings. Chill champagne for 2 hours before serving, and serve at 40°F. to 50°F. for the best flavor and bouquet. If you prefer the bubbles to last longer, serve in flutes. To open a champagne bottle, remove the foil, untwist the wire cage over the cork, hold the bottle at a 45-degree angle with the cork pointed away from anyone, hold the cork with one hand, and *gently turn the bottle* (not the cork) with your other hand. If opened properly, the bottle should poof, not pop, when opened. If champagne has no bubbles or tastes flat, it's probably old and should not be drunk.

COCOA

Cocoa is delicious and easy to make. Mix 2$\frac{1}{2}$ Tbsp. unsweetened cocoa, 2$\frac{1}{2}$ Tbsp. sugar, and a dash of salt in a saucepan. Add $\frac{1}{2}$ cup water and heat over medium heat. Stir and continue to heat until mixture is thick and bubbly. Slowly stir in 1$\frac{3}{4}$ cups milk. Continue stirring to prevent burning, until thoroughly heated, but do not boil. Once ready, remove the pan from the heat and pour the cocoa into cups and top with a marshmallow. This will make 3 servings. To make cocoa foamy, beat it with a rotary or electric beater right before serving. If serving adults, for another special touch, add 1$\frac{1}{2}$ tsp. or 1 Tbsp. peppermint schnapps or $\frac{1}{2}$ tsp. crème de menthe plus $\frac{1}{2}$ tsp. crème de cacao to each cup of cocoa.

COFFEE

One pound of coffee will produce 40 cups. Use freshly ground coffee for the best flavor, since old coffee tastes stale. Begin with cold water and never boil unless you prefer a very strong flavor; boiling brings out the tannic acid in coffee. When reheating, it will lose some of its flavor and probably taste bitter. Always wash your coffeemaker regularly by "making" a pot of commercial coffee pot cleaner or a solution of $\frac{1}{4}$ cup vinegar and 6 cups water. *Always* use a clean pot to make coffee. If coffee is perked too long and tastes bitter, add a dash of salt. Use the chart below to determine strength:

FOR A PERFECT CUP OF COFFEE

	Weak	Medium	Strong
Coffee	1 Tbsp.	2 Tbsp.	3 Tbsp.
Water	1 cup	1 cup	1 cup

To make iced coffee: Double the amount of coffee normally used, make coffee, allow it to cool, and add ice. Serve with milk or cream and sugar. Great after-dinner coffees can be made easily. For a cup of **demitasse**, use 3 Tbsp. coffee for 1 cup water, and serve in demitasse cups with cream and sugar. For **liqueur coffee**, fill a demitasse cup ¾ full of coffee and add 1 Tbsp. any liqueur. **Mocha coffee** can be made by combining equal parts of coffee and hot chocolate; top with a small spoonful of whipped cream and a few shavings of chocolate. To make **café royale**, place a jigger of brandy into a cup of strong black coffee, and serve with cream. Fill a coffee cup ⅔ full of hot coffee, add ⅓ cup hot milk, and top with whipped cream and sprinkle with ground cinnamon for **Viennese coffee**.

FRUIT DRINKS

Lemonade or Limeade: For old-fashioned fresh-squeezed lemonade or limeade, combine ⅓ cup of fresh-squeezed lemon or lime juice, 1 cup water, and 5 tsp. sugar, mix well, and pour over ice. For pink lemonade, add 2 tsp. grenadine syrup and a dash of red food coloring to the recipe above.

For **fruitade**, save the juices from canned, frozen, and fresh fruits in a closed container in the refrigerator. Once you have saved 3 to 4 cups, place the juice in an ice cube tray and freeze. Remove and beat in a blender or with an electric mixer until the frozen pieces are fine. Serve with a straw. For a special touch, add liqueur when blending.

ICE-CREAM DRINKS

Place 1 to 2 scoops of ice cream in a glass and fill with any of the following: cold milk, cola, root beer, coffee (cold), or fruit juice. Make a great drink by placing 1 scoop of orange sherbet in a tall glass and adding equal parts of ginger ale and orange juice. To make a **Black Cow**, place 2 scoops vanilla ice cream in a tall glass and fill the glass with cola or root beer. To make an **Ice Cream Soda**, place 2 Tbsp. of your favorite syrup, 2 Tbsp. milk, and 2 scoops ice cream in a tall glass. Slowly add carbonated water until mixture is 1½ inches from the top of the glass. Stir. Top with whipped cream and a maraschino cherry. Instead of syrup, you may substitute 2–3 Tbsp. fruit juice or fruit-flavored drink. To make a **Malt**, place 1 Tbsp. syrup, 1 cup milk, 1–2 scoops ice cream, and 1 tsp. unflavored powdered malt in a blender. Blend for 45–60 seconds. To make a **Milk Shake**, place 2–3 scoops ice cream in a blender and cover with 1 cup of cold milk and 1 Tbsp. syrup. Blend well for 45 seconds. The degree of thickness depends on the amount of milk you add. If milk shake is too thick made with 1 cup milk, add a little more. You may use half-and-half instead of milk for even thicker shakes. Also, you may add syrup, jam or preserves, fruit, instant coffee, or flavorings.

LIQUOR

Ingredients for the klutz's basic bar:

ALCOHOL	NON-ALCOHOL	AFTER-DINNER
Bourbon	Club soda	Amaretto
Gin	Colas, diet colas	Brandy
Rum	Cranberry, orange juices	Cognac
Scotch	Ginger ale	Frangelico
Sherry	Grapefruit juice	Grand Marnier
Tequila	Lemons, limes	Kahlúa
Vermouth	Olives	
Vodka	Tonic water	
Whiskey		

It's a good idea to keep a small bartender's guide on hand. For a party, remember to allow 1 lb. of ice per person. All liquors vary in their alcoholic content, which is referred to on the label as the "proof." The proof of a liquor is twice the amount of its alcohol content. For example, if a liquor is 90% proof, then it consists of 45% alcohol.

There are a few rules to remember when making mixed drinks. Always place ice in the glass first, if serving a cocktail on ice. To stir a drink means to mix the ingredients together. Some drinks need to be stirred more than others, while carbonated mixed drinks need little stirring. When fixing a pitcher of drinks, stir for at least 10–15 seconds. Remember, stirring causes the ice to melt more quickly, thus diluting the drink faster.

To shake a drink you may use a shaker purchased at a cookware or liquor store, an electric blender, or a tall glass with a lid. Always shake drinks made with cream, eggs, fruit juices, or sugar, and always place eggs or fruit juices in the shaker before adding the liquor.

To strain a drink use a coil-rimmed bar strainer. Drinks will taste better and dilute less if you chill the glass before filling it. To chill a glass, place it in the refrigerator or freezer until it feels cold. Another way to chill a glass is to place ice (crushed or chopped) in the glass until it's chilled. Then pour the melted ice out before adding your mixed drink.

Simple sugar syrup may be substituted for powdered sugar. To make simple sugar syrup, place 2 cups granulated sugar and 1 cup water in a pan and heat on *low,* stirring constantly, until the sugar dissolves and the liquid is clear. This should take about 5 minutes. Pour the syrup into a bottle and refrigerate until ready to use.

To frost a glass or the rim of a glass, place the glass in the freezer until the glass has a frosty appearance. Burying a glass in ice will also produce the frosty look. After it's frosty, rub the slice of a lime or lemon around the rim of a glass. Then dip the glass rim into a bowl of powdered sugar or coarse salt, depending on your preference.

To crush, crack, or chop ice, place it in a sealed plastic bag and either hammer the ice or slam it several times on a hard surface. You may also chop with an icepick (be careful!), or place in a blender to crush.

PUNCH

Allow 2 servings of 4 ounces per person. One gallon of punch will produce 32 servings of 4 ounces each. **To make basic punch:** Take any type of ice cream or sherbet and pour ginger ale over it right before serving. If using a punch bowl, place the ice cream or sherbet in the bowl after you have poured in 1 liter of ginger ale. Add the ice cream or sherbet and then finish adding the ginger ale.

To make clear ice molds: Use a round ring mold and distilled water for best results. You may also use water that has been boiled and then cooled to room temperature. First, add whatever you like to the mold—fresh fruit, sprigs of mint, grapes, red or green cherries, or flowers. To add flowers, wash them first and place the face of the flower down in the mold. You may use roses, carnations, etc. Add enough water to the mold to fill it 1/3 full or to cover the fruit or flowers, and place the mold in the freezer. After the mold is frozen, remove it from the freezer and fill it with water so the mold is 3/4 full. Then place the mold back in the freezer until ready to use. When ready to use, remove the mold from the freezer and place the solid metal mold side in warm water for a few seconds. The ice mold should slide out easily and should then be placed in the punch bowl with the fruit or flowers showing. **Tip:** Freeze punch in a ring mold and use instead of ice to prevent diluting your punch as much. You may add berries to the mold for a little zest.

To make Tea Punch (a Southern favorite): Place 2 cups water and 2 cups sugar in a pot and bring to a boil. Boil the mixture for 10 minutes. Be sure to stir the sugar and water until all of the sugar dissolves. After the sugar mixture has boiled for 10 minutes, add 2 handfuls of fresh mint (which is easy to grow in your yard) and 5 family-size tea bags to the pot. Remove from heat and steep the mixture for 20 minutes. Then strain (to remove the mint) and pour the strained liquid in a gallon jug (a plastic milk container works great!). Add the following: a 6-ounce can of frozen lemonade and a 6-ounce can of frozen orange juice. Fill the jug to the top with water and shake jug well to mix. You may use decaffeinated tea bags if you are concerned about caffeine.

TEA

Usually light teas have a milder flavor, and dark teas have a stronger flavor. "Pekoe" refers to the size and type of leaf, not the flavor. When buying, remember 1/4 pound of tea will make 35 to 45 cups. Store in a dark, airtight container up to 6 months.

To brew delicious tea, begin with a clean pot and cold water. Rinse the teapot first with hot water. Use 1 tea bag or 1 tsp. tea per 3/4 cup or 6 ounces of water. Place tea bag or tea into a cup, and add boiling water. If using loose tea, use a tea diffuser, which may be purchased at a cookware store. Let it steep (this means to let the tea stand in the water so the water will absorb the taste of the tea and will change color) for 3 to 5 minutes, remove, and stir. If using loose tea without a tea diffuser, pour the tea through a strainer before drinking. Add lemon, milk, honey or sugar according to your taste. Use a nonmetal teapot for serving good tea. If you do not have a teapot, use a cup and place the saucer on top of the cup to steep the tea.

For clear iced tea, use 2 tea bags or 2 tsp. tea per 3/4 cup or 6 ounces of water. Allow the tea to cool to room temperature, pour in a glass, and add ice. Remember that ice will dilute the tea.

To make herbal tea, add 1 tsp. dried herbs or 3 tsp. fresh herbs for every 6 ounces of tea. Herbs that are wonderful in tea are mint, thyme, rosemary, bay leaves, marjoram, anise, sage, parsley, and savory.

TEA TIPS FOR THE KITCHEN KLUTZ

- Place a spoon in the cup when carrying tea or coffee. The spoon will help keep the liquid from spilling.
- If preparing a large amount, let the tea steep for 5 additional minutes.
- To prevent cracking a china cup when pouring in hot tea, place a spoon in the cup first to absorb the heat.
- Heat the cup first by rinsing with hot water.
- If your tea is cloudy, pour in a small amount of hot water to make the tea clear.

WINE

When selecting wine, choose according to your taste or ask your local liquor dealer for suggestions. Store wines in an area that maintains a constant temperature and, if possible, store at 55° to 60°F. but never higher than 75°F. Always store corked bottles on their sides to keep the cork moist and tight. A wine rack is ideal because it positions the bottles at a slight angle so the corks stay covered with wine. The only exception to storing corked bottles on their sides is port, which may be stored upright. Turn stored wine a quarter of a turn occasionally to reduce sediment buildup.

In general, white wines ready to be enjoyed may be stored unopened in the refrigerator up to 3 months. Once opened, wine should be used within a few days for the best flavor, and after 5 days it should only be used for cooking.

In general, allow 1/2 to 2/3 of a 750-ml. bottle per person if serving wine as the main beverage and allow 2- to 2 1/2-ounce servings of dessert wine per person. A standard wine glass generally holds 4 oz., and a 750-ml. bottle of wine will pour 6 glasses.

BASIC WINE SERVING CHART

Types of Wine	Temperature for Serving	Glass for Serving
Sparkling	Very well chilled—40°F.	Flute or flat, wide-rimmed (champagne) glass
White wine	Well chilled—50°F.	Tulip-bowled, narrower rim, less rounded
Rosé	Well chilled—50°F.	Same as for white
Red wine	Room temperature—65–70°F.	Round-bowled, stemmed glass
Dessert (port, Madeira)	Room temperature—65–70°F.	Small wine or cocktail glass

Allow 2 hours to chill a bottle of wine in the refrigerator. To chill quickly, place wine bottle in a bucket or sink full of ice and water for 20 minutes.

Before uncorking a bottle of wine, hold it up to the light to make sure that it's bright and clear. Murky, cloudy wine indicates a problem. However, any sediment or cork in the wine is fine but should be removed before drinking. Sometimes white wine may contain tiny crystals but this is not a problem.

If you don't have a corkscrew, run hot water over the *neck* of the bottle to expand the glass and cause the cork to pop out. If the cork crumbles when you are trying to remove it, pour the wine through a strainer and into a decanter for serving. Don't worry if the cork breaks. This doesn't necessarily mean that the wine is bad; the cork might have broken because the cork was old or the wine was stored improperly.

Fill the wineglass 1/2 to 2/3 full so the aroma can concentrate in the upper part of the glass. After pouring wine into a glass, twist the bottle to the right or to the left while bringing the bottle to an upright position in order to avoid drip stains.

Choosing Wines for Accompanying Food

Red wine is generally heavier-bodied and thus many prefer it with heavier foods such as red meat. In addition, red wine contains tannin, a chemical in the grape skin that helps with digesting fatty meats such as beef. Likewise, many prefer a lighter-bodied wine—white wine, for instance—with lighter meats such as poultry or fish. Wine should not be served with artichokes, asparagus, marinated foods, or salads made with vinegar, since these foods affect the taste of the wine. In addition, if serving fine wine with dinner, try not to serve cocktails before dinner. The strong liquor taste will deaden the taste buds and desensitize them for the delicate wine flavors. If you are serving chocolate for dessert, it is best to serve champagne, since most wines don't go well with chocolate.

Cooking with wine

Cooking with wine imparts a wonderful flavor and smell. The alcohol evaporates during the cooking process, leaving only the flavor of the wine. Leftover wine is great for cooking, and should be used instead of "cooking wine."

Wine acts as a tenderizer when added to marinades for meat. Wine intensifies the salt flavor in food when you use it in cooking. It is better to use too little rather than too much wine in cooking. Wine may be substituted for part of the liquid in a recipe. Always use a dry wine for cooking. Vermouth is a good substitute for white wine when cooking. With **beef** recipes, use a Chianti or burgundy. With **dessert**, use a port. With **fish**, use vermouth or any white table wine. With **game**, use any red table wine. With **lamb**, use any white table wine. With **poultry**, use Chablis, sherry, vermouth, or any white table wine. With **soups**, use sherry for onion soup, Chablis for consommé, vegetable, and chicken soups, and Burgundy for beef stew and minestrone. A delicious sauce for basting **pork** is made by mixing together $3/4$ cup Marsala wine and $1/4$ cup Cointreau.

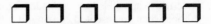

BREAD

Nothing smells better when you walk into your home than a loaf of bread baking! Bread is fun to make as well as to share with friends and family. The "quick" breads that use baking powder or baking soda are easy and, like their name, quick to make. Yeast bread is more difficult, but don't let that deter you. If you've never made bread before, you might want to make a quick bread such as pumpkin or banana first and then move on to make a yeast bread. Pay special attention to the tips given below for making extra-delectable bread!

STORING BREAD

Homemade bread will generally last 2 to 7 days. After baking bread, make sure it is completely cool before storing. Wrap loaf in aluminum foil (tightly so that it cannot come undone) and store in a cool, dry place.

To freeze bread, wrap the cooled loaf tightly in plastic and then in freezer paper. Bread may be frozen up to 6 months, although the flavor is best when eaten within 2 months. To thaw frozen bread, leave at room temperature for several hours or wrap in aluminum foil and heat for 30 minutes at 350°F.

QUICK BREADS

Quick breads, which include biscuits, pancakes, waffles, dumplings, muffins, popovers, and some rolls, are a great way for a kitchen klutz to begin baking bread. They are normally made using baking powder, baking soda, eggs, or steam as the leavening agent rather than yeast and thus are much easier to make. As their name implies, they are "quick" in cooking because kneading is not usually required and they rise during the baking process. Your quick bread recipe will tell you whether to use baking powder or baking soda. They are two very different ingredients, so make sure you use the correct one. While both leaven bread by releasing gas into the mixture, baking soda releases gas as soon as it is combined with liquid whereas baking powder releases part of its gas when combined with liquid and the remainder when heated. Although you will need to follow a particular recipe precisely, use the tips given below to ensure success when making each type of quick bread.

Biscuit Tips

When making biscuits, always finely cut the shortening into the flour mixture. For flaky biscuits, use shortening that is cold. Soft wheat flour makes the best biscuits. Add liquid at the same time and quickly mix with a fork until the mixture becomes a round ball, and there's none left on the sides of the bowl. Place the dough on a lightly floured surface and knead gently. Use a rolling pin to roll the dough out or you may pat the dough to flatten. Make the dough layer as thick as you want, but remember that the biscuits will double in size when they bake. Try to cut as many biscuits from the first rolling as possible because overworking the dough will produce tougher biscuits.

To make biscuits that will "slice" easily in half once cooked, roll the dough out to 1/4 inch thickness and gently fold it over before cutting the biscuits. Cut biscuits with a floured cutter, and place on an ungreased baking sheet. For butter biscuits, brush the rolled dough with melted butter (before cutting). If you place biscuits close together when baking, they will be soft, if farther apart, they will be crusty. For soft sides as well, bake biscuits close together in a pan with sides.

Leftover cooked biscuits can be wrapped in aluminum foil and stored up to 3 days at room temperature, or wrapped in freezer foil and frozen for up to 2 months.

Cornbread Tips

This quick bread is easy to make! Always beat mixture until smooth. Use white cornmeal if you want an uneven texture and yellow cornmeal for a smooth texture. You may flavor cornbread by adding 1 cup of chopped onion and/or peppers or grated cheese. There are many excellent commercial cornbread mixes available.

Dumpling Tips

Mix dumpling dough as little as possible—just blend the ingredients together. Don't drop them directly into boiling meat stock, but lay them on the chicken or vegetables that are cooking in the stock. Always simmer dumplings for about 10 minutes uncovered and then for 10 minutes covered, using a dome lid—this prevents them from becoming soggy.

Muffin Tips

The batter for muffins should be lumpy. Just mix to combine—never overmix. Soft wheat flour makes the best muffins. To bake, use baking cups or a greased muffin pan. Muffins are done when you insert a toothpick into the center and it comes out "clean." For perfectly rounded muffin tops, grease the bottoms and 1/2 inch up the sides of each cup in the muffin pan.

Pancake and Waffle Tips

When making pancakes and waffles, always use low heat. Blend the batter—do not overbeat or overmix. The mixture should be lumpy. Always test the temperature of the griddle before you pour the batter. To test temperature, sprinkle a few drops of cold water on the griddle. When the water beads and dances, the griddle is ready. If the water just sits and boils, the griddle is not hot enough. If the water evaporates immediately, the griddle is too hot. You do not have to grease the griddle if you cook your pancakes over low heat. If you feel it is necessary, you may lightly grease your griddle.

For pancakes, it is time to turn them over when the batter bubbles. The second side will cook in less time. Turn them over only once. To keep pancakes warm, do not stack them. Place them between tea towels on a baking sheet in a 200°F. oven.

For great waffles, cook until no steam comes out of the waffle iron. Do not raise the lid during baking. Use a fork to remove waffles and don't stack them. To keep warm, place on a cookie sheet in a 200°F. oven. If the waffles stick, brush the waffle iron off, removing any remaining waffle bits before pouring the next batter.

To season a waffle iron, follow the manufacturer's directions. If no directions are provided, and the iron does not have a nonstick surface, you will need to "season" the iron so your waffle will not stick. To do this, brush liquid vegetable shortening on the waffle iron while it's cold. Turn on the iron and after it heats up, turn it off and let it cool. Wipe off the excess oil after it cools. Reheat and test with water before using. Never eat the first waffle after you have seasoned your waffle iron. Once it has been properly seasoned, you do not have to wash or grease your waffle iron again—just wipe it with paper towels.

Popover Tips

Popovers, a bread that is crusty on the outside and hollow on the inside, are made without baking powder or soda. They may be eaten plain or stuffed with a filling. Beat the mixture just enough to blend the ingredients, do not overbeat. Although the batter may seem thin, the oven temperature and the liquid will create steam, which will make the batter rise.

Melba Toast

To make melba toast, toast both sides of a thin slice of bread (1/4 inch thick). Then carefully split the toasted piece with a sharp knife so that you now have two slices and retoast the bread. You may use an electric toaster or place on baking sheet in an oven set on broil. If desired, cut the bread in decorative shapes for a fancy look.

STEPS FOR MAKING YEAST BREAD

While not as easy as baking a quick bread, baking yeast bread is easier than you think. In order to bake yeast bread, you need to understand the process. Always assemble your ingredients and utensils first. After you have made the dough according to the recipe, you knead the dough to distribute the gas bubbles evenly throughout. After kneading, let the dough rise once or twice, depending on the recipe. Then shape the loaves and bake according to the directions. The following information will help you when baking yeast bread.

Step 1: Assemble Your Ingredients. The main ingredients for yeast bread are flour, a leavening agent, salt, sweetener, liquid, and shortening. Any type **flour** may be used, although hard wheat flour (known as "all-purpose" flour) is the most preferable.

A **leavening agent** makes the bread rise and expand. Common leavening agents are yeast, baking powder, and baking soda. Yeast may be bought in two forms: compressed/fresh and active/dry. Compressed/fresh yeast comes in cakes and will last 10 to 14 days in the refrigerator. You can freeze it, but you must thaw it completely at room temperature before using, and then you must use it immediately after thawing. Active/dry yeast comes in packets containing 1 Tbsp. or 1/4 ounce and can be kept on a cool, dry shelf, although it is best kept in the refrigerator. Be sure to check the expiration date on the package. There is a third type of yeast used in making sourdough bread—wild yeast. This is yeast that has been fed flour and water and kept alive in the refrigerator.

To dissolve yeast, sprinkle the yeast in warm water (about 110° to 115°F.) and allow it to sit a few minutes, then stir with a fork until the yeast is dissolved. To make sure the yeast is good, add 1 tsp. sugar to the yeast/warm water mixture. If it bubbles quickly, the yeast is good; if nothing happens, the yeast must be discarded. If the yeast is good, you may still use it after adding the sugar.

Salt is used to slow the yeast action and bring out the bread flavor. A **sweetener** is used for flavor as well as food for the yeast.

The following types of **liquid**—skim milk, whole milk, prepared instant nonfat dry milk, buttermilk, sour milk, water, and beer—are used in making yeast bread. Skim milk and whole milk may be used interchangeably. If using dry milk, make the milk according to the directions on the box. Also, buttermilk and sour milk may be used interchangeably. If you have only fresh milk and the recipe calls for buttermilk or sour milk, add 1 Tbsp. vinegar per cup of fresh milk and let it stand for a few minutes before using.

Shortenings such as emulsified vegetable shortening (like Crisco), butter, or margarine are used to make the bread smoother and flakier. To substitute shortening for 1 cup butter or margarine, use 7/8 cup shortening plus 1/2 tsp. salt.

Step 2: Mixing. Before you start mixing ingredients, you should rinse the mixing bowl with hot water and dry the bowl. Add the yeast/warm water mixture, then the salt, sweetener, and shortening, then beat with a wooden spoon or an electric beater until the mixture falls from the beater in sheets. Next follow the recipe for adding the proper amount of flour to make a dough that will stand clear of the bowl and not stick to the fingers. Now you are ready to knead the dough.

Step 3: Kneading. The goal of kneading is to make the dough rounded, smooth, satiny, and elastic. Kneading evenly distributes the gas bubbles formed by the yeast. Always lightly sprinkle flour over the surface where you place the dough. You will need to repeat this process as you knead the dough. Lightly dust your hands with flour also.

To knead, shape the dough into a ball. Press the ball flat with the palms of your hands. Then take the edge of the dough that is farthest away from you and fold it towards you. Then take the heels of your hands and press the fold down while pushing the dough away. Then give the dough a one-third turn and repeat the preceeding steps of pressing and folding in a rhythmic motion. Keep folding, turning, and pushing, until the dough is no longer sticky and looks smooth. This process will take 5 to 15 minutes. If using a mixer, knead the dough for 15 minutes with a mixer and then 5 more minutes with your hands. Dough that has been kneaded enough will spring back when you press the dough with your finger.

Step 4: Rising/Shaping/Baking. Always place dough to rise in a bowl at least twice the size of the dough itself—the dough will double in size as it rises. The bowl should be lightly greased, and if the bowl is very cold, warmed first by rinsing the bowl out with warm water. Dough will rise faster in a warm bowl. After placing dough in the bowl, you may brush some melted butter (at room temperature) or vegetable oil on the top. Cover bowl with a clean cloth and let rise in a warm place, but never in direct sunlight. The ideal temperature for rising is 80° to 85°F. A good place for rising is an unheated oven, with a pan of hot water on the shelf below the bowl. You will know the dough has risen enough when you can lightly press it with your finger and leave an imprint. If you stick your finger in the dough about 1/2 inch and the imprint disappears, the dough will need to rise more. Usually, the rising process takes 2 hours.

When the dough has finished rising, punch down its center. Next, fold the edges over into the center and completely turn the ball over. Divide the dough according to what you need by using a large sharp knife. Your recipe will tell you how many pieces to shape the dough into. Next, shape the pieces into rolls or loaves of bread. Remember to place the edges of the dough under to make rounded loaves or rolls. Place on a greased baking pan. After shaping, let the dough rise again until it doubles in bulk, about 1 hour. To test for readiness, make an imprint near the bottom or edge. If the imprint remains, the dough is ready to be baked. Preheat the oven and bake according to the recipe directions.

Step 5: Test for Doneness. After baking, to make sure the bread is done properly, tap the bottom of the pan—it will sound hollow. Likewise, when you tap the top of the loaf of bread with your knuckles, it will sound hollow. Like a cake, bread pulls away from the sides of the pan when it is done.

MAKING ROLLS

The dough for rolls is made in the same way as bread. They can be made from any basic sweet dough. Yeast dough may be kept in the refrigerator for 3 days before you roll it out and use it. Keep in mind that white yeast rolls double in size when rising, whereas dark rolls do not. In general, rolls take 45 to

60 minutes to rise and only rise half of their original size. Shape rolls into any style you wish—twisted, crescent, dinner, or cloverleaf—and any size from small to large. Rolls normally take 18 to 30 minutes to bake and should be baked at 375° until lightly browned. If you make rolls from bread dough, they may be baked at the same time you bake your bread.

BREAD TIPS FOR THE KITCHEN KLUTZ

- Bread made with milk is finer in texture than bread made with water.
- Always use a preheated oven because bread rises in the first 15 minutes.
- For an arched loaf, fill the pan 2/3 full; for a flat loaf, fill the pan 1/2 full.
- Do not use too much yeast because it will coarsen the bread and cause it to go stale more quickly.
- Bake bread in a dark-colored pan, it absorbs the heat better than a light colored pan.
- Line your oven with unglazed tiles to form a steady, even heat.
- Throw a handful of ice cubes in the oven during baking to cause steam for a crustier bread.
- To keep the crust from getting hard, place a small shatterproof bowl of water in the oven while the bread is baking.
- Use a hot serrated knife for cutting bread.
- The weather affects breadmaking! The temperature and humidity affect the absorption of the flour and the yeast action, causing flat bread.
- If bread does not rise, dissolve a new package of yeast and wait 5 minutes, until bubbles start to form. Knead mixture into the dough and try again.
- For a crispy, shiny crust, brush the dough with milk, water, or a beaten egg before baking. For a hard crust, use an egg white mixed with a small amount of water.
- For a soft and glossy crust, brush bread with melted butter after baking.

DAIRY

Dairy products are items most of us use or eat daily since so many of our favorite foods contain them. Cookies, cakes, pies, sauces, salad dressings, ice cream, and casseroles just are a few examples of dairy-based items. Keep in mind these foods are perishable and must be stored properly. Today most dairy products have expiration dates on their packaging, so be sure to check the date before purchasing them.

Eggs or egg substitutes are among the easiest items to cook, so don't hesitate to fix them in some of the many varied ways listed in this chapter. Eggs may be hard-cooked, poached, or fried as well as cooked over toast or in the oven. Eggs are also used in recipes to hold the other ingredients together. If you watch what you are doing and follow the directions, it's hard to ruin an egg when cooking.

Cheese is another versatile food that can be prepared in many ways. It may be used as an appetizer, main dish (such as cheese soufflé), or for dessert. In addition, it's delightful in sauces, casseroles, dips, as well as on its own with crackers, fruit, and wine. Enjoy its versatility!

Nothing compares to the delicious taste of butter, cream, or whole milk. These products are included in this chapter, although many cooks today use dairy and nondairy substitutes that are often lower in fat and cholesterol.

BUTTER

BUYING

Butter is the emulsified fat from cream that is made by churning or vigorously stirring cream to separate the liquid fat ("whey") from the solid fat ("butter"). Butter may be purchased in **regular (salted)** or **sweet (unsalted)** forms. **Whipped butter**, which comes in both salted and unsalted varieties, is regular butter with air beaten into it so that it is softer and easier to spread.

STORING

Butter should be stored tightly wrapped or covered in the refrigerator. Check the expiration date on the package for length of storage. Opened salted butter will last up to 1 month in the refrigerator, but unsalted butter will last only 2 weeks. All butter may be frozen for a period of up to 6 months.

COOKING

Always use regular salted or unsalted butter in your recipes. Whipped butter usually contains 30% air and will ruin your recipe if it is used instead of regular butter. If you substitute salted butter in a recipe that calls for unsalted butter, be sure to reduce the salt in the recipe accordingly. Each stick of salted butter contains approximately 1/4 tsp. salt.

Unsalted butter should be used for greasing pans since salted butter can cause the food to stick. To soften a stick of butter, place it on a microwave-safe dish and microwave it for 15 seconds on low power. You can also leave it out at room temperature for 20 to 30 minutes or pop it into the oven on very low heat for a few minutes (watch carefully). To whip butter, place it in a bowl and beat with an electric mixer until it is light and fluffy.

Butter burns easily, so always cook it over low heat and watch it carefully.

Clarified or drawn butter is made by melting butter in a heavy saucepan or in a microwave oven on high (level 10) for 1 minute. Remove the butter from the heat and let it stand for a few minutes. A clear, clarified layer will float to the top while the salt and milk curd will settle to the bottom. Pour off the clear liquid—this is the clarified or drawn butter—and use it in your recipe. If you are serving clarified butter with lobster, you may want to add lemon juice.

There are several easy-to-make flavored butters that add a gourmet touch to bread. Use any brand of unsalted butter and prepare it according to the following instructions.

To make Fines Herbes Butter, combine 1/2 cup softened butter, 1 Tbsp. chopped chives, 1 Tbsp. minced parsley, 1/2 tsp. tarragon, 1/2 tsp. chervil, 1/4 tsp. salt, and a dash of pepper. Beat until fluffy.

To make Garlic Butter, combine 1/2 cup softened butter, 2–3 minced garlic cloves, and 2 Tbsp. minced parsley. Beat until fluffy. Add 1–2 tsp. grated Parmesan cheese for additional flavor.

To make Herb Butter, combine 1/2 cup softened butter, 1/4 tsp. grated onion, 1/4 tsp. oregano, 2 tsp. minced parsley, 1/8 tsp. cayenne pepper, 1 clove minced garlic, and 1 Tbsp. lightly toasted sesame seeds.

CHEESE

Cheese is a versatile ingredient that will help any kitchen klutz. It enhances everything from soups to pasta to salads to vegetables, and may even be used for dessert. It may be consumed at breakfast in an omelet, at lunch on a sandwich, or at dinner as an appetizer or in soup.

Cheese can be categorized as natural ripened (such as Cheddar, Monterey Jack, Brie), processed (such as cheese spread), or fresh (such as cream cheese and cottage cheese). Natural cheese is considered either hard or soft, depending on its water content. The composition of cheese affects its flavor, texture, and its use. The chart at the end of the chapter will help if you are unsure about a particular cheese's texture, taste, or serving instructions.

BUYING

When buying packaged cheese, always check the expiration date. Also, check the wrapping or packaging to make sure there are no tears, mold, moisture, or cracks (which could indicate dryness). If you buy unpackaged cheese from a deli, supermarket dairy department, or cheese store, always ask the clerk about its freshness.

STORING

Store all cheese in the refrigerator double-wrapped tightly in plastic, aluminum foil, or waxed paper to prevent the cheese from becoming hard and dry. Unopened processed cheese and natural cheese will keep for 3 months. Opened processed cheese and natural cheese will only keep for 6 weeks. For hard cheeses, cut off any mold that has grown on the cheese before using. Cottage cheese and cream cheese should be thrown out when moldy. The mold is not harmful (moisture causes the mold to form). Always check the date on the wrapper before buying and eating!

You can freeze cheese by double wrapping it with freezer paper. Hard cheeses will keep up to 6 months, and soft and semisoft cheeses will keep in the freezer up to 4 months. Always thaw frozen cheese in the refrigerator and use it within a few days of thawing.

PREPARING

When grating or slicing, remember that cheese will grate more easily if it is chilled. A 1/4-pound chunk of cheese will yield 1 cup grated cheese. Processed cheese will not grate easily because of its softness. To slice hard or firm cheese, run the knife under hot water first to warm the knife, which will then soften the cheese slightly. Before serving natural ripened cheese, unwrap and blot dry with a paper towel. Rewrap in plastic and leave at room temperature until you are ready to serve.

COOKING

Always cook cheese over low heat—high heat will make it tough and stringy—and stir frequently. Cheese should only be cooked long enough to melt. Grate or chop cheese first before adding it to a sauce so it will melt more easily. If you are afraid of burning cheese, melt it in the top of a double boiler or in the microwave. Low-fat cheeses will not melt as well because of their low fat content. On the other hand, processed cheese is creamy, melts easily, and is less stringy, so it's great for cooking. An additional tip, add grated Cheddar cheese to a casserole during the last 5 minutes of cooking to keep the cheese from becoming hard.

The chart on pages 30–33 lists many different varieties of cheese and their characteristics.

CHEESE TIPS FOR THE KITCHEN KLUTZ

- Always serve hard and semihard cheese at room temperature for fuller flavor.
- Always serve soft cheese slightly chilled.
- In choosing a wine to complement the cheese, remember the stronger the cheese, the fuller-bodied the wine choice.
- Do not buy cheese that has a wet or sticky wrapper.
- Use a different knife for each cheese served so that the different flavors don't mix.
- Use mild unsalted crackers when serving mild cheese so that the flavor of the cheese is not overpowered by the crackers.
- As an appetizer, 2 ounces of cheese generally is enough for 1 serving.
- Remember, mold on hard cheeses is not harmful, but does need to be cut off before eating or using the cheese.

CREAM

There are five types of cream available for purchase. **Whipping cream** (heavy cream) contains at least 30% butterfat and is used in sauces, soups, vegetables dishes, and desserts. **Regular Cream** contains 18% to 30% butterfat and is used in coffee and tea. **Half-and-half** is a mixture of half cream and half whole milk; it contains approximately 11.5% butterfat. **Light cream** contains between 18% and 20% butterfat. **Créme fraîche** is the French version of heavy cream. It is usually not available for purchase commercially but may be made by adding 2 tsp. sour cream or 1 tsp. buttermilk to 1 cup whipping cream. Shake the mixture well and let stand uncovered at room temperature for 24

CHEESES AND SUGGESTED WINES TO ACCOMPANY THEM

Type	Origin	Texture	Taste	Serve with
American	American	firm	varies from mild to sharp	sandwiches, in casseroles, soufflés, creamy sauces, with fruit
Beer	American	smooth, soft	similar to Limburger but milder	dark bread and beer, or Zinfandel
Bel Paese	Italian	semisoft	mild	dessert, crackers, fruit, light bread, and Beaujolais or Chenin Blanc
Bleu	French	semisoft, sometimes crumbly	spicy	dessert, in salads and dips, with crackers, with pears or apple slices and dry red wine such as a Pinot Noir or Cabernet Sauvignon
Boursault	French	soft and creamy	delicate, mild	serve as dessert with French bread and red wine
Boursin	French	soft	rich, creamy with a slight tartness; may be flavored with herbs and garlic	serve as dessert with fruit and wine or as an hors d'oeuvres
Brick	American	medium firm	strong, sweetish	serve in salads, with peaches, cherries, or melons or plain with Zinfandel or beer
Brie	French	soft	sharp	with fruit and crackers and with red wines such as Cabernet Sauvignon, Pinot Noir, Merlot
Caciocavallo	Italian, Balkan	hard	smoky, salty	used in cooking and grating
Camembert	French	semisoft	distinct, full, rich flavor	for dessert with apples, pears, peaches, toasted walnuts, and a rich red wine such as Pinot Noir or Merlot, in salads
Cantal	French	firm	piquant	snacks, appetizers, and beer

30

Type	Origin	Texture	Taste	Serve with
Cheddar	English	hard	mellow and rich, tastes from mild to sharp	snacks, mellow Beaujolais or beer
Chèvre	French	soft	smooth, creamy, mild	Chardonnay, Cabernet Sauvignon, or Sauvignon Blanc Beaujolais
Cheshire	English	hard	mellow and rich, similar to Cheddar	in salads, dips, with canned or fresh fruits
Cottage	American	soft	mild	in dips, cheesecake, sandwich spreads—adds body and richness to dishes
Cream	American	soft, buttery texture	very mild	
Edam	Dutch	semisoft to firm	mild, nutlike flavor	has a red rind; serve with grapes or oranges and dry red wine or beer
Emmentaler	Swiss	hard, smooth	sweet, nutty	in fondue, snacks, with fruity Zinfandel or Beaujolais
Feta	Greek	semisoft	mild, crumbly to dry, salty	great in Greek salads
Fontina	Italian	semisoft	mild, nutty	with light brown rind, serve in fondue, as dessert with bread or fruit, with beer or red wine
Gjetöst	Norwegian	hard	sweet	as dessert or an appetizer, with bread
Gorgonzola	Italian	semihard	streaks of mold	salads, dressings, dessert
Gouda	Holland	hard	mild, nutty, similar to Edam	dessert, appetizer (comes round in a red wax)
Gruyère	Switzerland	firm to hard	mild, nutty, slightly sharper than Emmentaler	has tan crust and tiny holes, use in fondue, serve with red wine such as Beaujolais
Havarti	Danish	semisoft to firm	mild and sweet to strong	sandwiches, crackers

CHEESES AND SUGGESTED WINES TO ACCOMPANY THEM (*Cont.*)

Type	*Origin*	*Texture*	*Taste*	*Serve with*
Liederkranz	American	soft and creamy	strong flavor similar to Limburger but milder	on rye bread or crackers with beer and dark bread, with Tokay grapes, or with Pinot Noir or Cabernet Sauvignon
Limburger	Belgium	soft and creamy	strong flavor and odor	in sandwiches made with dark bread, with beer or strong Pinot Noir or Cabernet Sauvignon, appetizers
Livarot	French	soft	strong, piquant	similar to Camembert but stronger and smellier; serve with rich red wine
Monterey jack	American	semisoft to firm	mild	excellent for grating, with bread, crackers, or in salads
Montrachet	French	soft	mild	souffles, dips, sandwiches
Mozzarella	Italian	semisoft	mild, milky	popular with eggplant; also used in pizza, appetizers and snacks, and on sandwiches
Muenster	German	semihard	mild	in sandwiches, appetizers, with melon and cherries; serve with Merlot or Beaujolais
Neufchâtel	French	soft and creamy	mild	in sandwiches, salads, as appetizer or dessert
Parmesan	Italian	hard	sharp, piquant	excellent for grating, on pasta, pizza, garlic bread, soups, salad, popcorn; serve with Chianti, Zinfandel, or Bardolino
Pecorino	Italy	hard	pungent	often used for grating, in pizza, pastas, soups, salad; serve with Chianti or Bardolino
Port du Salut (Oka)	French, made in Canada	semisoft	usually strong but ranges from mild to strong according to age	popular for dessert, with fresh fruit, apple pie, on a snack tray and with port wine

Type	Origin	Texture	Taste	Serve with
Processed	American	soft	varies	ideal for soufflés, sauces, grilled cheese sandwiches, casseroles
Provolone	Italian	hard	ranges from mild to strong according to age	young cheese for snacks and desserts and aged for grating; serve with Merlot or Beaujolais
Ricotta	Italian	soft	mild and creamy	used in such Italian dishes as lasagna, ravioli, and manicotti
Romano	Italian	hard	mild to sharp	serve young cheese with bread and fruits, use aged romano in cooking; serve with Chianti, Zinfandel, or Bardolino
Roquefort	French (made from ewe's milk)	semisoft	sharp, pungent, blue-veined	as dessert with strong Cabernet Sauvignon or Pinot Noir, excellent used in salad dressings, good for appetizers mixed with cream cheese
Swiss	Switzerland	semihard	mild to sharp	used in sandwiches, salads, in cooking (fondue)

hours until it is thick. After it has thickened, cover and refrigerate. It will last up to 2 weeks.

STORING

Cream is highly perishable and should be stored in the refrigerator as soon as possible after purchase. Check the expiration date on the carton for storage life. You may freeze cream well wrapped in freezer paper or plastic for up to 6 months. Make sure there is a small space between the top of the carton and the cream. To defrost cream, place it in the refrigerator. Be sure to shake it after defrosting.

PREPARING/COOKING

Cream may be substituted for milk in a recipe to add extra richness. Many sauces, custards, pies, soups, gravies, dips, and homemade ice cream are normally made with cream instead of milk. Be careful when boiling cream because it may curdle. If a recipe calls for boiling cream, it is best to just cook it right below the boiling point. Crème fraîche will not curdle when boiled. If you need a quick substitute for a cup of heavy cream, use 3/4 cup milk plus 1/3 cup butter. To substitute for a cup of light cream, use 7/8 cup milk plus 3 Tbsp. butter.

To whip cream, first determine the amount of whipping cream you need. 1 cup liquid will produce 2 cups whipped cream, as the whipping cream will double in size when you beat it. Ultrapasteurized whipping cream does not produce as much volume. Pour whipping cream into a chilled bowl and use cold beaters to beat. **Tip:** Place the bowl and beaters in the freezer for a few minutes before whipping cream; the bowl and beaters should be icy to the touch. Start at low speed and then beat on high until stiff. Watch the cream carefully because it will turn to butter if you beat it too long. If the whipping creams separates, beat it with a wire whisk.

To sweeten whipping cream, beat the cream for approximately 1 minute and then add 1 to 2 Tbsp. of sugar and 1 tsp. vanilla or almond extract. Continue to beat until stiff. (Powdered sugar works best but granulated sugar will do.) Here are other sweeteners you can add to make different flavored whipped creams:

Chocolate: Add 4 Tbsp. sugar, 1 Tbsp. cocoa, and 1 tsp. vanilla extract
Cinnamon: Add 2 Tbsp. sugar, 1/2 tsp. cinnamon, and 1 tsp. vanilla extract
Coffee: Add 2 Tbsp. sugar and 1 tsp. instant coffee
Lemon: Add 2 Tbsp. sugar and 1 tsp. lemon juice
Peppermint: Add 2 Tbsp. sugar and 1/2 tsp. peppermint extract
Rum: Add 2 Tbsp. sugar and 1 tsp. rum extract

Tip: If you're in a pinch and do not have whipping cream at hand, a *chilled* 6-ounce can of evaporated milk will work equally as well.

EGGS

BUYING

There are four grades of quality for eggs; these ratings are based on the yolk, the white, and the shell: Grade AA and Grade A are the highest quality, almost perfect in shape with clean and nice shells, firm and thick whites, and yolks well-centered and high standing. They are good to use when hard-cooking, frying, or poaching. Grade B and Grade C are the lowest quality and usually are not found in stores. Their shells may be rough or have ridges, the whites are not as thick, the yolks may not be centered and are flatter. They are good for cooking, scrambling, and baking. Remember that all grades of eggs have the same nutritional content. The color of the eggshell is determined by the breed of the mother hen and has no effect on the taste or nutritional value of the egg.

There are six sizes of eggs; the size is determined by the weight per dozen eggs.

EGG SIZE AND WEIGHT

Size	Weight (minimum for each size)
Jumbo	30 ounces per dozen
Extra Large	27 ounces per dozen
Large	24 ounces per dozen
Medium	21 ounces per dozen
Small	18 ounces per dozen
Peewee	15 ounces per dozen

Always check the expiration date on the egg carton you are buying. Always purchase size "large" eggs when buying eggs to be used in recipes. Egg size does make a difference in how a recipe turns out. Recipes always use "large" eggs unless otherwise specified.

SERVING YIELDS FOR LARGE-SIZE EGGS

1 yolk = 1 Tbsp.
14 yolks = 1 cup
1 white = 2 Tbsp.
7 whites = 1 cup
5 whole eggs (yolk and white together) = 1 cup

STORING

Store eggs in the refrigerator in the carton in which you buy them. Do not store near strong-smelling food, because the eggshell is porous and will absorb its smells. Store with the "point" end down and the broad end up, so the yolk will center. It's important to have the yolk centered aesthetically if you are hard-cooking or frying an egg. There is no need to wash eggs, as they are washed before packaging. Eggs will keep 1 to 3 weeks, depending on how fresh they are when you buy them. Remember to check the date on the carton. To store egg whites, place them in an airtight jar in the refrigerator; they will keep for up to 10 days. They may be frozen for up to 6 months by placing them in ice cube trays, and covering the frozen trays with freezer foil or plastic. To store yolks, place them in an airtight jar, cover with water, and refrigerate; drain before using. The yolks will only keep for 2 to 3 days. They are more perishable than egg whites.

Tip: To determine if an egg is fresh, place it in a bowl of cold, salted water. If the egg lies on its side on the bottom, it is fresh. If the egg stands at an angle, it is 3 to 4 days old. If the egg stands on end, it is at least 10 days old. If the egg floats, it is rotten. Fresh eggs have a dull shell. Also, the thicker and whiter the white membrane cord in the egg (it's the small stringlike piece), the fresher the egg.

BEATING

To beat eggs, use a fork, whisk, or an electric mixer and beat until you cannot tell the difference from the yolk and the white. **Slightly beaten eggs** are beaten only until the whites are combined with the yolks. **Beaten** means that the eggs are beaten until the whites and yolks are well blended. **Well-beaten eggs** are beaten until the whites and yolks are fully blended; the mixture will look light and frothy.

Often, a recipe will require you to beat only the egg whites or only the yolk. To separate the yolk from the white, you may: 1. Crack the egg in half on the counter edge, break it open over a bowl so that the yolk will fall into one of the shell halves, move the yolk back and forth between the shell halves and let the white run out until only the yolk is left; 2. crack the egg in your hand and let the white run through your fingers until the yolk is separated; or 3. buy a gadget that separates eggs. Remember cold yolks will not break as easily as those at room temperature. If some of the shell gets in the yolk or white, use another piece of shell to remove it.

To beat egg whites, separate the white from the yolk. Egg whites will beat much better and yield more volume if they are at room temperature. You must remove all the yolk from the egg white in order to beat the egg white stiff. If any egg yolk gets in the egg whites, use half a broken eggshell or paper towel to remove it. *Egg whites will not beat well if even a speck of yolk gets into them.* Eggs whites will increase in volume about six times so make sure you use a bowl that is large enough. Also, make sure the beaters are clean.

For "stiff but not dry" or "beaten stiff" whites, beat egg whites until the whites stand in peaks when you lift the beaters out. The peaks will slide if the bowl is tilted, and the points on the peaks will droop a little as well as appear glossy. For "stiff and dry" or "beaten very stiff" whites, beat egg whites until the whites stand in peaks that will not move when the bowl is tilted or will not droop when you lift the beaters out. The peaks will look dry and will stand up.

To beat egg yolks, separate the yolk from the egg white first. Egg yolks, well beaten, will be thick and lemon in color. The longer you beat, the lighter the color and the fluffier the yolks.

METHODS OF COOKING

Hard-Cooked and Other "Boiled" Eggs

Hard-cooked eggs are often called "hard-boiled," but this is a misnomer since you don't actually boil the eggs, just simmer them. To help prevent cracking, warm eggs to room temperature before cooking. There are two ways to hard-cook eggs: simmering or letting them stand in hot water.

To simmer hard-cooked eggs, place the eggs, which have warmed to room temperature, in a single layer in a pot and add enough cold water so that there is 1 inch of water on top of the eggs. Bring the water slowly to boiling point, and reduce the heat to simmer—meaning the water is barely bubbling.

To soft-cook eggs—meaning the white is softly set, and the yolk is runny—simmer for 3 to 4 minutes from the time the water comes to a boil.

To medium-cook eggs—meaning the white is solid, and the yolk is liquid—simmer for 4 to 5 minutes.

To hard-cook eggs—both the white and yolk are solid—simmer for 12 to 15 minutes.

After you have simmered the eggs for the chosen length of time, immediately plunge the eggs into cold water, which will stop the cooking and prevent the yolk from changing color.

To hard-cook eggs by the standing method, place the eggs in a pot, add enough cold water so that there is at least 1 inch of water above the eggs, and bring the water slowly to a boil. Remove the pot from the heat and cover with a lid. Next follow the instructions below to "cook" the eggs to the desired state.

To Soft-cook eggs:
for very soft—let stand in the pot for 2 minutes;
for medium soft—let stand in the pot for 3 to 3½ minutes;
for firm soft—let stand in the pot for 4 minutes.

To medium-cook eggs, let stand for 8 to 10 minutes.

To hard-cook eggs, let eggs stand for 15 minutes.

After the eggs have been in the hot water for the chosen length of time, plunge them into cold water to stop the cooking and prevent the yolk from changing color.

To serve a soft-cooked egg, crack the shell at the large end and place the soft-cooked egg in an egg cup. You may also crack the shell in the center with a knife, pull the shell apart at the crack, use a spoon to remove the egg, and place it in a cup. Season to taste.

To remove the shell of a hard-cooked egg, crack the entire shell by tapping it with a knife or rolling it on the counter. Take the egg and roll it between the palms of your hands to loosen the shell and make it much easier to peel. Start at the large end of the egg and begin peeling. If you are having a hard time peeling the egg, place the egg under cold water and continue.

Ways to serve hard-cooked eggs include **Creamed Eggs**, which are made by cutting peeled hard-cooked eggs into quarters or slices and placing them in a cream sauce (*see* "Sauces") and then serving over toast, rice, biscuits, or asparagus and topping them with bacon, ham, cheese, or whatever you like. To make **Deviled (or Stuffed) Eggs**, peel 1 hard-cooked egg and slice it length-wise into two halves. Gently remove the yolk, being careful not to break the whites. Mash the yolk in a bowl, using a fork, until it is mashed fine. Add 2 tsp. mayonnaise, 1/4 tsp. prepared or Dijon mustard, salt, pepper, and mix together. You may also add any of the following in 1/16 to 1/4 tsp. portions: minced onion, minced sweet pickles, anchovy paste, chopped ham, curry powder, American or Parmesan cheese, Worcestershire sauce, or celery. Refill the "holes" in the

---

TIPS FOR HARD-COOKING EGGS

- To cook a cracked egg, place 1 Tbsp. salt into the water. Rub the crack with salt, and place the egg into simmering water. This will prevent the white from bubbling out.
- To test for doneness, hard-cooked eggs spin around easily on a countertop.
- Fresh eggs that are hard-cooked are more difficult to peel.
- If eggs are especially difficult to peel, place them in a bowl of ice water for 2 minutes, drain, and place them in a pan of almost boiling water for 10 to 20 seconds.
- If preparing deviled eggs, or stuffed hard-cooked eggs, slice a small piece off the bottom side of the egg half to form a flat surface for the egg to sit on while you stuff it.
- Watch the cooking time! Overcooking will make the egg yolks dark, tough, and discolored.

egg white halves with the yolk mixture. Garnish the top with any of the following: sliced pimientos, onions, green pepper, olives, paprika, parsley, or capers. Increase the recipe to make as many portions as desired.

To hard-cook an egg yolk, place it carefully in a strainer and lower it into a pan of simmering water with just enough water to cover the yolk. Cook over low heat until the yolk is done. Remove the yolk and use on sandwiches or in salads. If you wish to store it, it will keep up to a week refrigerated.

Fried Eggs

Heat a skillet over medium heat and add 1 Tbsp. butter, margarine, butter substitute, or bacon grease per 2 eggs. After the butter melts, lower the heat and crack one egg into a saucer or bowl to make sure no shell gets in the egg—if it does, it will be easier to remove. Then repeat for the second egg. Gently slide the eggs into the skillet one at a time. Never cook more than 2 eggs at a time when you are frying. Cook slowly, basting the eggs with the butter. To speed up the cooking time, place a lid on the skillet. It will take 3 to 6 minutes to cook 2 eggs, depending on how you like them set. You may also cover the skillet with a lid for 1 minute or longer if you do not want to baste, which will also make the whites firm. To keep eggs softer, add 1 Tbsp. of boiling water before covering with a lid. To reduce the amount of grease, before adding the eggs pour all of the excess butter/oil out, crack the eggs into the skillet, add a little hot water, cover tightly, and cook over low heat.

Omelets

To make an omelet, beat the eggs with a blender, mixer, or egg beater until fluffy. Do not prepare more than 3 eggs at a time. For moisture, beat in 2 to 3 Tbsp. of liquid such as milk, cream, water, or sherry per egg. Add salt and pepper to taste. Next melt 1½ Tbsp. butter, margarine, or butter substitute in a suitable pan over medium heat. Once melted, turn the heat to low and add the egg mixture. Gently swirl and shake the pan over low heat until an egg pancake forms. As the omelet cooks and begins to set at the edges, use a spatula or fork to lift the edge and move the uncooked mixture under the bottom to cook. Add filling on ½ of the "pancake" and then fold the pancake over with a spatula, fork, or large spoon to form the omelet/moon shape. Use any one or a mixture of the following ingredients to fill an omelet (make sure the "filling" items are at room temperature before adding to your omelet):

bacon (cooked)	jam, preserves, jelly
cheese (any type)	mushrooms (sliced)
chives(chopped)	peppers (chopped)
cottage cheese	sausages (cooked)
garlic (minced)	spices
ham (chopped)	sprouts
herbs	tomatoes (chopped or sun-dried)

Poached Eggs

Heat 1½ to 2 inches of water in a saucepan on medium heat and bring to a boil. Lower the heat and simmer (remember: to simmer means to let the water barely bubble). Crack an egg into a small cup (do not let the yolk break) and then gently pour the egg into the simmering water. Simmer 3 minutes for soft yolks, 4 minutes for medium yolks, and 5 minutes for firm yolks. When egg is ready, remove it from the water with a slotted spoon or spatula and place on your serving plate. Season with salt and pepper and serve by itself, on toast, an English muffin half, spinach, cornbread, or whatever else strikes your fancy.

To Make Eggs Benedict: Take half a toasted English muffin, place a thin slice of cooked ham or Canadian bacon on top, then top with a poached egg, and cover with Hollandaise sauce (*see* "Sauces").

To Use an Egg Poacher: Pour an inch of water in a pan and bring to a boil. Place 1 tsp. butter in the metal egg cup, break an egg into a bowl, and then gently pour the egg into the metal cup. Place the egg cup in the holder of the egg poacher, and simmer over water. Cover and cook for 3 to 4 minutes. This method poaches the egg with steam.

TIPS FOR POACHING EGGS

- Add 1 tsp. vinegar or lemon juice per egg to the water to prevent the whites from separating.
- Use fresh Grade AA eggs because they have a stronger yolk and thicker white.
- Slide the egg to the side of the pan to cook, in order to keep the yolk in the center of the egg.
- Poached eggs may be cooked in advance and reheated in boiling salted water for about 30 seconds.

Scrambled Eggs

Break an egg into a bowl and add a dash (1/16 tsp.) of salt and pepper and 1 Tbsp. milk or cream. Beat with a fork or whisk until well mixed. Heat 1 Tbsp. butter, margarine, bacon grease, or nonstick cooking spray in a skillet or saucepan over medium heat. To test the skillet's heat before adding the egg mixture, add a few drops of water to the skillet—it should sizzle. When ready, pour the egg mixture into the skillet, reduce the heat, and cook slowly and gently. Stir the egg gently (but not too frequently) and cook until the egg is set, but still glossy and moist, about 4 to 8 minutes. Remember that the egg will continue to cook from the retained heat of the skillet, so remove from heat and serve at once.

Final tips to remember: always use a low temperature when cooking scrambled eggs; a high temperature will make your eggs tough. For moisture, you can also add 2 to 3 Tbsp. water or sherry (instead of milk) per egg. Garnish scrambled eggs with sautéed mushrooms, onions, grated cheese, chopped peppers, or sun-dried tomatoes.

Shirred (Baked) Eggs

Preheat the oven to 350°F. Butter an individual shallow baking dish (ramekin), add 1 egg, 1 tsp. butter, and 1 Tbsp. milk or cream. Put the ramekin in a baking pan with boiling water about halfway up the sides of the pan. Bake for 12–16 minutes until the egg is set. Serve in the baking dish if you like—it will save on cleanup time! You may garnish shirred eggs with chives, parsley, or watercress.

To make Shirred Eggs Florentine, line a greased dish with cooked spinach that is well drained and buttered, and place the egg on top of the spinach. For other variations, you may use cheese, bacon, or ham in place of the spinach.

"Bird-in-a-Nest" or "Picture Frame" or "Egg-in-a-Hole"

This type of egg dish has many names. It is very good and children seem to love it. Take a piece of bread and with a biscuit cutter or knife cut a round hole in the middle of it. Spread butter on both sides of the bread. Place 1 Tbsp. butter or margarine in a skillet on low heat, and let it melt. Add the bread to the skillet, and crack the egg into the hole. Cook slowly over low heat until the egg is set, and the bread is light brown on the bottom side. Turn over and brown the other side. Once the second side is light brown, or the egg is cooked to your taste, remove from pan, season, and serve.

French Toast

Melt 1 to 2 Tbsp. butter or margarine in a skillet (or coat with a nonstick cooking spray) over low heat. In a bowl, mix together 2 eggs and 1/2 cup whole milk, skim milk, or cream. The richer the milk used, the creamier the toast will be. If desired, 1/2 tsp. sugar and 1/2 tsp. vanilla extract may also be added. Take a slice of bread (preferably sourdough, French, or any thick bread) and place in the bowl to let it absorb the egg mixture. Remove the egg-soaked bread and place it in the prepared skillet. Cook uncovered over low heat. When the egg mixture looks like it has begun to "set," flip the bread over. If you wish, sprinkle with cinnamon or cinnamon-sugar while it is cooking. Once the bread is golden brown on each side, remove and serve on a warm plate with syrup (warm the plate in the microwave on high for 45 seconds or for 2 minutes in a 175°F. oven).

Cooking with Eggs For the More Advanced Kitchen Klutz

When following a recipe, always use "large" eggs unless otherwise specified. In recipes for cake, custard, and salad dressings, you may substitute 2 egg yolks for 1 egg. In recipes for cookies and yeast dough, you may substitute 2 eggs yolks plus 1 Tbsp. water for 1 egg. When adding egg yolks to a hot mixture, beat 1 tsp. water in the egg yolks first. This will help combine the two mixtures. Also, always place a small amount of the hot mixture into the egg yolks before adding egg yolks to the hot mixture.

A soufflé is a delicate dish based on eggs. They may be served hot or cold, as the entrée, or as dessert. Make sure the cream sauce is thick and firm, and make sure the egg whites are stiff but not dry before folding them into the soufflé mixture. After you beat the egg whites for the soufflé, quickly put the soufflé together. Since the egg whites combined with the steam in the oven cause the soufflé to rise, you want to proceed quickly before the egg whites deflate. Always add an extra egg white if you are doubling a soufflé recipe. When adding liqueurs for flavor, add an extra egg yolk for every 2 Tbsp. of liqueur added. To make a soufflé lighter, you may add an extra egg white for every 2 whole eggs.

It is best to use a straight-sided soufflé baking dish in order to achieve the best form. Souffles will rise in an ungreased pan but will rise higher if the pan is greased. In addition, the crust on top will not stick to the edge if the pan is greased. Dust the greased sides and bottom of the soufflé dish with flour for non-dessert soufflés, and with sugar for dessert soufflés. To make a crown or high hat for the soufflé, take a spoon or spatula and form a shallow path or groove around the pan, about 1 inch from the edge, before placing the dish in the preheated oven. (see next page)

EGG TIPS FOR THE KITCHEN KLUTZ

- Always cook eggs at low to moderate temperatures because high heat toughens eggs and makes them curdle.
- Always crack the egg (yolk and white) into a bowl or cup before placing it in your pan. This way, if you break the yolk or get shell in the egg, you will be able to correct the problem easier.
- Do not use salted butter when cooking eggs because it can cause them to stick. Use unsalted butter, oil, or nonstick cooking spray instead.
- If possible, use eggs at room temperature. They will cook more evenly. You may set the eggs out on the counter 30 minutes before using or gently place them in a bowl of warm, not hot, water for 5 minutes.
- Do not eat raw eggs. There is a chance that bacteria and salmonella could be transmitted.
- The white membrane cord will not interfere with the taste of the egg. It can cause lumps in custards, sauces, or other cooked mixtures, however, so you may want to remove it.
- Egg substitutes may be purchased in the dairy and frozen food section of your grocery store. They are made primarily with egg whites and contain no cholesterol. Egg substitutes may be used in most recipes containing eggs. Read the container for serving size information. Dairy-case egg substitutes should be kept in the refrigerator until their expiration date or may be frozen for several months for longer storage; frozen egg substitutes must be used within seven days after defrosting.

While the soufflé is baking, do not open the oven door. To test if a soufflé is fully cooked, insert a silver knife into the center of the soufflé and remove it. The knife will be dry if the soufflé is well-done and moist if the soufflé is underdone. Serve the soufflé immediately in the dish in which you have baked it.

MILK

BUYING

There are many forms of milk available that are used in cooking. Be sure to pay attention to your recipe to use the correct type. **Buttermilk**, often used in breads and cakes because of the texture it imparts, is made from pasteurized skim milk that has a lactic acid bacteria culture added. It has a tangy taste and can be used in place of sour milk in a recipe. Many recipes call for **evaporated milk**, which gives a creamier taste to foods. It is whole milk with 60% of the water removed and Vitamin D added, then homogenized and canned. If buying evaporated milk, look for it on the shelf in a can—it does not come refrigerated. Most milk purchased today is **homogenized milk**, which has no film on top because the cream (fat) is spread throughout the milk by a mechanical process called homogenization. **Low-fat milk** (available as 1% or 2% milk) is a wonderful substitute for whole milk if you are concerned about fat content. It is whole milk with most or much of the cream (fat) removed. A small amount of cream is left in low-fat milk. **Powdered milk** is great to keep in your pantry in case you run out of milk. It is whole milk that has had the water removed. It usually comes in an airtight box and should be stored in a cool, dry place. To make milk from powdered milk, you add water. **Shelf-stable milk** is also great to keep in your pantry—it is sold in rectangular containers in skim, 1%, 2%, and whole milk varieties and can be kept for 6 months unopened. **Skim milk**, milk without the cream (fat) but still with vitamins and minerals, is wonderful to drink, or eat with cereal but is not as satisfactory when used in cooking because of its low fat content. Recipes without sugar often use **Sweetened condensed milk** in place of sugar. It is whole milk with a lot of the water removed and sugar added and comes canned and not refrigerated. **Whole milk** contains 4% butterfat and should be used in recipes that call for regular milk. Whole fresh milk straight from the cow has a cream line. A cream line is a line on top of the milk that contains the cream that rises to the top (like oil rises to the top of water).

STORING

Fresh milk is very perishable and should be refrigerated as soon as possible after purchasing. Always check the date on the container for storage life.

COOKING WITH MILK

Make sure you use the type of milk called for in your recipe. Also watch when cooking with milk to make sure it does not boil. It is better not to substitute a different milk than what is called for in a recipe unless you have no other choice. The one exception is that sour milk and buttermilk may be used interchangeably.

YOGURT

Yogurt is made from fermented milk and is rich in calcium, protein, and vitamins. It is available in nonfat or low-fat varieties as well as plain, strawberry, blueberry, lemon, and many other flavors. You can make your own flavored yogurt by adding chopped nuts, fruit, granola, spices, or extract flavorings to plain yogurt. Plain yogurt is often substituted for sour cream in recipes to reduce the fat content. Yogurt is also used in recipes for salad dressings, sauces, casseroles, and as a topping for fruit and baked potatoes. Be sure to store yogurt in the refrigerator and check the expiration date on the carton before purchasing.

MEATS

Although beef, chicken, lamb, turkey, and veal are all available in different cuts, don't let this overwhelm you. There are delicious ways to cook every type and cut of meat. Find a method of cooking that you prefer, as well as one that fits the cut of meat, and prepare it in that way. Meat is easy to prepare, if you follow the recipe. The only way you can go wrong is to overcook it or choose the incorrect method to cook that type of meat.

Chicken is easy and inexpensive to prepare and will become a favorite of the kitchen klutz because of this. It can be baked in Italian dressing or sprinkled with seasonings and baked, both of which produce delicious yet effortless chicken.

Lamb, which is widely available in the fall and early spring, adds variety to your meals and is relatively easy to prepare. Lamb chops are cooked just like pork chops and can always be served with mint or pepper jelly if you happen to overcook them.

Turkey, a long-time holiday favorite, is as easy to cook as chicken and may be substituted in any chicken recipe. The kitchen klutz will find instructions in this chapter for cooking a whole turkey and should not be afraid of this task.

Veal, which is baby beef, is more difficult to cook than other meats because it contains less fat and can dry out easily. However, don't let this keep you from making veal dishes—just follow the tips in this chapter.

Be daring and try varieties of meat that you normally don't purchase such as organ meats. They are rich in nutrients and you will be amazed how enjoyable they are.

BEEF

Beef contains all 21 amino acids and is a rich source of nutrients for your diet. On the average, beef is composed of 60% water, 18% protein, and 22% fat.

CUTS OF BEEF

There are many different cuts of beef, each with a different degree of tenderness determining the method of cooking. The **brisket** is a less tender cut from the breast and foreleg that is ideal for slow cooking or barbecuing. Brisket, which is used for **corned beef**, should always be marinated before cooking. **Chuck** is a less tender cut from the shoulder, neck, blade, or upper leg and is often used for pot roast, stew meat, braised steak, and hamburger. Like brisket, chuck needs to be slowly cooked. **Flank** is a less tender cut from the belly and is also best marinated before cooking. Flank is used for fajita meat, braised flank steak, and London broil. The **heel of round** is a less tender cut from the rear legs and is used for stew meat. The **loin end** is the most tender cut—it is from the front of the hips. The **filet of tenderloin** is the most choice and tender cut that is the long muscle that lies inside the rib bone. The thick end is used for filet mignon and tournedos, and the middle part is used for chateaubriand. The **neck** cut is less tender and is also used in stews. The **rib** is a tender cut from behind the shoulder along the backbone. Cuts from the rib include rib eyes, rib steaks, rib roasts (standing rib and rolled rib). The **round and rump** are less tender cuts from the rear and hind legs. Both are used for pot roasts and braised steaks. Round and rump cuts need slow cooking. Rump and round may be used for country-fried steak, Swiss steak, beef Stroganoff, chicken-fried steak, hamburgers, and stews. The **shank** cuts are from the front of the beef and are good for stews and beef stock. **Short loin** is a tender cut and is used for porterhouse, T-bone, and club steaks. The **tongue** is considered a delicacy.

The less tender cuts such as round and chuck are often ground to make hamburger meat. Ground round has the least amount of fat and ground chuck has the highest amount of fat. **Remember:** Less tender cuts should be cooked with a lid and tender cuts should be cooked uncovered.

BUYING

Meat is usually the most expensive item on your grocery list. Be aware of the different grades, brand names, inspection stamps, and its appearance when you are buying beef. Quality beef has a fine-grained marble texture. The marbling results from veins of fat running throughout the beef. The top grades are red with white fat, and the lower grades are deeper red with creamy yellow fat. Beef is classified and graded according to the quality of the cut. The different classifications are prime, choice, lean, standard, commercial, utility, cutter, and canner. **Prime** is the most tender, expensive, and highest quality. It is red and richly marbled with white streaks of fat and may be purchased from meat markets. **Choice** is the most common variety and is usually the highest grade found in a grocery store or supermarket. It is marbled with streaks of fat, is tender, and has good flavor. **Lean**, which has very little fat, is economy beef and is also called **good**. Lean is not as tender as prime or choice but is still good-quality beef. **Standard, commercial, utility, cutter,** and **canner** are lower grades that need long, slow cooking. Marinating always helps with the lower grades of beef.

An inspection mark, indicating wholesomeness, is stamped on the meat with a harmless vegetable dye after the meat is inspected by a veterinarian. You may want to trim off the stamp for appearance. The Federal Grade stamp indicates classification and is also harmless.

SERVING

Remember to consider the bone and fat loss when buying beef. Cuts with a lot of fat and bone yield less meat.

BEEF CUTS SERVING SIZES

Type of Beef	Amount to Purchase Per Serving
Beef round, with bone	1/4 pound
Ground beef	1/4 pound
Filet of beef, tenderloin	1/2 pound
Filet mignon, 1 inch thick	4–6 ounces
Lunch meats	1/4 pound
Chuck, rump, rib roasts	1/2 pound
Pot roast, boneless	1/4 pound
Pot roast, with bone	1/3 pound
Ribs	1 pound
Roasts, boneless	1/4 pound
Round steaks	1/2 pound
Steaks, without bone	6–8 ounces
Steaks, with bone	10–16 ounces
Stew meat	1/4 pound

STORING

Meat to be served within two days after buying may be kept in the meat compartment of the refrigerator, which is usually the coldest area of the refrigerator. Remove the store wrapper, and loosely rewrap meat with plastic wrap, plastic bags, or wax paper. Consult the following chart for refrigerator storage.

TYPE OF BEEF	REFRIGERATOR STORAGE
Rib roast	6–7 days
Pot roast	5–6 days
Corned beef	7 days
Stew meat	2 days
Steaks	3–5 days
Hamburger meat	2 days
Brains and kidney	1 day
Liver, heart, tongue	2 days
Smoked tongue	7 days
Cooked sweetbreads	2 days

*Storing Meat in the Freezer:*When freezing meat, never use the wrapping paper from the grocery store. If you freeze meat in the store wrapper, it will only keep 1 to 2 weeks. If will last much longer if you rewrap the meat in heavy foil or freezer paper (to keep the beef from drying out and to prevent freezer burn). Consult the following chart for freezer storage of most types of meats.

Meat	Freezer Life
Beef	6–12 months
Lamb	6–9 months
Veal	6–9 months
Pork	3–6 months
Ground beef, lamb and veal	3–4 months
Ground pork	1–3 months

Storing Cooked Meat: You may first cool the hot meat before refrigerating (no longer than 1 to 2 hours outside the refrigerator) or place it in the refrigerator while it is still hot. Neither way will affect the flavor. Store cooked meat in the coldest part of the refrigerator, and wrap or cover it. A cooked roast will keep for 4 to 5 days.

To freeze cooked meat, wrap the meat well in freezer paper or heavy foil. Frozen cooked meat will store for 2 to 3 months. Do not cut, grind, or slice cooked meat until ready to use.

Storing Processed Meat: Store processed meat (canned, cured, or ready-to-serve) in the meat compartment of the refrigerator. Luncheon meats will keep 1 to 2 weeks; however, always check the date on the wrapper to be safe. Unfortunately, freezing is not suitable for processed meats such as luncheon meats or canned hams because of their salt content.

Defrosting

Thaw meat in the freezer wrapper in the refrigerator, if possible. If not, you may defrost it in the kitchen sink or microwave. The method used for defrosting beef will not affect the flavor, juiciness, or tenderness of the meat. Never thaw beef in water, however, unless the meat is to be cooked in liquid. Always fully defrost before cooking. Once meat is defrosted, refrigerate it until you are ready to cook. The time for defrosting beef cuts varies—thin cuts of beef require less time to defrost than thick cuts. Remember, do not cook meat until it has *fully* thawed.

METHODS OF COOKING

All beef is muscle from the animal. If the muscle is used a lot, the meat will be less tender than meat from muscles used seldomly. Because cooking toughens beef, the tenderness of the meat determines the method of cooking. Dry-heat methods, such as pan-frying, pan-broiling, broiling, and roasting are most suitable for tender cuts. Moist-heat methods are most suitable for tough cuts of meat.

USING A MEAT THERMOMETER

A meat thermometer is a great purchase and will ensure that your meat is cooked to your liking. There are two types: a **regular** meat thermometer is inserted before cooking and left throughout the cooking process; an **instant** meat thermometer is inserted for a quick reading and left in a few seconds.

For the most accurate reading, insert the meat thermometer in the thickest part of the meat without touching any bone, fat, or the bottom of the pan. To test your thermometer for accuracy, place it in a pan of boiling water for 2 to 3 minutes. The temperature should read 212°F.

Broiling

Suitable cuts of beef for broiling are ground beef, steaks (club, T-bone, porterhouse, tenderloin, sirloin). All thin and tender cuts are also suitable.

Directions: Turn oven to "Broil" or 550°F., and preheat. If your meat is very lean, brush it lightly with vegetable oil to prevent it from drying out while cooking. Trim off any fat, if you prefer, or use scissors or a knife to make a cut every 2 inches in the fat. This will cause the steak to remain flat while it's cooking. Place meat in a pan (on a rack if you have one) and put it in the oven about 2 to 3 inches from the broiler (top burner) for a thin or 1-inch-thick cut, and 3 to 4 inches from the broiler for a thick or 1½-to-2-inch thick cut. If the beef is really thick, place it 6 inches from the broiler, and broil until the top side is brown. Remove the pan from the oven. Season the top side with salt, pepper, seasoning salt, and/or Worcestershire sauce, if desired, and turn the meat over. Place the pan back in the oven and brown the other side. To test for doneness, slice the meat near the bone. If meat is boneless, make a slice in the center of the cut. When the color inside meets with your taste, season as desired. **Note:** Tenderloin is so tender it is sometimes difficult to tell when it's done. Serve the meat quickly on a warm plate since broiled meat cools quickly. **Tip:** Place a slice of bread in the pan to absorb the grease and to prevent splatters.

BROILING TIME CHART

Cooking times given are approximate because ovens vary as do cuts of beef. The amount of fat and bone as well as the shape and size of the meat all contribute to cooking time variations.

Cooked	1 Inch Thick	2 Inch Thick	Meat Temperature
Very rare	3 minutes each side	9 minutes each side	130°F.
Rare	5 minutes each side	16 minutes each side	140°F.
Medium	6 minutes each side	18 minutes each side	160°F.
Well done	8 minutes each side	20 minutes each side	170°F.

Pan-broiling (or frying)

Suitable cuts of beef for pan-broiling include ground beef, steaks (Club, T-bone, minute, cube, porterhouse, tenderloin, sirloin). All thin and tender cuts are also suitable. Pan-broiling requires the same amount of time as broiling in an oven, so refer to the Broiling Time Chart for proper cooking times. Do not, however, pan-broil steaks that are more than 1 inch thick because they will not cook well. **Note:** Minute or cube steaks need only 2 to 3 minutes on each side.

Directions: Lightly grease the skillet with oil (vegetable) or butter. Heat over medium until hot. Next, place the meat in the skillet. Gradually brown, uncovered, over medium heat (approximately #5 on an electric stove). Once brown, lower heat, and continue cooking. Turn periodically to cook evenly. Skim fat as it accumulates. Cook until done, and season as desired.

Braising

Suitable cuts for braising are the less tender cuts of beef, such as brisket, shoulder and rump roasts, and short ribs. This method takes time if you want the meat to be tender.

Directions: Optional—First dredge or sprinkle beef with flour (**Tip:** Place flour in a bag, put in meat, close, and shake). Brown on both sides in a hot skillet in about 2 Tbsp. vegetable oil. Season to taste with salt, pepper, herbs, spices, and add vegetables to the skillet as desired. Add liquid (stock, water, bouillon, tomato juice) and cover. Alternately, you may place the meat in a covered pot and cook it in the oven at 350°F. until tender. Whether braising in the oven or on the stove, it can take 45 minutes to 3 hours, depending on the size of the cut. Cook at a low temperature (simmer) until tender.

Roasting

Any tender cuts of beef such as rolled rib roast, tenderloin, or standing rib roast are suitable for roasting. Roasting gives meat a wonderful flavor. The meat is basted with the flavors of its own fat while slowly cooked.

Directions: Season to taste. (Seasoning may be done during cooking as well.) The meat will only absorb the seasoning to a depth of 1/2 inch during roasting. If you want, you can make slits in the meat and insert slivers of garlic or other seasoning to get it deeper. Place the meat on a rack in a shallow pan, to keep the meat out of the juices. The bottom will brown faster without a rack because the rack allows the heat to circulate evenly around the meat. The meat should be positioned so that the fat is on top. The fat will baste the meat as it cooks. If the roast does not have any fat, apply a thin coat of oil to it. If you do not have a rack, use a row of carrots or canning jar lids to elevate the meat. Insert the meat thermometer so that is does not touch any bone or fat (omit this step if you have an instant-read meat thermometer). Place the roast in a preheated oven at 325°F., uncovered. If you wish to brown the roast before cooking, turn the oven up to 500°F. and place the meat in the oven for 15 minutes, then turn the oven down to 325°–350°F. and continue cooking. Roast the meat until done as desired (according to the Roasting Time Chart); also use a meat thermometer to determine doneness. The internal temperature of the roast will continue to rise for about 20 minutes after taking the roast out of the oven, so it is best to remove the roast from the oven when the meat thermometer is 5°F. from the desired final temperature. Let roast stand for a good 15 minutes before carving; it will retain the maximum amount of juice.

Tip: Roasting at the low temperature of 325°F. produces juicier meat and reduces the amount of shrinkage. Using a good heavy roasting pan also helps. You may make a few small gashes in the meat and insert pieces of garlic before you cook the roast if you like.

ROASTING TIME CHART

This chart assumes meat is at room temperature before cooking. The times are approximate because ovens vary, as do the shape, size, and fat content of the roasts.

Cooked	*Minutes per Pound*	*Meat Temperature*
Rare	22–26 minutes	140°F.
Medium	26–30 minutes	160°F.
Well Done	33–35 minutes	170°F.

Note: Add 10 minutes per pound for rolled roasts. Roasts with bone require less time because bones conduct heat.

Roasting Tenderloin

If you really want to impress your guests, purchase a beef tenderloin and roast according to the following easy instructions, which are different than regular roasting. For 4 to 6 pounds, roast at 450°F., brush with oil, butter, or bacon fat, and cook uncovered according to the following directions.

Rare	30 minutes
Medium	40–45 minutes
Well done	50–60 minutes

You may also roast tenderloin at 325°F.—22 minutes per pound for rare, 25 minutes per pound for medium-rare, 30 minutes per pound for well done.

Pot Roasting

Suitable cuts of beef for pot roasting are blade-bone chuck, or round-bone chuck, boned rump, and sirloin tips. Remember, with bone-in, allow 1/3 pound per serving, and with boneless, allow 1/4 pound per serving.

Directions: Place roast in a large pot with a small amount of oil (omit the oil if the meat has a lot of fat), brown on all sides either on top of the stove over medium heat (#7 on an electric stove) or in the oven at 450°F. without a lid. Turn the meat as it browns. Once roast has browned on all sides, add whole or sliced onions, garlic cloves, 1 tsp. salt, and 1/4 tsp. pepper, and put a lid on the pot, making sure it fits tightly. If you are adding vegetables, add them approximately 45 minutes before the roast is done. You may also add 1 to 3 Tbsp. water if it seems dry. Turn the oven to 350°F. and cook the roast according to the Pot-Roasting Time Chart.

Another quick and easy way to cook a pot roast or round steak is to place the roast on a large, heavy piece of aluminum foil. If you don't have heavy aluminum foil, double two pieces of regular foil. Sprinkle dried onion soup mix over the meat, wrap foil tightly so that no air is able to penetrate, and place meat in an uncovered pan. Roast in a preheated oven at 300°F. for 3 hours. After meat has cooked for 2 hours, you may add potatoes, carrots, and the like and continue cooking for another hour. Be careful when you open the aluminum foil—hot steam will be released, which can burn.

POT ROASTING APPROXIMATE TIME CHART

Size of Roast	Thickness	Roasting Time
3-pound, boned	2 inches thick	2½–3 hours
5-pound, boned	3 inches thick	3½–4 hours

GROUND BEEF

Ground beef has many uses and is easy to cook. It is used for hamburgers, spaghetti sauce, soups, and in many casseroles. There are at least four varieties that are graded according to their fat content: ground beef (30% fat), ground chuck (24%–30% fat), ground round (20%–24% fat), and ground sirloin (15% fat). When buying ground beef, look for meat with good color that is moist in appearance. Remember, the leaner the ground beef, the less moist your hamburger patty or dish will be. Ground beef is very perishable. Rewrap loosely and store in refrigerator for 1 to 2 days. If you will not be using it within 1 to 2 days of purchase, wrap well with freezer plastic, paper, or foil and freeze for up to 3 months. You may prepare the patties before freezing and separate each with a sheet of wax paper—they will thaw more quickly this way and you can remove patties as you need them. As previously mentioned, always thaw meat in the refrigerator whenever possible.

Hamburgers

To shape a hamburger patty, use your hands to form a ball with the hamburger meat. Lightly flatten the ball into a patty shape. You may also use a hamburger press, which may be purchased at a kitchenware store. Add meat to a lightly greased skillet (unless meat has a lot of fat—then use an ungreased skillet). Cook over medium heat. Turn patties occasionally. A thick patty should take 4 to 8 minutes and a thin patty should take 2 to 6 minutes, depending on how well you like yours cooked. For cheeseburgers, add the cheese 1 to 2 minutes before the patties finish cooking. To cook hamburger patties in an oven, preheat the oven on the "broil" setting. Place the meat patties on a rack in a shallow pan and place in the oven 3 inches from the broiler (top). Turn the patties over once while cooking. Cook for 8 to 12 minutes, or until done as desired. For cheeseburgers, add the cheese 1 to 2 minutes before the patties finish cooking. To cook hamburger patties on a grill, make sure the grill is hot, then place the meat on the grill and cook, turning occasionally. Season the meat when it is almost cooked. Add cheese, if desired, at the last minute. See "Grilling" for additional tips.

TIPS FOR COOKING HAMBURGERS

- When shaping hamburger patties, poke a hole in the center to help the meat cook more quickly. The hole will close during cooking. Also, frying a strip or two of bacon in the pan before cooking your patties will give the beef an extra delicious flavor. Don't pour the bacon grease out before cooking the beef.
- For a barbecued hamburger, brush with barbecue sauce halfway through the cooking.
- Do not overcook hamburger meat and never cook it on high heat. High heat will harden and dry out the meat.
- Do not use a spatula and press down on the meat unless you want to press out all of the juices and fat.
- Only salt and pepper meat when it is almost through cooking. Salt will draw the juices out.
- Try these great garnishes: salsa, bacon, chili, jalapeños, guacamole, sautéed onions, sliced mushrooms, and sliced bell peppers.
- Place a slice of uncooked bacon on the bottom of the pan to keep meatloaf from sticking.

Cooking ground beef for other dishes (such as spaghetti): Place beef in a skillet and use a spoon to "chop" the beef up. Cook over medium heat, stirring often. Make sure meat is thoroughly cooked. It should be brown, not pink or gray, when cooked. Drain the fat by placing the meat in a colander after the meat has cooked. To remove more fat after cooking, pour hot water over the meat to "wash" the fat off.

BEEF TIPS FOR THE KITCHEN KLUTZ

• To tenderize meat, soak it in any of the following or in a mixture of any of them: melted butter, soy sauce, salad oil, Worcestershire sauce, or a mixture of vinegar and olive oil. Meat will be tender, but drier, if a tenderizer is used.

• For a quick way to tenderize steak, cover with beer and refrigerate for several hours, drain, pat dry, and cook.

• Searing (or browning) meat first *does not* retain the juices more than any other method of cooking. Searing does, however, give the meat a distinctive flavor (the high temperature causes the juices to brown, which flavor the meat).

• Season beef with thyme, marjoram, basil, savory, or rosemary.

• The more fat (marbling) there is in beef, the juicier the beef will be. The fat melts during the cooking process and permeates the beef.

• If possible, use tongs when turning meat. This will prevent poking unnecessary holes in the meat and causing loss of juices.

• Do not wash meat—use a damp cloth or damp paper towel and wipe if necessary.

• If you buy a large cut of beef, such as a roast or saddle, you may want to try "aging" the beef in your refrigerator to improve the taste and texture, as well as tenderize the cut. After purchasing, unwrap and place on a broiling rack over some paper towels in your refrigerator. Leave uncovered in refrigerator for 3 to 4 days. Do not age fillets or tenderloin more than 1 to 2 days.

CHICKEN

Chicken is approximately 65% water, 30% protein, and 5% fat, which makes it one of the most healthful meat choices. There are six different classifications of chicken: broiler or fryer, capon, Cornish hen, poussin, roasting chicken, and stewing hens. They vary in size, weight, tenderness, and, consequently, methods by which they should be cooked.

Broilers or fryers are 9-to-12-week-old chickens. Their skin is soft and pliable and their meat is tender. They usually weigh 2 to 3⅓ pounds. Because they are tender, you can bake, broil, boil, fry, or barbecue and the meat will remain tender.

A **capon** is a young desexed male chicken weighing 4 to 7 pounds that has tender meat and great flavor. The capon has a high proportion of meat to bone and generally has more white meat than roasting chickens have. Capons are good for roasting.

A **Cornish hen** is produced from a Cornish gamecock and a Plymouth Rock Chicken. It has delicate meat that is all white. Each weighs about 1 to 1½ pounds.

A **poussin** is a 4-to-6-week-old chicken whose maximum weight is 1 pound. **Roasting chickens** are usually 3 to 5 months old. Their skin is soft and smooth-textured, while their meat is tender. Like their name implies, they are ideal for roasting. Roasting chickens usually weigh 4 to 6 pounds.

Stewing hens are mature hens that are usually large and have lots of fat and stringy meat. They are less tender than roasting chickens, so you will need to cook them with "moist-heat" methods (cover hen with water or liquid when cooking). Stewing hens are best used in soups, stews, and casseroles. Each hen weighs approximately 2¹/₂ to 5 pounds.

BUYING

Before buying chicken, know if you will need whole vs. cut-up, skin vs. skinless, bone vs. boneless, or white meat vs. dark meat. Buy chicken with moist and tender skin, plump bodies, and short legs. Avoid dry, hard, and bruised skin. Don't worry about skin color—it does not affect taste.

SERVING SIZES FOR CHICKEN

Purchase	Amount Per Serving
Broiler or fryer	¹/₂ pound
Capon	²/₃ to ³/₄ pound
Cornish hen	1 bird
Whole chicken with bone	³/₄ to 1 pound
Breast	¹/₂ breast
Drumsticks	2 drumsticks
Thighs	2 thighs

Note: 5 pounds of poultry will produce approximately 3 cups of cooked, diced meat.

STORING

Correct storage for chicken is crucial! Place the poultry in the refrigerator or freezer soon after buying. Remember, fresh chicken should not smell. If it does, rinse it with cold water; if it still smells, do not use it. Poultry should be loosely wrapped in wax paper or plastic wrap and stored in the coldest section of the refrigerator for up to 3 days. Fresh poultry will only last 1 to 3 days.

Frozen cut-up poultry can be stored in the freezer for up to 6 months, but do not remove it from the freezer until ready to thaw and use. Whole chickens may be frozen up to 1 year. Never freeze a chicken that has been stuffed.

Always thaw chicken in the refrigerator and allow at least 1 day to thaw a small bird. Thawing chicken at room temperature increases the chances of bacteria growing, which can cause food poisoning.

Never refreeze poultry! Leftover, cooked chicken should be refrigerated as soon as possible and will only last a few days. Whole birds usually come with a giblet package in the cavity of the bird. The giblets are the neck, liver, heart, and gizzard. Be sure to remove the giblets before storing!

STORAGE CHART FOR CHICKEN

Type of Chicken	Refrigerator Storage	Freezer Storage
Whole	uncooked—up to 3 days cooked—up to 2 days	uncooked—up to 1 year cooked—3 to 6 months
Cut-up (breast, leg, thigh, etc.)	uncooked—up to 2 days cooked—up to 2 days	uncooked—up to 6 months cooked—3 to 6 months
Giblets (neck, liver, heart, gizzard)	uncooked—12 hours cooked—up to 2 days	uncooked—up to 6 months cooked—3 to 6 months
Chicken cooked with liquid	up to 2 days	3 to 6 months
Chicken cooked without liquid	up to 2 days	3 to 6 months

To Thaw/Defrost Frozen Chicken

Thaw frozen chicken in the refrigerator, on the counter, or in a bowl covered with cold water. You will need to change the water periodically to keep it cold. To thaw frozen chicken in the microwave, use the defrost/low setting and microwave as follows.

Type of Chicken	Microwave Time
Chicken Breast, boneless	9–13 minutes per pound
Chicken pieces, boneless	4–8 minutes per pound
Cornish game hens	8–10 minutes per pound
Whole chickens	5–8 minutes per pound

Cutting and Boning a Chicken

Make sure the chicken is not frozen (should be tender when touched). You may use either kitchen scissors or a sharp knife to cut and bone a chicken.

To *cut up a whole chicken*: First, cut off the tail. Then, cut off one of the wings, where it is attached to the body. Set the wing aside. Cut off the other wing. Press legs downward and outward until the joints crack, and remove the legs. (The joints may have to be cut with a knife.) Cut around the backbone and pry the meat from the breast. Breasts may then be cut into pieces or boned.

To *bone chicken breasts*: Turn the chicken with the skin-side down and push against the ribs of the breast until the joints break. Push the meat away from the bones, until only attached at the top. Pull out the cartilage and the breast-bone, and carefully cut the meat away until reaching the wishbone. Remove the ribs and wishbone and fold the skin over the meat.

METHODS OF COOKING

Barbecuing

Place the chicken on a barbecue grate with the skin-side up, approximately 6 inches from the heat. Cook for 5 to 10 minutes first, then brush with barbecue sauce and slowly grill. Turn often, and continue to brush on barbecue sauce. Barbecuing should take 45 to 60 minutes, depending on the size of the chicken pieces.

Boiling

Place a 4½-to-5 pound fowl (whole or cut-up) in a pot, and cover with cold water from the faucet. Add a peeled onion, several pieces of celery, a peeled carrot, some parsley sprigs, and a dash of pepper. Bring the water to a boil, cover, and simmer over low heat for 1½ to 2½ hours, until the chicken is tender. Chicken is tender when you can pierce it with ease with a fork and no pink or red juice comes out. **Tip:** Let the chicken cool in the liquid for juicier and tastier chicken.

Broiling

Preheat oven on "Broil." Pour melted butter, cooking oil, lemon juice, or barbecue sauce over the chicken, and place it with the skin-side down on a lightly greased pan. You may season the chicken with fresh or dried herbs, salt, pepper, paprika, onion powder, garlic powder, seasoned salt, or whatever else you like. The pan should be placed in the oven as far away from the heat as possible. If you cannot place the chicken at least 7 inches from the broiler, lower the heat to 350°F. Broil each side for 15 to 20 minutes at either temperature. Be sure to brush the chicken with liquid when turning over. Larger pieces may need longer to cook. **Tip:** If you line the pan with aluminum foil, it will save you clean-up time.

Frying

Cut the chicken into pieces, wash, and dry. Dip the pieces in cold buttermilk, sweet milk, cream, or water. You may also dip in a mixture of 1 beaten egg and 2 tsp. water. Next, dredge the chicken in a mixture of 1 tsp. salt, ¼ tsp. pepper, and 1 cup flour. Add ½ inch of oil to the skillet and heat on medium-high. Test to see if the skillet is hot enough by adding a small drop of water to the oil in the skillet—if it sizzles, the skillet and oil are ready. Add chicken with skin-side down and brown on both sides over moderate heat. Reduce the heat to low, and cook covered for 10 to 20 minutes on each side. Uncover the pan during the last 10 minutes to make the chicken crispy. Remove the chicken pieces and drain on paper towels. To keep chicken hot, place it in a covered pan with a few drops of water and keep in a 350°F. oven. Remember to allow ⅔ to ¾ pound or 2 pieces per serving.

TIPS FOR FRYING CHICKEN

- Cook the meaty parts (thigh, legs, breast) first, and cover with a lid for 15 minutes. Uncover, turn, and finish cooking.
- Cook the wings, backs, and gizzards uncovered on low heat.
- Place the flour-coated chicken in the refrigerator for 1 hour before cooking for better adhering.

Note: Be careful! Oil will splatter when you place the chicken in the frying pan. If the oil catches on fire, dump a bag of flour, sugar, or baking soda in the frying pan to smother the fire (do not use water!).

Poaching

Heat seasoned water/broth to a low simmer, measuring enough liquid to cover the entire bird. Add the chicken, cover, and cook until tender. Do not boil or the chicken can easily overcook.

Roasting

Preheat oven to 325°F. to 350°F. Place the chicken (on a rack if possible) in a shallow pan with the breast-side up. Brush with melted butter, margarine, or vegetable oil on the top and sides. Place the pan in the oven. (**Note:** Stuffing should not be added until you are ready to roast the bird. Loosely place the stuffing in the bird; never pack stuffing in because it will expand during the cooking process.) While the chicken is cooking, do not add water, do not turn the chicken, and do not cover the pan. To keep it from drying out, you may baste (coat the chicken) with drippings from the pan. Generally roasting time should be figured at 20 minutes per pound if stuffed, 15 minutes per pound if unstuffed. Begin testing for doneness during the last 15 minutes of cooking. Slice into the bird between the leg and the body to see if the juices run clear. Any sign of pink juice in the bird means it needs to cook longer. If possible, use a meat thermometer. The meat thermometer should read 170°F. for breast meat and 185°F. for thigh meat.

Sautéing

Heat about 4 Tbsp. butter, oil, or bacon grease in a large skillet over medium heat. Add the chicken pieces. You may lightly dust the chicken with flour, cornmeal, and salt and pepper, if you like. Brown the chicken on all sides over medium heat, uncovered. Turn the heat down to low and add any seasonings you like, such as garlic, onion, salt, pepper, curry powder, basil, or chives, and any vegetables, such as carrots, broccoli, celery, or snow peas. Place a lid on the skillet and cook the meat slowly, until tender. Chicken normally takes 35 to 45 minutes to sauté, depending on the size of the pieces. Be sure to turn the pieces occasionally while they cook. If you would like your chicken crisp, uncover for the last 10 minutes of cooking.

Smothering

Brown the chicken first, then smother the chicken in any sauce you like (*see* "Sauces"). Cover and bake at 350°F. for 1 hour.

Cooking Giblets

Giblets are the neck, heart, liver, and gizzard of a bird. They are very tasty, contrary to popular belief. These may be used to make gravy or eaten alone. After cooking giblets, they may be stored up to 2 days in the refrigerator. To cook giblets, thoroughly rinse them with cool water. Trim off any visible fat, if you desire. Place the gizzard, heart, and neck in a saucepan. You may add any of the following to the pan: a sliced, small onion or a whole, small onion (peeled first), 1/3 bay leaf, 1 carrot (peeled first and cut in half), 1/4 cup chopped green pepper, or 1 tsp. thyme. Cover with 4 to 6 cups water and add 1/2 tsp. salt. Place a lid on the pan and simmer over low heat until you can pierce the giblets easily with a fork. Giblets will be tender when done. The simmering process should take between 30 minutes and 2 hours, depending on the size of the chicken.

If you wish to use the liver, add it during the last 15 to 30 minutes of the cooking process since the liver has a very strong flavor and can overwhelm the other giblets. You may also cook the liver separately (see next page).

CHICKEN TIPS FOR THE KITCHEN KLUTZ

- For easier skinning, skin chicken when it's slightly frozen.
- Stick a fork into your cooked chicken to see if it is tender and ready. Clear, not red juice, should come out if the chicken is cooked thoroughly.
- If cut into pieces, white meat cooks more quickly than dark meat.
- For an easy chicken seasoning, mix together 2 Tbsp. parsley flakes, 1 Tbsp. oregano, 1 Tbsp. marjoram, 1 Tbsp. thyme, 1 Tbsp. rosemary, 1 Tbsp. ground ginger, 1 Tbsp. celery salt, 1 tsp. sage, and 1 tsp. white pepper. This recipe will make 1/3 cup and should be stored in an airtight container.
- Soak chicken in buttermilk for several hours before you cook.
- Add 1 tsp. lemon juice or a pinch of baking soda when boiling to make the chicken tender.
- Use dental floss to truss the bird. It's very strong and doesn't burn. Also, be sure to use unwaxed floss because the wax will melt.
- Remove the white tendon running lengthwise in chicken breasts to reduce shrinkage during cooking.
- Use tongs to turn chicken so you won't lose the juices from the bird.
- If you overcook boneless breasts, add a splash of wine, water, or chicken broth and simmer until tender.
- For tender boneless breasts, cook very quickly or long and slowly.

After cooking the giblets, save the broth and remove the giblets. You may use the broth for the liquid in a gravy recipe and add the giblets to it, cut up, if you prefer. If you are not going to use the broth and giblets immediately, you may refrigerate them for up to 2 days.

To sauté chicken livers: Rinse them well with cool water, then cut in half. Place 2 to 3 Tbsp. butter or margarine in a heavy skillet over medium heat. Add the chicken livers and sauté until they are brown on all sides. Remove them from the skillet and season with salt and pepper. You may serve them on toast or with rice or any other way you prefer.

GAME

If you are lucky enough to have a friend or family member who hunts and will give you game, accept it happily and don't worry about how you will fare. Game is easy to prepare and cook and the final result is very gratifying. Game refers to wild animals used for food. Game are different than domesticated animals: wild animals tend to be leaner, and their muscles are stronger, which means that game usually need to be marinated or tenderized. In addition, game should never be overcooked since it will toughen too much. Game tends to have dark meat for the breast as well as the thigh and leg, because game use their wings to fly more than domesticated chickens and turkeys do. Marinate with buttermilk, wine, olive oil, or brandy. Wash game well inside and out with cold water and dry thoroughly. For better flavor and more tenderness, age by hanging in a cold place, or placing in the refrigerator with the fur and feathers still attached, before preparing to cook. Consult the following chart for aging times.

Game	*Age for*
Dove	5 to 10 days
Duck	2 to 3 days
Pheasant	5 to 10 days
Quail	3 to 8 days
Turkey	2 to 8 days
Venison (deer, elk, moose)	2 to 3 weeks

SERVING SIZES FOR GAME

Game	*Per Serving*
Duck, with bone	1 pound
Geese, with bone	1 1/2 pounds
Grouse (partridge)	1 bird
Guinea hen/squab	3/4 to 1 pound
Pheasant, with bone	1 pound
Quail (Bobwhite)	1 bird
Squab	3/4 to 1 pound

Game	Per Serving
Rabbit	1/2 large rabbit
Squirrels	1 large squirrel
Squirrel stew	2 or 3 squirrels for 6 servings
Venison (deer, elk, moose):	
Ground—for stew, soup, chili	1/2 pound
Liver	2 slices
Loin Chops	1 chop
Roast	3/4 pound
Ribs	1 1/2 pounds
Rump—for pot roast	1/2 pound
Shoulder—for pot roast	1/2 pound
Shoulder—grilled	1 pound
Steaks	1 steak

Removing Feathers from Fowl

"Wet picking" (while bird is wet) is the most effective method for retaining the appearance and flavor. The bird should be dipped in water heated according to the following specifications.

Duck	Heat water to 150°–160°F.
Goose	Heat water to 130°F.
Pheasant	Heat water to 130°F.
Quail	Heat water to 130°F.

Dip the bird up and down until the tail and wing feathers can be pulled out easily. Before pulling out the feathers, wrap the bird in cloth, and let it steam for 2 minutes, then pull the feathers out. To remove pinfeathers, singe first and use tweezers to pull out the feathers.

DUCK

Wild duck is very lean, so cook it carefully. Domesticated duck is usually very tender. Duck meat is usually all dark. Thaw frozen duck in the refrigerator. A duck raised to be eaten will take 24 to 36 hours to thaw, depending on size.

To cook wild duck, preheat the oven to 500°F. Clean the duck well and pat dry with a dish towel. Sprinkle inside and out with salt. Place a peeled raw apple, celery, and onion inside. Cover the outside breast with strips of uncooked bacon and place the bird in a shallow pan. Place the duck in the oven, uncovered, and bake at 500°F. for 30 minutes. Reduce the heat to 350°F. and bake for another 30 minutes. Add 1/4 cup red wine per duck to the pan and bake at 350°F. for 15 minutes more. **Note:** Sprigs and teal ducks cook more quickly than mallards and probably will not take the full 1 hour 15 minutes to cook, so check for doneness sooner when cooking these types. After the duck is done, remove the apple and onion and serve with lots of wild rice.

To glaze baked duck, you may brush with a mixture of one of the following during the last few minutes of baking: melted currant jelly and orange juice mixed together or wild plum jelly (melt the glaze in a heavy saucepan on low heat).

To roast wild duck, preheat the oven to 425°F. Clean the bird well and rub with lemon juice, inside and out. Place on a wire rack in a shallow pan in the oven and roast for 10 minutes per pound of duck. While roasting, baste frequently with melted butter. When done, take 1 cup juice from the pan, add 1/2 tsp. flour, 1 Tbsp. wine vinegar, 2 tsp. brown sugar, 1/4 cup orange juice, and 1 tsp. grated orange rind, and heat over low heat. Pour over duck and serve. If the duck becomes brown too fast, lower the temperature to 375° or 350°F. Note: large ducks should bake at 350°F for 1 1/2 hours or until done.

To roast duck in a browning bag, purchase a disposable browning bag at the grocery store. Preheat the oven to 350°F. Clean the bird well, place 1 cup of sliced apples and 1 cup of sliced celery in its cavity; and place it in the browning bag. Sprinkle 2 to 3 Tbsp. flour in the bag according to the directions on the bag, make a few slits in the top of the bag with a knife, add 1/2 cup melted butter, 1/2 cup frozen orange juice concentrate, and 1 cup chicken broth, tie the bag with the enclosed tie, and cook for 1 1/2 hours. Roast until tender and juicy—the leg meat should feel soft and the leg joint should move easily and be loose.

To roast domesticated duck, preheat the oven to 325°F. Prick the skin around the tail area with a fork so that the fat will drain out while roasting. Place the duck on a wire rack in a shallow pan, sprinkle with salt and pepper, and bake uncovered for 1 to 2 hours, depending on size. You may pour out fat that will drain into pan as the duck roasts or use a basting bulb to suction it out. Baste with hot water or olive oil several times while roasting. After the duck has cooled some, baste with juices in the pan. Roast until tender and juicy.

To glaze roasted duck, brush with a mixture of currant jelly and orange juice during the last few minutes of roasting. Melt the glaze first in a saucepan over low heat.

For stuffed duck, serve with a mixture of chopped carrots, onion, and celery sautéed in butter. **Note:** The vegetables will absorb the wild duck's flavor.

To make gravy, place 2 Tbsp. of pan drippings in a heavy saucepan over low heat with 2 Tbsp. flour. Brown slowly, remove from heat, and slowly add 1 cup hot water. Place back on the stove and cook until mixture is bubbly, then cook 1 minute or until thick. Season as desired.

GEESE

Geese are best served roasted. A 6-to-8-pound bird will take 3 to 3 1/2 hours at 325°F. A 10-to-12-pound bird will take 3 3/4 to 4 1/4 hours at 325°F. Add 5 to 10 minutes per pound for well-done goose.

Cook goose the same way as wild duck. Thoroughly wash inside and out in cold water. If the bird is really fat, add 1 tsp. baking soda to a pot of cold water and wash bird well in this solution. Then rinse the bird with clean cold water before cooking. Be careful! Geese are full of bones. Fresh meat can be removed from the bones and cooked in a roasting pan with a lid. Season cooked goose with onion, garlic, bell pepper, parsley, salt, pepper, butter, or red wine. Slice and serve with gravy. Apples can be added as well.

GUINEA HEN

Prepare these delicate and tender game birds as you would chicken, but keep in mind that guinea hens are drier than chicken. After cleaning, a guinea hen usually weighs 1½ to 2¼ pounds. One hen will usually produce 2 servings. Guinea hen is good braised, roasted, or fried. To roast, roast a 2½-pound hen at 425°F. for 30 minutes, then at 350°F. for 30 minutes per pound.

PHEASANT

Prepare as you would a chicken. Pheasant is delicious baked in cream!

QUAIL (BOBWHITE) AND GROUSE (PARTRIDGE)

Quail and grouse are the most delicate of all game and are usually small and tender. On average, 1 bird will produce 2 servings. Quail and grouse are mostly breast meat and are delicious roasted.

To pan-broil quail or grouse, split the bird in half and pan-broil uncovered, breast-side down, in a generous amount of butter or margarine. Baste frequently with liquid and a mixture of chopped onion, mushrooms, butter, and parsley. Quail or grouse are also good wrapped in bacon and baked at 350°F. for 30 minutes.

To cook quail or grouse in a roasting bag, mix 1½ Tbsp. flour and ½ cup wine and place in a bag with 1 cup chopped celery, 1½ cups sliced mushrooms, ½ cup chopped onions, 1 Tbsp. butter, and 1 Tbsp. fresh parsley. Place quail in the bag, make a few slits in the top of the bag, and close the bag with the enclosed tie. Place in a shallow pan and bake in a preheated 350°F. oven for 1 hour. The gravy in the bag may be served with the quail.

To broil quail or grouse, preheat the oven on the "broil" setting. Rub butter or margarine on the thoroughly cleaned bird, and sprinkle it lightly with salt and pepper. Place the bird with the skin-side up in a broiler pan or on a wire rack in a shallow pan. Broil for 11 minutes, turning the bird over after 6 minutes of broiling.

RABBIT AND SQUIRREL

Rabbit and squirrel are best in fall and early winter. American domesticated rabbit has mainly white meat that is mildly flavored; European rabbit is dark meat. To prepare for cooking: Remove the skin, intestines, and organs as quickly as possible. Clean inside and out thoroughly with cold water. Soak in a mixture of salt water, vinegar, and water or another marinade for several hours or overnight. **Note:** Rabbits have scent glands that must be removed before cooking. The glands are located on either side of the spine, under the forelegs, between the shoulders and in the back. Be careful not to cut the glands when removing. Cook rabbit and squirrel like chicken. They are both good grilled, fried, barbecued, baked, and in stew. The flesh is lean, so use extra fat during cooking. Young animals should be roasted or fried, older animals are better braised.

SQUAB

Squab are young pigeons that usually weigh about 1 pound each. Allow 1 squab per serving. Squab should be cooked like chicken and are delicious braised, roasted, broiled, or sautéed. To sauté, split squab in half and season with salt and pepper. In a skillet of hot butter, sauté until golden-brown on both sides—this should take 20 to 30 minutes.

VENISON (DEER, ELK, MOOSE)

Age meat at 38°F. accordingly: a young animal, which is more tender, should age for 1 week; an old animal, which is tougher, should age for 2 to 3 weeks. Before cooking, thoroughly clean. Refrigerate up to 2 to 3 days before cooking. A good tenderizer for meat from an older animal is buttermilk or plain milk. Older animals will need to be marinated to make the meat moist. A good and simple marinade is a bottle of Italian dressing. Soak the meat in the marinade for at least 24 hours before cooking. Marinating will not remove the gamey flavor. The fat produces a gamey flavor and should be cut off before cooking; use salt pork or beef suet for cooking instead. **Note:** Suet is another word for fat; you can usually get some from the butcher.

Don't overcook venison because it will dry out easily. Moose is relatively fat, so it should be cooked like pork. Elk and venison are leaner and should be cooked like tender cuts of beef. To pan-fry steaks, sprinkle salt or seasoned salt

---

QUICK AND EASY SAUCES TO SERVE WITH GAME

- Melt ¹/₂ cup currant jelly with 1 cup orange juice and 1 Tbsp. regular prepared mustard or Dijon mustard.
- Melt ¹/₂ cup currant jelly, then add ¹/₂ cup ketchup and ¹/₂ cup sherry.
- Melt ¹/₂ cup currant jelly, ¹/₄ tsp. Worcestershire sauce, 2 Tbsp. butter, and 4 Tbsp. undiluted frozen orange juice concentrate.
- Mix ¹/₄ cup French dressing, 2 Tbsp. orange juice, 2 tsp. dried onion soup mix, and 4 Tbsp. apricot preserves. Place in a saucepan and heat for a few minutes on low.

and pepper or lemon pepper on both sides of the steak. Place 1 to 2 Tbsp. butter, vegetable oil, or bacon grease in a skillet and melt over low heat. Add the steaks and cook for 1 to 2 minutes on each side. The meat will stick easily, so you may need to add more butter or oil while cooking.

Venison can be served rare, medium, or well done. It may be prepared like country-fried steak, barbecued, or roasted—just like beef.

LAMB

While lamb is available all year, it is most plentiful in the spring. Lamb, the tender meat from a sheep that is less than a year old, has a fine flavor and is tender and juicy. It is easy to fix and is great to serve company. The USDA grades are prime, good, cull, choice, and utility, with prime being the choicest cut and utility the least. The age of the lamb determines the type.

Type of Lamb	Age	Color of Meat
Milk-fed/baby	6–8 weeks old	pink meat
Spring	3–5 months old	red meat
Mutton	1 year old	dark red meat

Tip: The more the leg weighs, the older the lamb. The older the lamb, the stronger the taste.

BUYING

When buying lamb, look for pink to dark red color and fine-grained, smooth meat. Remember—the older the lamb, the darker the meat, the stronger the taste, and the larger and whiter the bones. Purchase thick, bone-in lamb chops. Types of chops include:

Rib chop—smaller than a loin chop; has a tender portion
English chop—from unsplit ribs (usually boneless)
Shoulder chop—has small, round bone
Shoulder bladebone chop—less tender; contains a lot of bone
Sirloin chop—large, meaty
Centercut loin chop—has T-shaped bone; tender and meaty; usually most expensive

Other cuts of lamb are leg riblets, strips of breast meat that are about 1 inch thick and connected to a rib bone, leg steaks, leg of lamb, crown roast, rolled shoulder, and rolled breast.

SERVING SIZES FOR LAMB

Type of Lamb	Amount per Serving
Lamb, with bone	1/2 to 3/4 pound
Lamb, without bone	1/3 to 1/2 pound
Leg of lamb	1 pound
Leg steak	1/3 to 1/2 pound
Chops	1/2 to 3/4 pound

STORING

Remove lamb from the store wrapper, wrap tightly in clean plastic wrap, and place in the meat compartment of the refrigerator. Lamb may be stored this way for up to 3 days. Ground lamb or stew meat purchased from the store must be cooked within 1 day of purchasing or may be frozen for up to 3 months. Other cuts of lamb may be frozen for up to 5 months.

METHODS OF COOKING

Lamb comes covered with a "fell," which is a paperlike covering. Beneath the fell is a layer of fat that ranges in color from clear white (younger) to yellow (older), depending on the age of the lamb. The fell may be left on for a stronger lamb taste, or removed for a milder one. Although many do not enjoy the "lamby" taste produced by the fell, leaving it on during cooking will help retain the juices and thus produce juicier meat. If cooking mutton, always remove the fell because mutton has such a strong taste. Removing the fell also makes carving easier.

Below is a helpful chart for determining how to cook each cut of lamb. You may pan-broil wherever it calls for broiling. Pan-broiling cooks the lamb in half the time of broiling. Remember to skim off the fat as you cook the meat. Frozen lamb chops will take twice as long to cook as fresh, so it is best to thaw them first in the refrigerator.

ROASTING TIME CHART

Desired Doneness	Meat Thermometer Reading
Rare	140°F.
Medium Rare	145°F.
Medium	160°F.
Well Done	170°F.

Here are some guidelines for cooking various cuts of lamb.

SUGGESTED METHODS FOR COOKING

Cut of Lamb	Method of Cooking
Leg chop, blade chop, Saratoga chop	Broil, pan-fry, braise
Shoulder, crown roast	Roast
Rib chops, patties	Broil, pan-fry
Riblets, neck slices	Braise, cook in liquid
Leg of lamb	Broil, pan-fry, roast, braise
Loin chop, English chop	Broil, pan-fry
Shanks	Braise, cook in liquid
Rolled shoulder, rolled breast	Braise, roast

Roasting

Suitable for the shoulder, crown roast, leg of lamb, rolled shoulder, rolled breast. The best lamb cuts to roast are the crown roast and the leg of lamb. Preheat the oven to 325°F. Remove the fell if you desire. Brown the meat in a small amount of melted fat that has been trimmed from the lamb. Place the meat in a shallow pan and bake uncovered at 325°F. for 30 minutes per pound, or until done to your taste. Turn the meat over halfway through baking. Let the roast stand 10 to 15 minutes after it's cooked to desired doneness before carving.

To Roast a Breast of Lamb: Preheat the oven to 400°F. Sprinkle the meat with seasonings of choice. Place the meat on a rack in a shallow pan or in a broiler pan with the ribs facing down. Roast for 20 minutes uncovered. Reduce the heat to 300°F. and cook for another 1½ hours, or until the meat is done as desired.

Broiling

Suitable for lamb chops and patties. Preheat the oven on the "Broil" setting. Place the meat on a rack in a shallow pan or in a broiling pan. Place pan uncovered in the oven 3 inches from the broiler. (Remember, the top of the food, not the pan, should be 3 inches from the broiler.) Turn meat over halfway through cooking and broil as follows:

BROILING TIME CHART

Cut of Lamb	Thickness	Medium	Well Done
English Chop	2 inches thick	24 minutes	30 minutes
Leg Steaks	1 inch thick	14 minutes	16 minutes
Loin	1 inch thick	12 minutes	14 minutes
Loin	1½ inches thick	18 minutes	22 minutes
Rib	1 inch thick	12 minutes	14 minutes
Rib	1½ inches thick	18 minutes	22 minutes
Shoulder	1 inch thick	14 minutes	16 minutes
Sirloin	1 inch thick	12 minutes	14 minutes

Pan-Broiling

Suitable for chops and patties. Cut some of the fat off the chops and place it in a skillet over medium heat. When the fat has melted some, add the chops and brown on both sides. Reduce the heat to low and cook the chops uncovered until done, turning occasionally. If using a meat thermometer to test doneness, the temperature at the center should read 140°F. for rare, 145°F. for medium rare, 160°F. for medium, and 170°F. for well done.

Roasting Mutton

Preheat the oven to 350°F. Remove the fell. Sprinkle the lamb with garlic powder or rosemary, or make slits in the meat and insert slivers or cloves of garlic. Brown the meat in a lightly greased skillet over medium heat. Once brown, remove the meat from the skillet and place it on a rack in a heavy pot. Add 1 cup water and 1 Tbsp. vinegar. Cover and cook until done, or about 30 minutes per pound. If more liquid is needed during roasting, you may add more hot water, tomato juice, or barbecue sauce.

You may also cook the mutton on top of the stove instead of roasting it in the oven. After browning, cover with 4 cups of water and simmer in a heavy pot for 30–40 minutes per pound. Mutton comes in chops that may be broiled or pan-fried. Tougher cuts, such as mutton leg and shoulder, should be slowly roasted in a covered pot in the oven.

LAMB TIPS FOR THE KITCHEN KLUTZ

- Lamb is best served hot or cold, not lukewarm.
- Lamb cuts with a bone will have more flavor than cuts without bone.
- Slice the fat on lamb every ½ inch to prevent meat from curling while cooking.
- Before cooking, rub lamb chops with olive oil or vegetable oil. Make tiny slits in the meat and insert slivers or cloves of garlic for extra flavor.
- Lamb may be aged to enhance the flavor and texture. If you buy a large cut of lamb, unwrap it and place it in your refrigerator on a broiling rack over some paper towels. Leave it in the refrigerator for 3 to 4 days in order to let it age. This will help tenderize the meat as well as improve the taste and texture. Be sure to leave the fell on until you are ready to prepare the meat for cooking.
- Season lamb with rosemary, savory, mint, or dill.

PORK

Pork, available year round, is tender and juicy and thus an ideal meat to cook. It has a distinctive flavor and comes in many forms—hams, sausage, bacon, pork chops, and spareribs, among them. There are many ways to prepare pork. The only thing you must remember about pork is to cook it thoroughly. The juice from well-cooked pork will be clear.

Buying

Always select pork with the least amount of visible fat, because even lean pork has some fat. Fresh pork should range in color from whitish pink to pink (pork fat is white in color and is firm). Lean and young pork is fine-grained, firm and pinkish-gray in color; pork from older animals will be a dark rose. Ready-to-eat pork is pork that is safe to eat without further cooking, although you may still heat it for further tenderizing. Tenderized pork is meat that has been prepared, not cooked, with a certain type of flavoring. Loin chops are considered to be the choicest cut of pork and are fine-grained, firm, and tender.

When buying ham, the cured and smoked legs of pork, make sure it has been stamped with the round U.S. inspection stamp to ensure that the meat has been prepared correctly; if incorrectly prepared, it can make you sick. Fully cooked, boned, and center cuts of ham are more expensive.

Sausage is a combination of ground pork, fat, and seasonings. It is available in links and patties. Other types of sausages that have been dried and seasoned are: salami, bologna, pepperoni, and hot dogs. Hot dogs, also called frankfurters and wieners, can be either all-beef or a blend of meat that includes pork and fat. Since most people consider hot dogs pork and their preparation doesn't vary, they're included in this chapter.

SERVING SIZES FOR PORK

Type	Amount per Serving
Boneless (strips, cubes, cutlets)	1/4 pound
Chops	3/4 pound or 1 chop
Spareribs	3/4–1 pound
Tenderloin	1/3 pound
Ham:	
uncooked, with bone	1/2 pound
uncooked, boneless	1/3 pound
cooked, with bone	1/3 pound
cooked, boneless	1/4 pound
Roast, with bone	1/3–1/2 pound
Roast, without bone	1/4–1/2 pound

STORING

Remove the store wrapping from pork, and rewrap tightly with clean plastic. Pork may be stored in the refrigerator according to the following recommendations.

PORK REFRIGERATOR STORAGE CHART

Type	Length of Time
Fresh pork	
Chops	2–3 days
Roasts	5–6 days
Sausage	2–3 days
Spareribs	3 days
Cured pork	
Bacon	6–7 days (or date on package)
Ham	1–2 weeks
Half	7 days
Whole	2 weeks
Picnic	2 weeks
Sliced	3–5 days (or date on package)
Sausage	
Smoked	2 weeks unopened or 1 week opened
Dried (pepperoni)	3 weeks

To store pork in the freezer, wrap it well with freezer paper, plastic, or foil and store according to the following recomendations.

PORK FREEZER STORAGE CHART

Type	Length of Time
Bacon	1 month
Ground pork	1–3 months
Ham, ham slices	2 months
Hot dogs	1 month
Sausage	2 months

METHODS OF COOKING

COOK PORK WELL! The internal temperature should register at a minimum of 160°F. (71°C.) on your meat thermometer. Remember to place the meat thermometer in the center of the cut so that it is not touching bone. When the pork is done, the meat will be grayish-white in color and the juice will run clear.

SUGGESTED METHODS FOR COOKING PORK

Cuts of Pork	Suggested Method of Cooking
Bacon	Broiling, baking, pan-broiling
Fatback (Salt Pork)	Flavoring with other foods
Feet	Boiling, frying, stewing, pickling
Hams (leg), fresh	Roasting, broiling
Smoked cuts	Boiling, baking, broiling (slices)
Loin chops, roasts	Roasting
Shoulder, fresh (also called Boston butt)	Roasting
Smoked	Boiling, baking, broiling
Spareribs	Boiling, baking
Tenderloin	Baking, braising, breading, broiling, pan-broiling

An easy way to determine the method of cooking is by the cut. Refer to the following chart for suggestions.

Cut/Shape	Suggested Method/Use
Chops—thin	Grilling, sautéing, frying, pan-broiling
Chops—thick	Baking
Strips	Stir-frying; use in salads or sandwiches
Cubes	Grilling; use in kebabs or stews
Roast—loin	Roasting
Roast—shoulder, leg	Braising
Cutlets	Frying, braising, sautéing
Ribs	Grilling, baking

LOINS, RIBS, AND SHOULDERS

Braising

Trim off excess fat, and lightly grease a hot skillet with the fat. Slowly brown chops on both sides (approximately 3 minutes on each side on medium heat). Next, if the chops are thick, add 1/4 cup water and cover tightly. If chops are thin, cover tightly but do not add water. You may either cook the chops on top of the stove on medium heat or in the oven at 350°F. Cook slowly until well done according to the following recommendations.

BRAISING TIME CHART

Cut	Thickness	Braising Time
Loin, ribs	1 inch	30–35 minutes per pound
Loin, ribs	1/2 inch	20 minutes per pound
Shoulder	1/2 inch	20 minutes per pound

71

Roasting: Preheat oven to 350°F. Wipe the pork with a wet cloth, then place on a rack in a shallow pan with the fat side facing up. For a crown roast, place in the pan with the bone end facing up. If you choose, rub the surface with salt, pepper, and spices. Grab your thermometer, and, in a crown roast, place it in the middle of a chop. Otherwise, roast it in the oven uncovered until the meat thermometer reads 185°F., or until the meat is no longer pink near the bone or the center of the meat. Do not add any liquid or baste or turn during cooking. When through cooking, remove the roast from the oven and let it sit a few minutes before slicing. **Tip**: When cooking a crown roast, cover the bone ends with foil to prevent them from burning).

Cooking a Pork Tenderloin: Preheat the oven to "Broil." (If you choose, you may marinate the pork tenderloin first.) Place strips of bacon or suet (fat purchased from the butcher) on top of the meat, and place the meat in a broiler pan or on a rack in a shallow pan in the oven 4 inches from the broiling element. Broil until the meat thermometer reads 185°F., or until the juice is clear and the meat is no longer pink near the center. It should take 6 to 8 minutes for each 3/4 pound. Depending on the size of the meat, you should bake a pork tenderloin at 350°F. for 30 to 55 minutes. Pork tenderloin is also excellent cooked on an outdoor grill.

Braising or Baking Pork Chops or Steaks: Cut fat off with kitchen scissors or a knife. Season, if desired, with salt, pepper, or seasoned salt. Place trimmed-off fat in a skillet and cook over low heat until melted. Push any extra to the side of the skillet or remove it. Brown the meat in the hot fat on both sides. For a 1-inch-thick piece of meat, browning will take 15 to 20 minutes. For thinner meat, it will take 5 to 10 minutes. Occasionally drain or spoon off any excess fat as the meat cooks. After the meat is brown on both sides, cover the skillet and cook over low heat, turning the meat occasionally until it is done as desired. If you need to add liquid, you may add a small amount (1/3 cup) of water, fruit juice (such as orange juice or tomato juice), or barbecue sauce. You may also add onions, garlic, or any other seasonings you like. After browning, it will take at least 30 to 45 minutes for a 1-inch-thick piece to cook thoroughly. When done, remove the pork from the skillet and serve.

Note: broiling pork chops is not a suitable way to cook them because it will make them dry and hard.

Roasting Spareribs: Preheat oven to 350°F. Place meat on a rack in a shallow pan. Season with salt, pepper, or whatever else you like, but do not add liquid. Cook uncovered for 90 minutes, or until done; the ribs should be tender, grayish in color, with clear juice.

Barbecuing Spareribs: Preheat the oven to 450°F. Place the meat on a rack in a shallow pan. Cook uncovered for 30 minutes, then reduce heat to 350°F., cover the spareribs with barbecue sauce, and cook for 1 to 2 hours. Baste with barbecue sauce every 20 minutes. If the ribs become too brown, cover the pan with aluminum foil.

HAM

Hams may be cured or smoked. A fresh ham is one that has never been cooked or processed. "Tenderized" does not mean the ham has been cooked but refers to a method of curing. Ready-to-eat hams are safe to eat without any more cooking, but cooking will further enhance the flavor and texture. All canned hams are ready-to-eat.

Baking a Fresh Ham

Preheat the oven to 350°F. Place the ham on a rack in a shallow pan. Roast in the oven uncovered until the ham is almost done, or until the meat thermometer reads 170°F. Remove the ham from the oven and cut off the rind, then cut lines in the fat with a knife (this is called scoring). Add glaze to the ham (see below) and bake at 400°F. for 15 to 20 minutes. Use the following chart as a guideline for cooking time and end temperature.

BAKING TIME CHART

Type of Ham	Cooking Time	Meat Thermometer Reading
Whole ham, ready-to-eat	10 minutes per pound	130°F.
Whole ham, uncooked	18–20 minutes per pound	160°F.
Half a ham, ready-to-eat	10 minutes per pound	130°F.
Half a ham, uncooked	22–25 minutes per pound	160°F.
Boneless butt	40–45 minutes per pound	170°F.
Picnic	30–35 minutes per pound	170°F.

Cooking a Picnic or Shoulder Butt (Fresh)

Place the meat in a large pot and cover with water. Add spices and/or vegetables as desired. Cover the pot and simmer on the stove until done. A 2-pound boneless shoulder butt will take 35 to 40 minutes per pound, a 5-to-8-pound picnic will take 30 to 35 minutes per pound. Remove the meat from the pan when done. If you wish to glaze, apply the glaze before serving, and place the meat in a preheated oven at 350°F. for 15 to 20 minutes, or until the glaze has cooked.

Baking Ham Steaks or Slices

Preheat the oven to 350°F. Place the ham in a shallow, heavy pan or iron skillet. Add a mixture of 1/4 cup brown sugar and 1 tsp. mustard. Pour 1/2 cup milk or fruit juices into the pan, making sure liquid only reaches top of ham. Bake at 350°F. until done, as follows:

• for 1-inch-thick steaks—1 1/4 hours
• for 1 1/2-inch-thick steaks—1 1/4 to 1 1/2 hours
• for ready-to-eat hams—cut the cooking time in half

DIFFERENT GLAZES FOR HAM

To prepare a glaze: Place the ingredients (choose from one of the combinations below, or one of your own) in a pan and cook on low heat until a liquid has formed, stirring frequently so the ingredients do not burn. Add the glaze to the ham and place the ham back in the oven for 15 minutes at 400°F.

SUGGESTED GLAZES

- 1 cup brown sugar, ³/₄ cup pineapple juice or crushed pineapple, and 1 tsp. dry mustard
- 1 cup currant jelly, 1 cup apple jelly, or 1 cup cranberry jelly
- 1 cup brown sugar, 1 Tbsp. dry mustard, and ¹/₂ cup pickle juice or fruit juice
- ³/₄ cup brown sugar, ¹/₂ cup orange marmalade, 2 tsp. dry mustard, and ¹/₂ cup orange juice

Pan-Broiling Ham Steaks or Slices

Brown the ham in a skillet over low heat without oil, covering the pan so the meat will be thoroughly cooked. A 1-inch-thick piece of meat will take 16 to 20 minutes (less time is needed for a thinner piece). Remember that precooked ham only needs to be browned before serving.

Remember: When cooked, the meat thermometer should read:

- 160°F. for a whole or half baked ham
- 130°F. for a ready-to-eat ham
- 170°F. for a boneless butt or picnic

How to Carve a Ham

Place the shank end (narrow) at the carver's right, if right-handed, or left, if left-handed. Cut a few slices from the side, and turn the ham on the cut, flat surface. Holding the ham with a fork, remove a small wedge 6 inches from the shank end, then cut thin slices down to the bone. Run the knife along the bone to release the cut slices.

Cooking a Country Ham or Cured Ham

Country ham needs to cook to at least 160°F. on the meat thermometer to kill all bacteria. There are two ways to cook a country ham:

1. Scrub and rinse the ham well with cold water, then place in a large pot and cover with cold water. Bring water to a boil over medium heat, reduce, and simmer until tender. This should take about 15 minutes per pound, and,

again, the juice should be clear when done. Remove ham from the liquid, and let cool to room temperature. Cut the skin and fat off; then the ham is ready to eat. If you wish to glaze, you may cover the ham with brown sugar, stick whole cloves in, and place the ham in an oven at 300°F. and cook for 1 hour or follow the alternate glaze suggestions given in this chapter.

If you live in an apartment, the following down-home method from Alva Wilk may not be your method of choice.

2. Scrub and rinse the ham well with cold water, then place in a large pot and cover with cold water. Place pot on the stove and bring the water to a boil over low heat (this may take 2 to 3 hours). Then boil the ham for 5 minutes. Turn the heat off, leaving the pot on the burner. Immediately wrap the pot in newspaper, making sure the newspaper does not touch the hot burner, and tape the paper on with freezer tape. Place a blanket over the pot, and leave overnight. The next morning, take the pot outside and pour out liquid (which will be a combination of water and grease). Your country ham is now ready to eat! Cut off the skin and fat before eating.

TIPS FOR COOKING PORK LOIN, RIBS, SHOULDER, AND HAM

- If boiling a ham, leave the ham in the water until the water is cold. This will make the ham juicier and more tender.
- Pork is good served with apples of any form—especially apple sauce. Other great seasonings for pork are marjoram, oregano, onions, paprika, sage, thyme, rosemary, garlic, or dry mustard.

BACON

Purchase bacon that is shiny-looking with good color, and always check the date before buying! You can store unopened bacon in the refrigerator for up to 7 days past the date stamped on the package. Unopened packaged bacon may be frozen; if wrapped well it will keep up to 1 month. Cooked bacon may be wrapped and refrigerated for up to 5 days, or frozen up to 6 weeks.

Methods of Cooking

The most common method is to place slices of bacon in a skillet (without oil) and heat slowly over medium heat, turning the pieces during cooking. Do not overcrowd, and drain well on paper towels. You may also place slices on a rack in a pan and bake at 400°F. for 10 minutes, without turning bacon, or place

---

TIPS FOR COOKING BACON

- Prick bacon with a fork in several places before cooking to help prevent curling.
- To minimize shrinkage while cooking, place the bacon in a cold skillet before turning the burner on, and cook over medium heat.
- For crisper, less fatty bacon, drain off the grease as it accumulates in the skillet. Remember to pour the grease into a jar or can and throw away when full. Grease will harden as it cools, which can clog up your sink drainpipes if you pour it down there.

---

slices on a broiling rack in the oven, 3 inches from the broiler, and cook, turning slices once. Remember, always drain bacon well on paper towels. You may want to check out the new microwave bacon rack—it eliminates much of the muss and bother and turns out nice, crisp slices.

Canadian bacon, which is from the loin and tends to be leaner and more expensive, may be baked like ham. After removing the covering, bake it on a rack in a shallow pan, uncovered, at 400°F. for 10 minutes. The meat thermometer should read 170°F. when done.

SAUSAGE

Buy sausage with a fresh odor and pink color. Fresh sausage should be stored in the meat compartment of the refrigerator for up to 2 days. Smoked sausage may be stored for up to 2 weeks unopened or 1 week opened. Dried sausage, such as pepperoni, will keep for 3 weeks. Sausage may be frozen for 1 to 2 months, well wrapped.

If cooking sausage links, place them in a cold skillet, add a little water, cover, and simmer for 5 minutes on medium heat, turning occasionally. If cooking patties, place them in a skillet and cook for 12 to 15 minutes over low heat until brown. Sausage is done when the juices run clear. Drain all sausage well on paper towels, and always use tongs, a spatula, or a spoon to avoid puncturing them.

Tip: Roll sausage links or patties in flour before frying to reduce shrinkage.

HOT DOGS (FRANKFURTERS, WIENERS)

An easy and inexpensive meat for the kitchen klutz is the hot dog, a perennial favorite. Topped with chili, cheese, and chopped onions, it makes a fast meal. Hot dogs may be heated (they have already been cooked) in many different ways:

Boiling

Drop hot dogs into a pot of boiling water. Bring the water back to a boil, remove the pot from the heat, cover, and let the hot dogs stand in hot water for 5 minutes. Remove the hot dogs from the water and drain on paper towels.

Broiling

Score the hot dogs diagonally every 1 inch (but do not slice completely through), dot with butter, and broil 3 inches from the top of the broiler element; turn occasionally until done.

Grilling

Cook them on an outdoor grill, turning several times until done.

Simmering

Drop the hot dogs into boiling water, reduce the heat, and simmer (right below boiling) for 5 to 8 minutes.

Microwaving

Place the wiener in a bun and wrap it in a paper towel, then place it in the microwave with the "seam" of the paper towel on the bottom. Microwave on High for 30 seconds per hot dog.

TURKEY

Female turkeys (hens) have a higher proportion of meat to bone, although both the male (tom) and the female are raised for the table. Turkeys are composed of 58% water, 20% protein, and 20% fat. They may be purchased whole, half, and cut up. When purchasing a whole turkey, you will find a giblet package tucked inside the turkey. This package will contain the neck, heart, liver, and gizzard. Buy turkey with moist, tender skin, avoiding dry, hard, and bruised skin. Whole turkeys are classified by size and age as follows:

TURKEY CLASSIFICATIONS

Size	Weight
Small	4–10 pounds
Medium	10–19 pounds
Large	20+ pounds

Type	Age
Fryer-roaster	4 months old
Young	5–7 months old
Yearling	1 year
Mature	more than 15 mos. old

Note: The younger the turkey, the more tender the meat will be.

Here are some guidelines to use when purchasing turkey.

SERVING SIZES FOR TURKEY

Generally buy 12 ounces or 3/4 pound per serving. 5 pounds of turkey = approximately 3 cups of diced meat.

Weight	Number of Servings
8–10 pounds	16–20 servings
10–14 pounds	20–28 servings
14–18 pounds	28–36 servings
18–20 pounds	36–40 servings
20–24 pounds	40–50 servings

STORING AND THAWING

Correct storage for turkey is crucial! Fresh turkey should be loosely wrapped in wax paper and stored in the coldest part of the refrigerator; it will last 1 to 3 days. Frozen turkey must be stored in the freezer until ready to use. After cooking, leftover turkey should be refrigerated as soon as possible and eaten within a few days. Remove the stuffing first and always store it separately from the meat.

Turkey may be thawed in the refrigerator or in cold water. To thaw a turkey in the refrigerator, consult the following chart.

CHART FOR THAWING TURKEY IN THE REFRIGERATOR

Weight	Thawing Time
8 pounds	1 day
8–12 pounds	1$\frac{1}{2}$–2 days
12–16 pounds	2–3 days
16–20 pounds	3–4 days
20–24 pounds	3–4 days

To thaw a turkey in cold water, place it in a bowl and cover completely with cold water. Remember to change the water frequently to keep it cold. Following are approximate thawing times for this type of process.

CHART FOR THAWING TURKEY IN COLD WATER

Weight	Thawing Time
4–12 pounds	4–6 hours
12–20 pounds	6–8 hours
20–24 pounds	8–12 hours

Remember, to avoid food poisoning, never thaw turkey at room temperature or allow it to sit at room temperature. After thawing, remove the giblet package, refrigerate it, and cook the giblets within 12 hours.

METHODS OF COOKING

Roasting

First, remove any feathers that may be left on the bird with tweezers and remove the giblets and any other intestines or dark-colored excess. Rinse the turkey with cold water inside and out and pat dry with a cloth or paper towels. Rub the cavity and the whole bird with butter or vegetable oil and lightly sprinkle the skin with salt (optional). Next decide if you want to stuff the bird or bake your stuffing separately.

Stuffing a Turkey: Add stuffing right before roasting and after you have rinsed the cavity and bird and patted it dry. Do not rub cavity with salt if stuffing the bird. Always stuff lightly because stuffing will expand during cooking. Use 1 cup of stuffing per pound of turkey. Roasting time will take an extra 3 minutes per pound of bird.

Trussing a Turkey: If you add stuffing or you have a large turkey, you will need to truss the bird so it will keep its shape while cooking. Remember, it does not really matter how the string is tied around the bird, as long as it firmly holds the bird together with the legs against the body. A trussing kit may be purchased at the grocery or supermarket or you may use ordinary string and follow the steps below.

1. With the breast-side down, tie a string around the tail end of the bird, leaving two long ends after the knot.
2. Take one side of the string and wrap it around the leg on the same side as the string. Wrap the other string around the leg on its side and bring the two strings together at the center of the bird.
3. Cross the strings over the middle of the turkey's breast, then wrap each string under and over the leg tips.
4. Pull both strings tightly to pull the legs in against the body.
5. Turn the bird over and tie the string in a bow on this side.
6. Once the bird is roasted, pull the bow apart and remove the string.
   Tip: If you don't have string, you may use *unwaxed* dental floss.

After stuffing and trussing (if you are doing so), decide how you want to cook the turkey. There are three different methods for roasting a turkey.

1. You may cook it in a browning bag, following the directions on the box.
2. You may wrap the bird in aluminum foil, to cook it more quickly.
3. You may roast the turkey uncovered.

If you are not using a browning bag but wrapping the turkey in aluminum foil, preheat your oven to 450°F. If you are roasting it uncovered, preheat the oven to 325°F. Place the turkey on its back on a wire rack in a shallow open pan. You do not need to use a wire rack, but it does help the heat circulate around the turkey more efficiently. You will need to baste while cooking in order to keep the bird moist if you are roasting it uncovered. Mix 2/3 cup water and 1/4 cup butter together in a pan, bring to a boil, and use a spoon or bulb baster to pour this mixture over the bird every 15 minutes. After the bird has roasted awhile, you may also use the pan drippings for basting.

If you are using a meat thermometer, insert it in the inside thigh muscle or the breast muscle (do not let the meat thermometer touch the bone). Put the turkey in the oven and cook according to the following recommendations.

COOKING CHART—FOR WRAPPED BIRDS

Weight	Oven Temperature	Cooking Time
6–8 pounds	450°F.	1 1/2–2 hours
8–12 pounds	450°F.	2–2 1/2 hours
12–16 pounds	450°F.	2 1/2–3 hours
16–20 pounds	450°F.	3–3 1/2 hours
20–24 pounds	450°F.	3 1/2–4 hours

Note: Uncover turkey for the last 30 minutes of cooking and baste with butter or oil to brown.

COOKING CHART—FOR UNCOVERED BIRDS

Weight	Oven Temperature	Cooking Time	Meat Thermometer
4–8 pounds	325°F.	1 3/4–2 3/4 hours	170°–180°F.
8–12 pounds	325°F.	3 1/2–4 hours	170°–180°F.
12–16 pounds	325°F.	4–4 1/2 hours	170°–180°F.
16–20 pounds	325°F.	4 1/2–5 hours	170°–180°F.
20–24 pounds	325°F.	5–6 hours	170°–180°F.

Remember: You only adjust the time, not the temperature, when cooking a turkey!

To Test for Doneness:

- Prick with a fork—the juice should run clear.
- Jiggle the leg/drumstick—the hip joint should be loose or break easily.
- Read the already inserted meat thermometer, which should read 170°–180°F when done.
- Insert an instant-read thermometer into the muscle on the inside of the thigh—the thermometer should read the same as above.

TIPS FOR ROASTING A TURKEY

• Grease the outside of the turkey with melted cooking oil.
• When roasting uncovered, cover the sides and top of the bird with a fat-moistened cloth (like cheesecloth) that is double-folded and soaked in liquid butter or oil. If the cloth dries during cooking, remoisten with oil or brush the bird generously with fat and baste frequently.
• For juicier white meat, cook breast-side down and then turn the bird breast-side up when it is 3/4 cooked. Large birds may be difficult to turn and should be cooked breast-side up from the start.
• Do not place the bird in the oven until the oven is fully preheated.
• Always remove the giblets and any dark-colored excess from the cavity before cooking!
• Sprinkle flour lightly over the surface of the turkey two or three times while cooking if you want a crust on the bird. For a thick crust, mix 2 Tbsp. flour and 3 Tbsp. butter until creamy. Spread this mixture over the breast and legs before cooking.
• If the turkey gets brown too quickly, cover it loosely with a tent of aluminum foil, with the shiny side facing the bird.
• For a glazed surface, only spread butter on turkey, and use only melted butter or pan drippings to baste.
• *Let the bird sit for 15 minutes, loosely covered, for easier carving.*
• For faster cooking, brush the turkey with oil or butter and double-wrap in aluminum foil, making sure to seal the edges of the foil airtight, or use an oven roasting bag from the grocery or supermarket.

Making Gravy

To make a great gravy, save the pan drippings. You will need to separate the fat from the stock. One way to do this is to refrigerate the pan drippings, so that the fat rises to the top. You may buy a special cup that removes fat from stocks and soups. Another way is to pour the pan drippings into a clear measuring cup. The oil will rise to the top and the stock will settle on the bottom. Use a spoon to remove the oil on the top.

Take 4 Tbsp. fat from the pan drippings, place it in a saucepan, add 4 Tbsp. flour, and brown the mixture over low heat. Add 2 cups juice from the turkey drippings (the stock which is the liquid without the fat) or from the giblet stock (*see* "Cooking Giblets" below) and cook over low heat until thick. You may add finely chopped cooked giblets if you like. **Note:** You may substitute butter or oil for the fat from the pan drippings, if necessary or desired.

Cooking Giblets

Giblets may be used to make gravy, dressing, or eaten alone. After cooking, they may be stored for up to 2 days in the refrigerator. To cook, first thoroughly rinse with cool water, and trim off any visible fat, if you desire. Place the gizzard, heart, and neck in a saucepan. You may add any of the following to the pan: a small sliced onion or a whole small onion (peel first), $^1/_3$ of a bay leaf, 1 carrot (peel first and cut in half), $^1/_4$ cup chopped green peppers, or 1 tsp. thyme. Cover with 4–6 cups water and add $^1/_2$ tsp. salt. Place a lid on the pan and simmer over low heat until you can pierce the giblets easily with a fork; giblets should be tender when done. The simmering process will take between 1 to 4 hours, depending on the size of the bird, and thus, the size of the giblets. You may need to add more hot water if you have to simmer the giblets for a long time.

If you wish to use the liver, add it during the last 15–30 minutes of cooking because the liver has a very strong flavor. You may also cook the liver separately by sautéing it in butter.

After cooking the giblets, save the broth and remove the giblets. You may use the broth for the liquid in your gravy recipe and add the giblets, cut-up, if you prefer. If you are not going to use the broth and giblets immediately, store them in the refrigerator for up to 2 days.

Carving a Roasted Turkey

Position the turkey so that a leg is at the right of the carver (on the left if left-handed). Bend the leg back with one hand and cut it off with the knife held in the other hand. Cut the thigh from the drumstick. Use a fork to hold down the turkey, and cut down sharply on the joint that joins the wing to the body. Slice thin pieces of turkey where the wing was, working up to the breastbone.

Leftover Roasted Turkey

After slicing and eating the roasted turkey, place the carcass (what's left of the bird) in a large pot. Cover the carcass completely with water, add 1 peeled onion, 2 peeled carrots, and a rib of celery. Bring the mixture to a boil, reduce the heat, and simmer. The turkey will cook apart, and the remaining meat will fall off. Drain, saving the liquid for use in other recipes. Separate the turkey from the bones, you are now ready to use it in any of these dishes:

- Turkey soup
- Turkey hash
- Diced in salads
- Turkey casseroles (may be used in place of chicken in any casserole)
- Turkey sandwiches

Other Methods of Cooking

Turkey may be cooked the same way as chicken and may be substituted for it in recipes. Ground turkey is now available at the grocery store and may be used in place of hamburger meat in foods such as spaghetti sauce, meatloaf, lasagna, and hamburgers. When making lasagna or spaghetti sauce with turkey, be sure to spray or coat your pan very well with oil or butter; turkey sticks to the pan since it has very little fat. In addition, if making hamburgers with ground turkey, you will need to add 1 egg per pound of turkey, in order to hold the meat together in the patty shape.

Broiling: Preheat your oven to "Broil." Take a young turkey weighing 4 pounds, split it in half, and break the hip, wing, and leg joints in two, so the bird will lie flat while broiling. Brush the bird with melted butter or vegetable oil and then salt and pepper the bird to taste if desired. Place the bird with the skin-side down on a wire rack in a shallow pan or in a broiler pan and place the pan in the oven so the turkey is 7 to 10 inches from the broiler element in the oven. Turn the turkey over frequently and brush with melted butter each time. The turkey should be ready in 1 hour. Be sure to use a meat thermometer or another method to test for doneness.

Tip: If you line the broiler pan with aluminum foil, it will save you time cleaning up the pan later.

Note: if you are cooking the turkey outside on a grill, hang it over the hot coals; do not place it directly on the grill grate.

Browning: Take cut turkey pieces and wash, pat dry, and lightly coat them with flour, salt, and pepper, or leave them plain. Place 1/2 inch of oil in a skillet on medium heat, add the turkey pieces, and cook uncovered until lightly browned. Remove the turkey and drain on paper towels.

Sautéing: Heat 4 Tbsp. butter, vegetable oil, or bacon grease in a large skillet. Add the cut turkey pieces, lightly dust them with flour or cornmeal, and salt and pepper to taste. Brown (uncovered) on all sides over medium heat. Turn the burner to low, then add any seasoning you like, such as garlic powder, onion powder, salt, pepper, curry powder, basil, or chives. Cover and cook slowly until tender. Turkey normally takes 35 to 45 minutes to cook, depending on the size of the pieces. Be sure to turn the the turkey pieces occasionally while cooking. If you would like your turkey crisp, uncover it for the last 10 minutes of cooking.

Stewing: Place the turkey in a large pot and add seasonings and enough water or liquid to cover the turkey. Simmer until tender (approximately 1 to 3 hours, depending on size and age of bird). **Note:** If not serving immediately, cool the turkey in the broth, then remove and refrigerate. For a good broth, add 2 to 3 pieces celery, carrots, onion, salt and pepper. For a juicier bird, let the turkey cool in the broth.

VEAL

Veal is a delicious meat to serve when entertaining a few guests or someone special since it is more delicate—and more expensive—than regular beef. It has a mild flavor and will be tender, moist, and juicy if cooked correctly. Veal is *never* broiled because it contains very little fat and a lot of connective tissue and will dry out easily during cooking. In this section you will learn several ways to prepare veal.

Veal is the meat from calves (young cows) that are approximately 4 to 14 weeks old. Many times the distinction is not made between veal and calf beef, and both are called veal, but calf meat is from calves 14 weeks to 1 year old.

Veal is white with a slightly pinkish tint and is usually less firm than beef. The whiter the meat, the more tender it will be because the white color indicates that the calf has been primarily milk-fed. Veal usually costs more than regular beef, but like regular beef, veal is classified as prime (best), choice, and good. Cuts include the **breast**, which is the least expensive cut and is wonderful prepared stuffed. The **leg** is often sliced for cutlets and steaks, and is good sautéed. The **loin** may be rolled loin or double loin and is good roasted; be sure to cover the loin with fat or suet when roasting or it will dry out. The **rib** section is cut into a rib roast and crown roast, both of which should be covered with fat or suet when roasting. The **rump** is good braised. The **shank** is also good braised and requires a longer cooking time because the shank cut is usually thick. The **shoulder** is often sliced for chops and roasts, and, like the rump and shank, it is good braised or even stewed.

Use the following chart to determine how much veal you will need for a particular occasion.

SERVING SIZES FOR VEAL

Type	Amount per Serving
Breast	1 pound
Cutlet	1 pound
Roast, with bone	$1/3$–$1/2$ pound
Roast, without bone	$1/4$–$1/3$ pound

STORING

Always remove the store wrapper, rewrap loosely in clean plastic, and refrigerate veal as soon as possible after purchasing. In general, veal will keep up to 3 days in the refrigerator after purchasing but consult the following chart for more specific storage time after purchase:

VEAL REFRIGERATOR STORAGE CHART

Veal Cut	Length of Time
Chops	3–4 days
Ground	1–2 days
Roast	5–6 days
Steaks	3–4 days
Stew meat	1–2 days

METHODS OF COOKING

Veal requires long, slow cooking, because it is very lean. Veal should be cooked more like poultry than beef, although it should not be broiled! In addition, butter, margarine, vegetable oil, or olive oil will improve the flavor. Rub a little on each side before cooking. Seasonings that are great with veal include basil, rosemary, sage, thyme, tarragon, and summer savory. One of several suggestions for cooking veal is to braise cuts from the shoulder. To determine doneness, use a meat thermometer and cook according to your taste.

Doneness	Meat Thermometer Reading
Rare	140°F.
Medium	160°F.
Well done	170°F.

ROASTING

This method is suitable for the loin, leg, rolled shoulder or rump, and rib section. Allow 1/3 to 1/2 pound per serving with bone, or 1/4 to 1/3 pound, without bone. To roast, the cut should weigh at least 3 pounds.

To Roast Veal: Preheat the oven to 325°F. Make slits in the meat with a knife and insert chopped pieces or slivers of garlic, if desired. You may also pour soy sauce or barbecue sauce on the veal. You will need to lay several strips of uncooked bacon or suet (purchase from the butcher) on top, and anchor them with toothpicks. Place the veal on a rack in a heavy pot, and in the center of the roast insert a meat thermometer, if you are using one, making sure it does not touch the bone. Do not add liquid, and do not baste while the veal is cooking because the bacon or suet on top of the meat will keep it moist. Bake the roast uncovered at 325°F. according to the following recommendations.

ROASTING TIME CHART

Cut and Weight	Cooking Time	Meat Thermometer	Oven Temperature
Leg—3 to 8 pounds	30–40 minutes per pound	180°F.	325°F.
Loin—4 to 6 pounds	35–40 minutes per pound	165°F.	325°F.
Rib—4 to 6 pounds	20 minutes per pound	165°F.	325°F.
Rolled, boned shoulder— 3 to 5 pounds	40–45 minutes per pound	180°F.	325°F.

Note: For easier carving, wait 15 minutes after removing from oven.

Pot Roasting

This is suitable for rolled, round, shoulder, and boned veal rump.

To Pot-Roast Veal: Preheat the oven to 350°F. Dredge the meat in flour. Using a heavy pot or Dutch oven, brown the meat over medium heat in several Tbsp. of melted butter, margarine, olive oil, bacon grease, or vegetable oil. Brown well on both sides—this may take 15 to 20 minutes. Remove the meat from the pan, then place a rack in the bottom of the roasting pan, place the meat on the rack, and add 1 cup water or tomato juice, salt, and pepper. You may also add a bay leaf, a clove of garlic, or whatever else you like for flavor. Cover the pot tightly and cook in the oven at 350°F. for 40 minutes per pound of veal. During the last 30 to 45 minutes of cooking, you may add vegetables, such as carrots and potatoes, to the pot.

Baking

This method is suitable for chops, cutlets, and steaks.

To Bake Veal: Dredge the meat in flour that has been seasoned with salt and pepper. Next dip the meat in a mixture of 1 beaten egg and 2 Tbsp. water. Next roll the meat in a bowl of finely crushed bread crumbs or cracker crumbs. Brown on both sides over medium heat in several Tbsp. of melted butter, margarine, olive oil, or vegetable oil. (This should take about 3 minutes per side.) Place the browned meat in a shallow pan in a preheated oven and bake at 325°F. until done. Turn once while baking. A 1-inch-thick piece will require about 40 minutes to cook. You may also test for doneness with a meat thermometer: 140°F. for rare, 160°F. for medium, and 170°F. for well done.

Braising

This method is suitable for chops, cutlets, and steaks.

To Braise Veal: Follow the directions for browning mentioned above. Add any desired seasonings and 1/2 to 3/4 cup of liquid such as milk, water, or tomato juice. Cover and simmer over low heat until tender, turning once. You may add vegetables such as onion, celery, or green beans. A 1-inch-thick piece of veal will require 30 minutes per side and a 1/2-inch-thick piece of veal will require 20 minutes per side. You may also use a meat thermometer to test for doneness: 140°F. for rare, 160°F. for medium, and 170°F. for well done.

VEAL TIPS FOR THE KITCHEN KLUTZ

- Season veal with sage, summer savory, thyme, basil, or tarragon.
- Because veal has a delicate and mild flavor, do not serve it with strong-flavored foods.
- Rub a clove of garlic over the meat's surface before cooking or make slits in the meat and insert slivers of garlic or spices such as marjoram.
- Rub a crumbled bay leaf over a roast before cooking.

OTHER MEATS

Variety meats are liver, kidney, brains, heart, tripe, tongue, oxtail, and sweetbreads. They are edible parts of an animal that are rich in vitamins and minerals. These "other meats" will add variety to your cooking, as their name implies. They are not hard to cook, so be sure to try them—your grandmother probably did.

BRAINS

Brains may be from beef, lamb, pork, or veal. Allow 1/4 pound per serving. Calf brains are considered the choicest, although all brains are very delicate and tender. They should be shiny, moist, pinkish, and plump. You will need to use them immediately after purchase or at least cook and eat within 24 hours. Brains may be frozen.

Methods of Cooking

Brains must be precooked before cooking. To **precook**, soak brains in salted water (1 Tbsp. of salt per quart of water) for 15 minutes. Then place in a pot of boiling salted water to which the juice of 1/2 a lemon has been added, cover the pot, and simmer for 15 minutes. Remove the brains from the boiling water and place in a bowl of cold water. After brains cool, remove them and take the membrane off with a knife.

Broiling: Preheat the oven to the "Broil" setting. After precooking, brush with olive oil, vegetable oil, or melted butter and broil 3 inches from the top burner for 10 to 15 minutes, turning occasionally. Serve with lemon slices, tartar sauce, or pickle relish.

Pan-Frying: Precook the brains according to directions above. Cut into 1-inch cubes and place in a bowl containing 1 beaten egg. Next, dip each cube into a bowl of finely crushed cracker crumbs. Melt 2 to 3 Tbsp. butter or vegetable oil in a skillet over medium heat. Fry until the cubes are brown on all sides, and serve with tomato sauce, ham, or bacon.

HEART

Heart has a mild flavor like liver. Of the various types of heart, veal has the most delicate flavor. The skin should be smooth, well-rounded with a firm texture.

SERVING SIZES

Type	Average Size	Per Serving
Beef	3–3¹/₂ pounds	¹/₄ pound
Lamb	¹/₄ pound	¹/₄ pound
Pork	¹/₂ pound	¹/₄ pound
Veal	³/₄ pound	³/₈ pound

Methods of Cooking

Trim off all fat and coarse fibers at the top and inside. Wash thoroughly and drain. Place in a pot, cover with water, add 1 tsp. salt and a peeled onion. Simmer covered on the stove until tender according to the following recommendations.

SIMMERING TIMES FOR HEART

Type	Length of Time
Beef	2 hours
Lamb	1–1¹/₂ hours
Pork	2 hours
Veal	1–1¹/₂ hours

When the heart is tender, you will be able to pierce it easily with a fork.

Cooking Chicken-Fried Hearts: Slice into ¹/₄-inch-thick pieces. Dredge each piece in a mixture of flour, salt, and pepper. Place in a skillet with 2 Tbsp. hot oil and fry until lightly brown. Add ¹/₄ cup water to the skillet, and simmer covered for 20 to 30 minutes.

KIDNEY

Kidney is considered a delicacy. A good kidney looks bright and shiny. Keep in mind that kidney is very perishable and must be used within 24 hours. Store it loosely wrapped in the refrigerator until ready to use.

SERVING SIZES FOR KIDNEY

Type	Average Size	Amount per Serving
Beef	1¼ pounds	¼ pound
Lamb	2 ounces	¼ pound
Veal	8-12 ounces	¼ pound

Cooking

Preheat the oven on the "Broil" setting. Wash the kidney with cold water. Cut away the membrane. Cut through the middle lengthwise and remove the fat and white tissue. Rinse the kidney and dry with paper towels. Brush with melted butter or oil. Place in a pan and cook 3 inches from the broiler element for 15 minutes, turning occasionally, or until brown. Serve on buttered toast.

To reduce the strong flavor found in beef and pork kidneys, soak them in salted water (1 tsp. per cup of water) in the refrigerator for at least 1 hour. If cooking veal kidney, remember that it is very tender and requires little cooking.

LIVER

Liver, the richest food source for iron, can be calf, beef, duck, lamb, pork, chicken, goose, and turkey. **Calf liver** is considered to be the best. **Beef liver** may be tender or sort of tough. It has a stronger flavor than other types but is less expensive. A dark-red color usually indicates toughness, so try to purchase light-colored liver. **Calf liver** is tender because the animals are milk- and grass-fed. It is light-colored and mildly flavored. **Chicken, duck,** and **goose livers** are tender and have a nice flavor. They are often used in pâtés. **Lamb liver** is tender and mildly flavored. **Pork liver** is less tender, has a stronger flavor than beef, and is less expensive. Like chicken, duck, and goose, it also is often used in pâtés. **Turkey liver** is tender but has a stronger flavor than other poultry livers. Buy liver that has a bright red color, shiny surface, and very little odor. You will need to eat liver within 24 hours of purchase or store it in the freezer.

Note: Allow ¼ pound of liver per serving.

Storing

Liver should be taken out of the store wrapping, wiped clean, and loosely wrapped with plastic. Store liver in the refrigerator up to 24 hours. To freeze, wrap well in freezer plastic, paper, or foil and freeze up to 2-3 months.

Methods of Cooking

Wipe liver with a damp cloth and remove the outside skin and veins. Calf, lamb, veal, and young beef liver may be pan-fried. Calf liver should always be cooked quickly on high heat, 1 minute on each side. Pork and beef livers may be tough, so they should be braised. Before using pork or beef liver in recipes, parboil for 5 minutes if sliced, or 20 minutes if whole. Liver should be tender when cooked. Do not overcook, because even a good piece of liver will become tough with overcooking.

Braising: This is a suitable method for beef or pork liver. Slice the liver into 1/2-inch-thick pieces and dredge them in flour. Brown slices in hot bacon fat or 1 to 2 Tbsp. vegetable oil. Add 1/4 cup wine, beef broth, or water. Heat to boiling, reduce heat, and season with salt and pepper. Cover and simmer for 20 minutes or until tender.

To braise with vegetables, braise as above except brown in hot bacon fat with chopped carrots, onions, and celery. Season and place in greased baking dish with the vegetables on the bottom and the liver on top. Add 1/2 cup liquid and bake for 30 minutes at 350° F.

Broiling: This is suitable for calf or lamb liver. Slice the liver into 1/2-inch-thick pieces and sprinkle with salt and pepper. Brush with melted butter, broil for 3 minutes (3 to 4 inches from the broiler element), turn once, and broil for an additional 2 minutes.

Pan-Frying: This method is suitable for calf, beef, or lamb liver. Slice the liver into 1/2-inch-thick pieces and dredge them in flour. Brown in hot fat, then reduce the heat, and season. Continue to cook over low heat for 8 to 10 minutes, turning only once.

For liver and onions, cook a sliced and separated sweet onion in bacon fat, or oil until golden and then cover and cook slowly until tender over low heat. In a separate skillet, pan-fry the liver. Serve the liver topped with the onions.

For liver and bacon, fry 2 pieces of bacon per serving of liver. Remove the bacon (keep it warm) and fry the liver. Crumble the bacon on top of the liver before serving.

Sautéing: Dredge a 1/2-inch slice through flour, sprinkle with salt and pepper, and sauté in butter over medium heat (2 Tbsp. butter per pound of liver). Turn frequently. It should take 1–2 minutes per side to cook.

LIVER TIPS FOR THE KITCHEN KLUTZ

- Rub a clove of peeled garlic over the pan before cooking liver.
- Sprinkle a few drops of lemon juice on the liver before serving.
- If liver is tough, you may tenderize it while covered in the refrigerator by soaking it in milk for 1–2 hours or tomato juice for 2–3 hours.

OXTAIL

Oxtail is the tail of a cow, and it is delicious, albeit a bit fatty. Allow 1/2 pound per serving. Store it loosely wrapped in the refrigerator for up to 24 hours or freeze it. Oxtail needs to be cooked long and slowly.

Cooking

Preheat the oven to 300°F. Dredge the oxtail in a mixture of flour, salt, and pepper. Place it in a hot skillet containing 3 Tbsp. melted salad oil or fat. Cook the meat over medium heat until brown. Place it in a casserole dish, cover, and set it aside. Brown 1 cup chopped onion in the skillet. Add the onions to the oxtail dish. Also, add 1½ cups canned beef broth, 1½ cups canned tomatoes, 1 Tbsp. vinegar, 1 tsp. minced garlic, 1 Tbsp. sugar, 1 tsp. salt and ⅛ tsp. pepper, and 1 bay leaf. Cover and bake for 3 to 4 hours, or until the meat is tender. If you need to add more liquid, add hot water. Remove bay leaf when done, cool, and then remove excess fat with a paper towel. Heat and serve.

SWEETBREADS

Sweetbreads are the thymus glands of a calf, cow, lamb, or pig. They come from around the heart, throat, and neck of the animal. Buy sweetbreads that are plump, firm, and white (which indicates they are from a younger animal and will be more tender). Use sweetbreads as soon as you purchase them, or you may keep them in the refrigerator and cook and eat them within 24 hours, or you may wrap and freeze them. Allow ¼ pound per serving.

Cooking

To precook sweetbreads, simmer them in boiling, salted water, covered, with a teaspoon of vinegar or lemon juice according to the following recommendations.

Type	Length of Time
Beef	35 minutes
Lamb	25 minutes
Veal	25 minutes

Drain the sweetbreads, place them in cold water, and remove the membranes. Place them in a covered container and store in the refrigerator until ready to cook.

Broiling

Preheat the oven to the "Broil" setting. After precooking, brush the sweetbreads lightly with olive or vegetable oil and place in a pan. Put the pan in the oven 3 inches from the broiler element and cook for 5 to 7 minutes on each side. When brown, remove the sweetbreads from the oven and serve with lemon butter or almonds.

Pan-Frying

After precooking, dip the sweetbreads in flour or finely crushed bread or cracker crumbs. Next dip in a beaten egg and then back into the crumbs. Place the sweetbreads in a skillet with 3 to 4 Tbsp. hot melted butter and fry over medium heat until brown on all sides. Serve hot with bacon, ham, or tomato sauce.

TONGUE

Tongue is available fresh, cured, pickled, and smoked. It requires long, slow, moist cooking. Fresh tongue may be stored loosely wrapped in the refrigerator for up to 24 hours, smoked tongue up to 3 days, pickled tongue up to 7 days. Pickled tongue must be soaked in cold water for at least 2 hours before cooking.

SERVING SIZES FOR TONGUE

Type	Average Size	Amount per serving
Beef	2–5 pounds	1/4 pound
Lamb	3–4 ounces	1/4 pound
Pork	1/2–1 1/4 pounds	1/4 pound
Veal	1/2–2 pounds	1/4 pound

Cooking

Cover tongue with cold water in a pot. Add 1 Tbsp. salt, 1 peeled onion, 1 bay leaf, 1 peeled carrot, and 1 rib of celery. Simmer covered until tender. Cooking time is 1 1/2 hours per pound. Beef tongue may take as long as 3 hours to cook. Once tender, remove the tongue from the pot and allow it to cool. Remove the bones, connective tissue, and skin. After removing the bone and gristle, make a slice on the bottom side of the tongue from the thick end to the narrow end. Next cut completely around the thick end to loosen the skin. Take the skin at the thick end and pull it off. It should come off in one piece. Serve tongue sliced, hot or cold, with any of the following sauces: barbecue, horseradish, or tartar. Tongue is also good served with spinach, beets, and potatoes.

TRIPE

Tripe is the muscular inner lining of the stomach of a cow. Good tripe is creamy yellow in color. Types include honeycomb, plain, pocket, and smooth. Tripe normally comes fresh, pickled, or canned. While all tripe has been cooked before it is sold, most needs to be cooked more to be tender.

Cooking

Place tripe in a pot of water. Make sure the water completely covers it. Add 1 Tbsp. salt and simmer covered over low to medium heat for 1 1/2 hours, or until tender when pierced with a fork. Drain and cut into pieces. Serve with a fresh tomato sauce.

SEAFOOD

There are many varieties of fish and shellfish available, so experiment and try them all. You will be amazed at the selection. Seafood is very quick and easy to prepare and cook, and is an excellent alternative to meat. It may be purchased fresh, canned, dried, or frozen.

There are many ways to prepare fish and shellfish that are delicious. Seafood may be broiled, boiled, pan-fried, deep-fried, poached, steamed, sautéed, or grilled. Since it cooks fast, it is best to cook it right before you are ready to serve. Remember not to overcook seafood since it will become tough and dry.

Sauces may be served with seafood to enhance their flavor. There are several sauces in this book (see "Sauces") that are delectable and easy to make. They will also help you hide a mistake if you accidentally overcook your seafood—just pour sauce on top and serve.

FISH

Some fish are high in fat while others are lean. "Fatter" fish (oily fish—5% fat) have oil throughout the flesh, and are best for baking, broiling, and grilling. Varieties include:

Amberjack	Carp	Rainbow trout	Shad
Barracuda	Eel	Rosefish	Sturgeon
Bluefish	Herring	Sablefish	Trout (lake)
Bonito blue	Mackerel	Salmon	Tuna (albacore)
Butterfish	Pompano	Sardines	

Medium-fat fish (2½%–5% fat) can be cooked by any method. Varieties include:

Anchovy	Redfish	Shark	Tuna (bluefin)
Bluefish	Salmon (pink)	Swordfish	Turbot
Catfish	Sea trout	Trout (rainbow)	Whitefish
Mullet			

Lean fish (less than 2½% fat) have most of their oil stored in the liver, and are thus much drier. Lean fish is good boiled, steamed, poached, or fried. If baking lean fish, add bacon strips, and if broiling, baste with melted butter. Varieties include:

Bass	Flounder	Perch	Sheepshead
Buffalofish	Gill	Pike	Sole
Cod	Grouper	Pollack	Triggerfish
Crappie	Halibut	Red Snapper	Tuna (yellowfin)
Croaker	Haddock	Rockfish	Walleye
Cusk	Monkfish	Scrod	Whiting
Dolphin			

BUYING

Fish may be purchased fresh, frozen, canned, salted, or smoked, or you may catch them fresh yourself. When buying **fresh fish**, remember the following guidelines: fresh fish does not smell "fishy" and should not leave an indentation when pressed. The eyes should be clear, bright, and full. The gills should be bright pink to red in color. Fresh fish should be on crushed ice and should have shiny skin. The scales should be close together and not slimy and the meat should stick close to the bones.

Terms to remember when buying fresh fish are drawn, dressed, and pandressed. *Drawn* means the insides of the fish have been removed. *Dressed* means the insides, head, tail, and fins have been removed. *Pan-dressed* means the fish is "ready for the pan."

When buying **frozen fish**, remember that frozen fish has no odor. The box the fish comes in should be firm and solid, and should not have ice on it. If it does, it means the fish has probably been thawed and refrozen, so do not buy it. Any discoloration of the flesh indicates freezer burn.

When buying **canned fish**, remember that it is ready-to-eat. Always check the can and never purchase a can that's been dented, is swollen, is leaking, or has an odor. The best canned salmon is the Red Sockeye; the pink salmon is not quite as good, and is less expensive. The best canned tuna is white solid (more expensive) versus dark flaky tuna (less expensive).

When buying **salted fish**, keep in mind that salting a fish preserves it, but not indefinitely. Salted fish is prepared in one of two ways: dry salting or pickling in brine. When dry salting, the fish is cleaned and then packed in dry salt. Firm fish, such as cod and haddock, are usually done this way. Fish "pickled in brine" has been cleaned and placed in salt water, and may also have been smoked. Fat and oily fish are often pickled in brine. When buying **smoked fish**, remember that smoked fish is usually eaten without cooking. Smoked fish may be salmon, whitefish, herring, and sturgeon.

SERVING SIZES FOR FISH

Type of Fish	Amount per Serving
Whole fish, with all organs	1 pound
Drawn fish, no organs	3/4 pound
Pan-dressed, scaled, no organs, no head, no fins, no tail	1/2 pound
Fillets	1/3 pound
Steaks	1/3 pound
Sticks	1/3 pound

STORING

To store frozen fish, place it at once in the freezer after purchasing. Thaw frozen fish in the refrigerator, draining often. Keep in mind that frozen fish should be cooked on the same day that it is thawed. If necessary, frozen fish that has been thawed will keep 1 day in the refrigerator. **Remember:** Never refreeze thawed fish.

Fresh fish will keep no more than 2 days in the refrigerator. To store, place crushed ice or ice cubes in a pan and cover the ice with plastic wrap. Place the unwrapped fish with the belly-side down on the plastic. Cover fish and pan loosely with plastic wrap and refrigerate for up to 2 days. You may also fill the inside of the fish with crushed ice. Replenish the ice as it melts, making sure the fish stays dry. Always clean and dress fresh whole fish before storing. Do not scale or bone the fish until you are ready to cook it. Leftover cooked fish will keep 2 days if well covered and placed in the coldest part of the refrigerator (usually the meat compartment).

Freshly caught fish should be cleaned and scaled in cold, salted water (2/3 cup salt per gallon of water) after catching. Then wrap it airtight in freezer paper, plastic wrap, or foil and freeze for up to 3 weeks. If eating within 2 days, follow previously stated refrigerator storage directions. Store smoked and canned fish in the pantry for up to 1 year if unopened.

Tip: Thaw frozen fish in milk for a fresh-caught flavor.

CLEANING

Fish are usually cleaned at the market. You will need to clean fish again, however, before cooking. If the fish has scales, always remove them before cooking. To scale, first soak the fish in water for a few minutes. Then, remove the scales by scraping a blunt knife over the fish in short strokes, starting at the tail and working toward the head. Next, slit the underside of the fish and remove the entrails (insides). Wipe the inside of the fish and use a paper towel or damp cloth to remove any blood clots adhering to the meat. The head and tail may be left on according to the size of the fish and the manner of cooking.

SKINNING

Remove the backfins with a sharp knife. Cut off a strip of skin on the back that runs the entire length. Work slowly to remove the skin with a knife. Fresh fish skin is usually removed easily.

BONING

First, clean and skin the fish before boning. At the tail, run a sharp knife under the flesh, close to the backbone. With the knife, follow the bone its entire length. Turn the fish over and run the knife along the other side to remove the remaining flesh. Use your fingers to pick out any small bones remaining.

PREPARING FILLETS

First, clean, skin, and bone the fish. Next, cut the fish into the desired size serving pieces.

IDENTIFYING THE DIFFERENT CUTS OF FISH

A **whole fish** is served as caught. **Drawn fish** is with the entrails removed. **Dressed fish** are with the head, tail, entrails, and fins removed. **Fillets** are usually boneless, sides cut lengthwise. **Butterfly Fillets** are double fillets held together by skin. **Fish sticks** are uniform pieces of fillets. **Steaks** are large, dressed fish sliced into cross sections.

METHODS OF COOKING

Fish do not have tough muscles, as swimming is easy! Thus, fish should only be cooked briefly, until the fish flakes easily with a fork. Overcooking causes fish to fall to pieces. Always serve fish as quickly as possible after cooking because fish has a tendency to become soggy when it stands a long time. In general, cook fish for 10 minutes per inch of thickness at the thickest part of the fish. The meat thermometer should read an internal temperature of 160°F. for medium-well to well-done fish or 125°F. for just cooked.

Before cooking salted fish, you must do one of the following to freshen the fish: 1. Wash the fish and then place it in a pan of cold water with the skin-side up. Make sure the water covers the fish. Soak the fish for 2 to 12 hours, depending on the amount of salt. Change the water several times while soaking—until the salt is gone. Or 2. Wash the fish and then place it in a pan. Cover the fish with cold water. Place the pan on the stove and bring the water to a boil. Drain the water. Repeat this process two more times.

Baking

This is suitable method for cooking any size or cut of fish.

Directions: Heat the oven to a moderate temperature (350°F.). Place the fish in a greased shallow baking pan, or on aluminum foil in a baking pan. You may also place the fish on a bed of sliced onions or celery in a pan. The onion or celery will prevent the fish from sticking to the pan. Sprinkle the fish with melted butter, salt and pepper, 1 Tbsp. lemon juice, and/or 1 tsp. minced onion, to taste. Bake for approximately (according to thickness):

- 30 minutes for steaks
- 20 minutes for fillets
- 15 minutes per pound of whole fish

Another way to bake fish is to cut the fish into the desired size cuts and let stand at room temperature for 15 minutes. Next, dip pieces in salted milk (1 tsp. of salt per 1 cup milk) and then in finely sifted bread crumbs. Place the covered pieces into a buttered or oiled baking pan, sprinkle pieces with melted butter, and brown for 10 to 20 minutes at 550°F.

Broiling

This is suitable for small, whole fish or fillets.

Directions: First clean, skin, and cut the fish accordingly. Dip the fish in olive or cooking oil, and place in a shallow baking pan or on a greased broiler. Sprinkle with salt and pepper. Broil fish (at 500°F.) 2 to 3 inches from the broiler element for 3 minutes. Remove the pan and pour 3 to 4 Tbsp. chicken broth (or dissolve one bouillon cube in water) over the fish. Place the pan back in the oven at 450°F. for the remaining time according to the following recommendations.

BROILING TIME CHART

Cut of Fish	Thickness	Total Broiling Time
Fillets	1/4–1 inch	6–10 minutes
Steaks	1/2–1 1/2 inches	6–16 minutes
Whole		10–16 minutes

Just before serving, pour over the fish a mixture of 1/4 cup melted butter and 1 tsp. lemon juice. **Note:** To turn fish on the cookie sheet, use two broad spatulas, or place a second cookie sheet over the first and invert both sheets together, then remove the first cookie sheet.

Boiling

This method is suitable for any type of fish.

Directions: Wrap cleaned and skinned fish in cheesecloth, and plunge it into boiling water containing a dash of salt and 1 Tbsp. vinegar or lemon juice.

After boiling for 5 minutes, add cold water and simmer until the flesh falls away from the bones.

Deep Fat Frying

This is suitable for fillets and really any type of fish, but it is particularly good for fillets.

Directions: Heat oil in a pot to a temperature of 350°F. or until a cube of bread browns in 50 seconds. Dip the fish in flour, egg, and then bread/cracker crumbs. Fry in hot fat until golden-brown, usually 3 to 6 minutes. Drain the fish on paper towels.

Pan-Frying

This method is suitable for trout, perch, crappies, sunfish, catfish—really any type of fish.

Directions: Drain thawed fish well, and blot it with a paper towel to remove excess water before frying. Sprinkle fish with salt and pepper, and dip in flour or cornmeal. Fry fish over medium heat in a hot skillet of fat 1/8 inch deep (add a little butter as well for excellent flavor). Fry until one side is golden brown, turn over, and brown other side. Frying should take a total of 10 minutes. Drain on absorbent paper.

Poaching

This is suitable for large pieces of fish and steaks.

Directions: Bring a pot of water (just enough water to cover the fish) containing 1 sliced carrot, 1 sliced onion, 1 Tbsp. parsley, 1 bay leaf, 2 whole cloves, 2 peppercorns, salt, and a little vinegar to a boil. Lower the fish into boiling water (or wrap fish in cheesecloth first). Simmer the fish for 6 to 10 minutes per pound.

To Poach Salmon: Place the salmon in a skillet containing enough water to cover the fish and add a little white wine, a few peppercorns, and a bay leaf. Simmer on low heat, covered, and turn the fish occasionally. Cook until the salmon is flaky (about 6 to 10 minutes per pound).

Sautéing

This method is suitable for any type of fish.

Directions: Clean small fish, but leave on the head and tail. Large fish should be cut into slices or fillets. Roll the fish in salted flour and place in a frying pan containing 2 to 3 Tbsp. butter or olive oil. Brown the fish over medium heat for 2 to 3 minutes, turn, and sauté the other side for 2 to 3 minutes until it's golden brown.

Steaming

This is suitable for large pieces of fish and steaks.

Directions: Cut the fish into pieces and sprinkle with salt. Wrap the fish in cheesecloth, and steam over boiling water for 10 to 15 minutes per pound, according to thickness. More flavor is retained with steaming than boiling. If piece is large, turn once. When done, remove the skin and bones and serve immediately.

FISH TIPS FOR THE KITCHEN KLUTZ

- To improve the flavor of fish, marinate it in 1 part vinegar or white wine to 2 parts oil.
- Recipes containing cooked seafood must be refrigerated and eaten within 2 days.
- Boil vinegar in pots and pans to take the fish odor out.
- Thaw frozen fish in milk for a fresh-caught flavor.
- Fillets or steaks will cook best when they are 1 to 1¼ inches thick. If necessary, lightly pound areas of uneven thickness to even them out. If steaks are thicker than 1½ inches, split the piece horizontally into two pieces.
- Place lemon juice on fish after cooking to keep it from becoming mushy.
- Coat hands with salt for easier gripping of fresh fish.
- If your fish appears dry after you have cooked it, top with store-bought onion dip and place under the broiler for a few more minutes to blend the flavors.
- A great way to serve tartar sauce is to cut a lemon in half, cut out the pulp, and fill the lemon cup with tartar sauce.
- For a delicious fish seasoning, combine 2 Tbsp. parsley flakes, 1 Tbsp. dried grated lemon rind, 1 Tbsp. dried celery seed, 1 Tbsp. dried thyme, 1 Tbsp. dried marjoram, 1 Tbsp. savory, 1 tsp. dried chives, and 1 crushed bay leaf. This recipe will make ½ cup seasoning mix, which should be stored in an airtight container.
- If you don't have a meat thermometer and want to test for doneness, insert a thin metal knife into the thickest part of the fish for 5 seconds. Remove the knife, and if it feels hot, then the fish is cooked sufficiently.
- When fish is overcooked, it becomes soft and mushy. All is not lost, though. You can make a delicious pâté by mashing and mixing it with whipped cream cheese, lemon juice, onion, sour cream, and dill.

CAVIAR

Caviar is the salted eggs of a large fish, usually sturgeon. Caviar is the Rolls-Royce of appetizers or can be used as a special ingredient in other dishes. Sometimes the eggs of other types of fish are used—such as salmon, lumpfish, and whitefish. The finest caviar, however, is from the beluga sturgeon (from the Caspian Sea in Russia). Caviar may be purchased fresh, canned, pressed, or pasteurized.

When buying fresh caviar, look for eggs that are shiny and separate and that smell salty. Because it is very perishable, refrigerate caviar as soon as possible. Don't let it sit in a hot car after purchasing.

Storing

To store fresh caviar, place the container in a plastic bag or other lidded container. Then surround the caviar container with ice, seal the bag or other container, and place it in the meat compartment of your refrigerator. *You will need to replace the ice as it melts.* Do not open the container of caviar until you are ready to use it. If unopened, fresh caviar will last up to 4 weeks. Once opened, caviar must be eaten within 3 days.

Canned caviar may be stored at room temperature or in the refrigerator until opened. After opening, store it wrapped in the meat compartment of the refrigerator for up to 3 days. Pressed caviar should be stored like fresh caviar. Pasteurized caviar may be stored at room temperature or in the refrigerator until opened. After opening, store in same fashion as canned.

Serving

Serve caviar *very* cold. To keep it cold while serving, place the caviar in a bowl and surround the bowl with ice. Serve it with crackers or toast points (a triangular piece of plain toasted bread) and lemon wedges, sour cream, shredded hard-cooked eggs, capers, or finely chopped onions. A great but expensive garnish is to place caviar on top of cooked fish you are serving.

SHELLFISH

Shellfish is so easy to fix and so delicious to eat that it will become a favorite to prepare. It may be served as an appetizer, in a casserole, or in soup. You may purchase shellfish year-round and store it in the freezer for emergencies.

Shellfish can be classified as either mollusks or crustaceans. Mollusks have no vertebrae but have a hard outer shell. Examples of mollusks are abalone, scallops, oysters, and clams. Crustaceans have hard shells and elongated bodies. Examples of crustaceans are lobster, shrimp, crayfish, and crabs. In this section you will find ways to cook all types of shellfish as well as how to store and buy it.

ABALONE

Abalone is a mollusk with a single shell and single muscle. The muscle is the edible portion. Abalone should be alive when bought fresh. Pick abalones without a fishy odor. Allow 1 steak per serving. If purchasing fresh abalone, refrigerate it immediately and cook it within 24 hours. Frozen abalone may be stored in the freezer for up to 3 months.

To remove the muscle from the shell, take a knife and cut between the shell and the meat. Cut off the dark part. Pound it to ¼ inch thickness to tenderize it. Dry it well.

To cook abalone, melt 2 to 3 Tbsp. butter and 1 Tbsp. oil in a heavy skillet. When the butter is hot, add the steak and sauté for 20 to 30 seconds per side. Season with salt, pepper, lemon juice, and parsley. To prevent abalone from curling while cooking, slice it approximately every ½ inch with a knife. Be careful, overcooking will toughen the fish. If you do overcook abalone, you can mince it and use it in chowder.

CLAMS

Clams may be soft-shell, hard-shell (from New England), or razor (from the Pacific) and are sold in the shell, by the dozen or quart, or out of the shell (shucked) by the quart in cans. Different clams are used differently in cooking. Canned minced clams can be used in dips, chowders, etc. Hard-shell clams, also called **quahogs**, are used in Manhattan clam chowder. The smaller hard-shell clams are called **littlenecks**, the medium-size are called **cherrystones**, and the large size are called **chowder**. Hard-shell clams are also used in cocktails. They are available in the spring, summer, fall, and early winter. Soft-shell clams are usually small and used in New England clam chowder as well as broths. Pacific Coast clams are good in stews and bisque. **Geoducks**, a type of Pacific Coast clam, weigh as much as 6 pounds each. Another type, **Pismo clams**, weigh as much as 1½ pounds each.

Buying

If purchasing clams in the shell, remember that the shell should be tightly closed, or close fast when touched, which indicates that the clam is still alive.

SERVING SIZES FOR CLAMS

Type	Amount per serving
In the shell	6–8 clams
Shucked (out of the shell)	½ cup
8 quarts in the shell = about 1 quart shucked	

Storing

Fresh clams should be cooked while alive, so they will need to be eaten quickly after purchasing fresh. You may store them uncovered in the crisper of the refrigerator for up to 24 hours. Fresh clams may be frozen up to 1 month, providing they are frozen when freshly caught. To freeze clams, first remove the shells, then strain the juices into a container. Wash the meat well with cold salted water, drain, and freeze in the container with the juices. Thaw in the refrigerator. **Remember:** Do not refreeze clams once thawed. Canned clams may be stored in the pantry or a cool place for up to 6 months.

Cleaning

Throw away any clams that are open or have cracked or broken shells. Scrub clams with a brush under cold water. Hold the clam by the tail under the faucet to wash out any sand. Soak in a pot of saltwater for 30 minutes, rinse, and drain again.

Methods of Cooking

Frying: Clean and dry shucked clams, dip in batter, fry in deep fat at 375°F., and drain on paper towels or brown paper. Fried clams are good served on toast and seasoned with salt, pepper, cayenne, and celery salt.

Roasting: This is a great outdoor way to cook clams at the beach. Wash the clams in seawater. Burn sticks of wood on a pile of stones and remove the ashes. Next, add a thin layer of seaweed to the stones, and pile the clams on top of the seaweed. Cover again with seaweed and a piece of canvas to hold in the steam.

Steaming: Clams to be steamed should always be bought live in the shell. Clean the clams first, then place them on a rack in a large pot or in a steamer. Add 1/2 inch of water, cover the pot and steam until the shells open partially. Serve with melted butter and a little lemon juice or vinegar. You may strain the broth (clam bouillon) and serve in cups as a dipping sauce.

Note: After cooking, throw away any clam shells that do not open—do not eat them.

CRABS

Buying

Crabs are either sold as soft-shell or hard-shell—it's the same crab, just at different stages of its molting cycle. Soft-shell crabs are in season from June to September, when crabs have just cast off their shells (molting). Crabs grow by shedding their shells and then making larger shells. Hard-shell crabs are available all year, although they are more plentiful in the summer.

Types of crab include **blue crab**, **Dungeness**, and **king crab**. Blue crabs are found in the Atlantic Ocean, Dungeness are found in the Pacific, and king crabs in the North Pacific. Dungeness are sweeter than blue crabs and are good for salads.

Look for moving legs when purchasing fresh crabs. Crabs may also be purchased cooked. If cooked, shells will be tinged with red and should not have an unpleasant odor. In addition, crabs may also be purchased frozen or canned.

SERVING SIZES FOR CRABS

Type	Per serving
Soft-shell	2 crabs
Hard-shell	2 crabs
Crab legs	1/2 pound
Crabmeat	3–4 ounces
Blue crabs	1 pound
Dungeness crab	1/2 to 1 whole crab

1 pound of crab meat = 3 cups crab meat
1 6 1/2-ounce can of crab meat = 1 1/4 cups

102

Storing

Keep crabs alive until you are ready to cook them. You may keep them in the container in which you purchased them or wrap them with damp paper towels. Fresh crabs must be eaten within 24 hours. Fresh water will kill crabs. Canned crabmeat should be stored in the pantry or a cool, dry place up to 6 months.

Methods of Cooking

When crabs are cooked the shells will be tinged with red and will not have an unpleasant odor.

Boiling: Place crabs in warm salted water for 30 minutes before boiling because if crabs are dropped directly into boiling water, they will shed their claws. Bring a pot of water containing lemon, celery leaves, and parsley to a boil. Dump hard-shell crabs into the boiling water, bring to a full boil, and simmer covered, approximately 15 minutes, until the shells are tinged with red. Drain, place the crabs in cool water, and drain again. Cool to room temperature and serve.

Serving: Break legs and claws off from the cooked crabs, crack the shell with pliers, a nutcracker, or seafood cracker, and remove the meat. Break off the tail, and force the shell apart. Throw away the spongy material and remove the meat.

CRAYFISH

Crayfish (pronounced crawfish) have a delicate, tantalizing, luscious flavor. The fat in crayfish is used in cooking them, which greatly enhances their cooked flavor. Crayfish, which look like miniature lobster, are wonderful in Créole and Cajun dishes. Discard any dead ones and only use live crayfish. Allow 1 dozen unpeeled per serving or 1/2 pound of peeled per serving. Keep crayfish alive until you are ready to cook them. You may keep them in the container in which you purchased them or wrap them in damp paper towels. Fresh crayfish must be eaten within 24 hours. Fresh water will kill crayfish. Wash live crayfish well with cold saltwater, changing the water several times.

Methods of Cooking

Prepare a pot of boiling water that has 1 Tbsp. salt and 1 Tbsp. caraway seeds. You may also add cayenne pepper, for more flavor. Next remove the stomach and intestinal vein of the crayfish by pulling the middle tailfin. Drop the crayfish into the boiling water, bring the water back to a boil, and cook covered for 5 to 7 minutes. Drain and eat. You may chill cooked crayfish before eating if you like. Serve crayfish in the shell.

Frying: Take 1 pound of peeled crayfish. Dip each piece in a mixture of 2 beaten eggs and 1 Tbsp. milk. Then roll the crayfish in a mixture of flour, salt, and pepper. Next, fry crayfish in a skillet of hot oil (any kind) over medium heat until brown. Remove and drain on paper towels. Fried crayfish may be served as an appetizer or as a main dish.

Eating: Use your fingers to eat crayfish. Using your thumbs and fingers of both hands, crack the tail open by pushing the tail back toward the body of the crayfish against the curve of the shell. Eat crayfish with melted butter. You may also add a little dill to the melted butter.

LOBSTERS

Buying

Lobsters are the largest shellfish, and are most plentiful from June through September. Look for a lobster that is heavy in proportion to its size. A 1-to-2-pound lobster is preferred. Two common types of lobster are Maine and rock. **Maine lobsters** are found along the eastern coast of the United States, from Maine to South Carolina, and are dark blue-green in color. **Rock lobster** is found off Southern California, Mexico, South America, and South Africa. It has a maroon or red-orange shell and is clawless.

COMMERCIAL GRADINGS OF LOBSTERS

Type	Size
Chicken	1 pound
Quarters	under 1 1/2 pounds
Large	1 1/2 to 2 1/2 pounds
Jumbo	over 2 1/2 pounds

If you are buying cooked lobster, test to ensure that the lobster has been boiled properly. Straighten the tail out, and the tail should spring back into place if the lobster was boiled correctly. Cooked lobster should be bright red and should not have an unpleasant odor.

If you are buying a live lobster look for movement in the legs. A live lobster will curl its tail under its body when picked up. (Be sure to leave sleepy lobsters alone!) In addition, make sure you find out how much the lobster weighs, so you will know how long to cook it.

Another fact to keep in mind when buying a lobster is that its meat shrinks more than any other seafood. Sometimes a female lobster is preferred, because the female finlike appendages are softer than the two on the male lobster.

BUYING LOBSTER

Type	Amount
Small, fresh	1 per serving
Large, fresh	1/2 per serving
2 1/2 pounds fresh	2 cups cooked meat
1 pound fresh	1 1/4 cup cooked meat
6-ounce can	1 cup meat
Rock lobster tails	1/2 pound per serving

Storing

Lobsters must be cooked, cooled, then frozen. Frozen lobsters may be stored in the freezer for several months. Live lobster should be cooked as soon as possible, but may be kept in the container in which you purchased the lobster or it may be wrapped in a moist cloth up to one day. Do not store live lobster on ice—fresh water will kill lobster. Remember that lobster purchased fresh must be kept alive until cooked.

Methods of Cooking

Fresh lobster must be cooked alive and should be boiled or broiled. Frozen lobster should be cooked like frozen lobster tails (see below). Lobster meat should be opaque when done and the shell should be bright red. Overcooking lobster will turn the meat stringy. Always add cooked lobster to a dish as the final step in process.

Boiling: Place the live lobster on its back and plunge a knife through the head, or if this is too gruesome for you, place it in a pot of vigorously boiling salted water and boil, covered, for 15 to 20 minutes. Lobsters should be completely immersed in the boiling water. Remove the lobster from the water and drain or wipe dry. To test if the lobster is done, cut into the underside of the tail with a knife to make sure the meat is no longer translucent. Serve with clarified melted butter and lemon juice. Use the following chart to determine boiling times:

LOBSTER BOILING TIMES

Weight of Lobster	Boiling Time
1–1½ pounds	10–12 minutes
1½–2 pounds	13–14 minutes
2–3 pounds	15–18 minutes
3–4 pounds	20–22 minutes
4–6 pounds	23–25 minutes
7–10 pounds	30–35 minutes

Broiling: First kill the lobster as described above. Next, split the lobster open from tail to head and remove the intestinal vein, liver, stomach, and lungs. Crack the claws with a hammer. Cut the tail crosswise to prevent curling. Place lobster in a broiling pan with the shell-side up 4 inches from the broiling element. Brush with melted butter and broil for 6 to 8 minutes. Turn over, brush again with melted butter, and broil for another 4 to 6 minutes until the meat and shell are pink. Serve with clarified melted butter and lemon (see p. 27).

Rock lobster tails are usually sold frozen, either 2 in a package—each weighing ¼ to 1 pound—or singly. To cook frozen lobster tails, boil the tails while still frozen in salted boiling water (1 tsp. salt per quart of water). **A rule of thumb:** Boil the tails 3 minutes longer than the weight of the tail. If the tails are thawed, boil for only 1 minute longer than the weight of the tail. To broil tails, broil the shell side for 5 minutes and the flesh side for 6 to 8 minutes. Once cooked, drain and cut away the undershell with scissors. Place your fingers between the shell and the lobster meat and pull the meat out in one piece.

Eating a Lobster

Twist off the claws and crack them with a nutcracker or seafood cracker (use a small hammer if you don't have a cracker). Separate the tail from the body. You might have to cut the thin shell portion under the tail to remove the meat. Remove the small intestinal vein from the tail meat that runs through the center. Hold the body shell and draw the body out. Leave in the feathery part (lungs), the stomach, and the liver—the tomalley (bright green in color). Some lobsters (females) will have roe (eggs), which is considered a delicacy. Break the body apart and dig out the meat between the bones. **Tip:** Take the liver of the lobster, mix it with mayonnaise, and serve it with crackers and bread as an appetizer.

MUSSELS

The only part eaten is the muscle that opens and closes the shell.

Buying Mussels

Mussels are available all year, although they are best in the winter months. Fresh mussels may be wild or cultured. Wild mussels are a dull blue-black color with erosion marks and often have seaweed or other matter attached. Cultured mussels are a shiny blue-black color and have no blemishes. Cultured mussels are larger than wild mussels.

Both wild mussels and cultured mussels are available when buying fresh. If you have a choice, buy cultured mussels because they are easier to clean and prepare and are usually more consistent in size. When buying live mussels, look for a tightly closed shell. If the shell is not tightly closed, tap the shell. Do not buy any that do not immediately snap shut, and do not buy any with a bad odor. Do not use if the mussel shell is open, or if the shell halves slide. Allow 12 mussels per serving.

Storing

Place mussels in a container in a single layer. Cover the container with a damp paper towel or cloth and store in the crisper of the refrigerator for up to 4 days.

Cleaning

Always scrub mussels well with a stiff brush. Scrape or clip the beards (or fringe) away. Cook immediately after cleaning since they spoil fast.

Methods of Cooking

Baking: Preheat the oven to 450°F. Place clean mussels in a large pan containing 2 Tbsp. olive oil. Place the pan in the oven and bake until the shells open. Remove the pan from the oven. Remove the upper shell of the mussel. Serve mussels on the lower shells with melted butter.

Steaming: In a large pot, melt 2 to 3 Tbsp. butter, margarine, olive or vegetable oil over medium heat. Add 1 cup chopped celery and 1/2 cup chopped onions or chives and sauté for 2 to 3 minutes until soft. Add 1/2 cup white wine and place the mussels in the pot, bring to a boil, reduce heat to medium, cover, and steam the mussels for 5 minutes, or until the shells open. Remove them from the pot and set aside on a warm plate. Strain the remaining liquid and place it back on the heat. Add 1 tsp. flour, and bring to a boil, adding salt and pepper. Serve this as a dip for the mussels or pour it over them.

OYSTERS

Buying

Oysters are in season from September to May. You may eat off-season oysters, but they have poor flavor and flabby texture. Shucked oysters should be plump and cream-colored and their liquid ("liquor") should be clear. Oysters bought alive should be tightly closed or should close quickly when tapped. If not, the oyster is dead and should not be used.

SERVING SIZES FOR OYSTERS

Type	Amount per Serving
In the shell	6–12
Shucked	1/2 cup

Note: 2 dozen shucked = 1 cup

Storing

Fresh oysters may be kept alive for several days in the refrigerator; store them covered with a damp cloth in the crisper section of the refrigerator. Store shucked oysters in a container with their liquor in the refrigerator for up to 2 days. If they are freshly caught, they may be frozen for up to 4 months. To freeze, remove the shells and strain the juices into a container. Wash the meat well with cold salted water, drain, and freeze in a container with the juices. Thaw oysters in the refrigerator. You may also freeze oysters in an ice cube tray—place one with some juice in each ice cube section. **Remember:** You cannot refreeze them once thawed.

Shucking

Insert a thin knife (if possible, use an oyster knife) under the back end of the right valve and push forward until it cuts the muscle that holds the shell together. The shells will separate. **Tip:** To open with ease, wash oysters with cold water and place them in a plastic bag in the freezer for one hour.

Cleaning

Place shucked oysters in a colander or strainer over a bowl. Pour cold water over the oysters to loosen bits of the shell. Remove any pieces of shell stuck to the muscle. **Note:** Many choose not to rinse oysters before cooking because the "liquor" from the oyster shell enhances their flavor.

Methods of Cooking

Oyster shells open when they are through cooking. Shucked oysters will curl when they are done. The liquor will be clear.

Frying: Clean shucked oysters and dry between paper towels. Sprinkle with salt and pepper, dip in flour, egg, and cracker crumbs, and fry in oil at 375°F. Drain on brown paper or paper towels. **Tip:** Add baking powder to the flour for fluffiness.

Oven-frying: Dip clean oysters in a mixture 1 cup of flour, 1 tsp. salt, and 1/4 tsp. pepper. Next dip oysters in 1 egg, slightly beaten, and roll in bread or cracker crumbs, then dip in olive oil and bake at 400°F. for 15 minutes.

Parboiling: Clean and drain the liquid from the oysters, then place them in a saucepan or a pot. Add enough water to cover, and bring it to a boil. Cook over medium heat until the edges begin to curl. Drain on a paper towel.

Eating Raw Oysters

Eat raw oysters in the shell . . .

• on a cracker
• on a cracker with cocktail sauce
• on a cracker with horseradish sauce

• dipped in cocktail sauce
• dipped in horseradish sauce
• with lemon juice

SCALLOPS

The only part eaten of this mollusk is the muscle that opens and closes the shell.

Buying

There are two types of scallops, **sea scallops** and **bay scallops**. Sea scallops are larger, usually 2 inches in diameter when shucked, and white to light pink to orange in color. Bay scallops are smaller, approximately 1/2 inch in diameter when shucked, and their color ranges from light tan to pink to creamy white. Bay scallops are more tender and delicate than sea scallops. Scallops are usually sold shucked. Look for a nice moist texture, good color, and nice odor (avoid any that have a strong smell).

SERVING SIZES FOR SCALLOPS

Type	Amount per serving
Shucked	1/3 to 1/4 pound
Sea scallops	1/3 pound
Bay scallops	1/4 pound

Storing

Scallops should be eaten within 2 to 3 days if purchased fresh, and may be stored in the refrigerator in a container surrounded by ice for a few days until ready to eat. Be sure to replenish the ice as needed. Scallops may be frozen for up to 4 months if frozen when they are freshly caught. To freeze scallops, remove the shells and strain the juices into a container. Wash the meat well with cold salted water, drain, and freeze in a container with the juices. To defrost, thaw scallops in the refrigerator.

Shucking

If you buy scallops in their shells, scrub the shells well with a brush. Preheat the oven to 300°F. Place the scallops in a pan with the deep-side down, then place the pan in the oven. Once the shells open, remove the meat. The coral matter inside may be prepared and eaten as well as the "scallop" meat. You may clean the shells well and use them as serving dishes for the scallops.

Cleaning

Place shucked scallops in a colander or strainer over a bowl. Pour cold water over the scallops to loosen bits of the shell, and remove any pieces of shell stuck to the muscle. **Note:** Many choose not to rinse scallops before cooking because the "liquor" (liquid from the scallop shell) enhances the flavor.

Methods of Cooking

Broiling: Preheat the oven to the "Broil" setting. In a shallow pan, arrange the scallops in a single layer and sprinkle with salt, pepper, and garlic salt. Place pan in the oven 3 to 4 inches from the broiler element and cook for 4 minutes. Turn the scallops often and baste with a mixture of butter or margarine and lemon juice. After cooking, you may sprinkle scallops with finely crushed bread or cracker crumbs or finely chopped onions, and broil for an additional minute. Scallops turn opaque white when done and are firm to the touch.

Sautéing: Melt 2 Tbsp. butter, margarine, olive or vegetable oil in a skillet over medium heat. Add salt, pepper, garlic, onion, or paprika to the skillet and stir. Increase the heat to high, and place the scallops in the skillet in a single layer. Cook over high heat until done—about 5 to 7 minutes. Scallops will become golden when done and will be firm to the touch.

Note: Scallops may be substituted for oysters in most recipes.

SHRIMP

The only part eaten of shrimp is the tail meat.

Buying

Shrimp may be bought fresh or frozen. If you are buying fresh shrimp, look for a close-fitting shell, gray-greenish color, no unpleasant odor, and firm flesh. Shrimp should be headless and dead when purchased. "Green" shrimp refers to raw shrimp. If you are buying frozen shrimp, look for shrimp that is ivory in color (not white—white color indicates freezer burn). Black spots on shrimp are a sign of aging and mean that the shrimp may be tough.

SERVING SIZES FOR SHRIMP

Size	Number of Shrimp per Pound	Amount per Serving
Jumbo	18–20 shrimp	4 shrimp
Large	21–25 shrimp	6 shrimp
Medium	26–35 shrimp	7 shrimp
Small	35+	10 shrimp

Remember: Shrimp lose one size when the shell is removed, and another size when they are cooked. Also, the larger the shrimp, the more expensive they will be.

Storing

Rinse shrimp thoroughly under cold water, drain, and place in a tightly covered container. You may then store them in the refrigerator for up to 2 days. Cooked shrimp may be refrigerated in a tightly covered container for up to 3 days. Shrimp may be frozen either raw or cooked. Thaw frozen cooked shrimp in the refrigerator. Uncooked frozen shrimp do not have to be thawed before cooking.

Cleaning

Shrimp may be cleaned before or after cooking, although they are easier to peel before they are cooked. To remove the shell, hold the shrimp tail in one hand and using your fingers on the other hand, break off some of the shell. Then pull the meat out while holding the tail. Remove the black vein with a sharp knife. The vein will not hurt you if you eat it—it's just not very attractive.

Methods of Cooking

Boiling: Place shrimp in boiling salted water (1 Tbsp. salt per quart of water). You may add sliced onion, peppercorns, parsley, celery salt, or bay leaves for additional seasoning. Cover and simmer for 2 to 5 minutes, depending on the size of the shrimp. It will usually take 2 minutes for smaller shrimp and 5 minutes for jumbo shrimp. Simmer until the shells turn pink. Drain shrimp and rinse with cold water to chill. Remove the shell and the dark vein along the back. **Note:** If shrimp are cleaned before cooking, simmer until the shrimp curl. Cleaned shrimp require less cooking time. While cooking, you may leave the shells in the pot with the peeled shrimp for more flavor. Serve with your favorite horseradish or cocktail sauce. Shrimp should be pink and firm when done. **Watch shrimp carefully when cooking, as they will overcook quickly.**

Sautéing: Clean the shrimp, melt 2 to 3 Tbsp. butter in a skillet or a saucepan set over medium heat, and add the shrimp. Cook over medium-high heat, turning once or twice until the shrimp are pink. It should take about 5 minutes to cook the shrimp, depending on size. Again, shrimp are done when they are firm and slightly curled. You may also add a chopped onion for flavor.

TIPS FOR COOKING SHRIMP

- Add several celery leaves or 1 Tbsp. caraway seed to your cooking pot to eliminate the odor of boiling shrimp.
- To help contain the odor, place shrimp remains (tails, heads, shells) in an airtight bag, and store in the freezer until the garbage collector comes.
- Shrimp should be firm and pink when done.
- For a shrimp-based broth, place clean shrimp shells in a pot of water and bring to a boil. Reduce heat and simmer covered for 30 minutes. Cool and strain the liquid. It may be frozen for up to 6 months and used in soup or gumbo containing shrimp or another type of shellfish.
- For a fresher taste, soak shrimp in a mixture of 1 Tbsp. sherry and 2 Tbsp. vinegar for 15 minutes before cooking.

SHELLFISH FOR THE REFINED KITCHEN KLUTZ

Snails (Escargot)

Eating snails goes back to ancient Rome. These small mollusks are considered a delicacy and are usually pricey.

Buying: You may buy snails that are canned or fresh. The best canned snails come from France, and they tend to be larger than American snails. The best size of snail to eat is one that is 1 to 1½ inches in diameter. If buying canned snails, buy a package of empty snail shells which you may use for stuffing.

- Allow 1 dozen snails per serving
- 1 pound of fresh snails = 44 canned snails

Storing: Store fresh snails in the refrigerator for up to 24 hours. Canned snails can be stored in the pantry in a cool, dry place for up to 6 months.

Cleaning: If using fresh snails, place them in a pan and cover completely with lukewarm water. Soak for 10 minutes. Throw away any snails that haven't started coming out of their shells yet. Drain water, then cover again with cold water, and add salt ($1/2$ cup salt per 50 snails). Moisten the edge of the bowl with water and coat with salt to deter snails from crawling out. Let the snails sit this way for 1 hour. Drain and scrub the shells with a toothbrush under cold water.

If using canned snails, place them in a colander and rinse with cold water. Then, place them in a bowl, fill it with water, add 1 tsp. salt and 1 clove of garlic, cover tightly, and refrigerate for several hours (preferably overnight if possible). After soaking, drain and blot dry with a paper or cloth towel.

Methods of Cooking: Use canned snails in recipes. To cook fresh snails, bring a pot of water to a boil. Add the snails, reduce the heat slightly so the water is simmering, and cook for 5 minutes. Drain into a colander. Use a cocktail fork or a snail fork and pull snails out of their shells. Cut the head, the black tail, and any green off with a sharp knife or kitchen scissors. Rinse again. Place in a pan, and add enough water, wine, or beef broth to cover. Place on the stove over low heat and simmer until tender (up to 2 hours). You may add chopped celery or carrots or a bay leaf to the pot if you like. Once snails are tender, turn the heat off and allow them to cool to room temperature in the pot. Eat according to your choice.

Eating: To eat snails, grip the shell in one hand using special snail tongs and with the other hand use a cocktail fork to extract the meat from the shell.

To make a delicious snail butter, place the following in a saucepan and simmer for one minute: 8 Tbsp. melted butter, 1 minced clove of garlic, dash of red pepper sauce, 1 tsp. of chopped onion, a drop of Worcestershire sauce, and 1 Tbsp. of fresh lemon juice.

VEGETABLES

With fresh vegetables available at the market year-round, you will find the buying chart in this chapter indispensable. It not only tells you what to buy and how much, but also what you should avoid when buying vegetables. The storing chart for vegetables will also be helpful because correct storage is crucial for maintaining maximum flavor and freshness.

Vegetables are easy to fix—whether raw or cooked—and add to any meal. In fact, meals containing only vegetables and no meat cannot be beat; they are delicious. For an extra-scrumptious meal, go to your local farmers market, select four or five of your favorite vegetables, then prepare and cook them in homestyle fashion, as mentioned later in the chapter.

Vegetables either grow in or above the ground and consequently they need to be rinsed well before cooking to remove dirt and grit. After rinsing well, you may cook them in numerous ways—boiling, steaming, broiling, baking, stewing, and grilling. Then you can serve them plain, with butter or cheese, with sauces, or with other vegetables mixed together for a colorful and unique flavor. Remember, cooking, serving, and eating vegetables is not only good for you, but delicious and fun as well.

BUYING

Consult the following chart when buying vegetables.

VEGETABLE BUYING CHART

Vegetable	Buy	Avoid
Artichoke	looks fresh, plump, heavy for its size; green leaves are close together and without blemishes (the rounder the artichoke, the larger the heart—the smaller the artichoke, the more tender)	spreading or loose leaves

Vegetable	Buy	Avoid
Asparagus	green (or pale ivory if white asparagus), straight, and firm stalks; choose stalks similar in thickness for even cooking	soggy, opening tips; too large can indicate toughness
Beans, green (including snap and string)	smooth, bright pods; small in size; fresh, green; should break with a "snap"	shriveled, blemished, dry-looking pods; discoloration
Beets	small, rich color (very dark reddish-purple)	broken skin, bruised
Broccoli	firm, compact clusters; dark green	tough stems, yellow clusters, black spots
Brussel sprouts	firm, compact; deep green color	smudgy and dirty appearance, yellowing, wilting
Cabbage	solid, firm; stem cut close to head	yellowing leaves, bursting heads with outer leaves separated from the stem, small holes indicate worms
Carrots	small, firm, smooth; bright orange	cracked, shriveled
Cauliflower	white, clean, firm, compact	dirty, bruised, spreading clusters
Celery	brittle; light green color	soggy, stringy stalks; yellow tops
Chives	young, tender; fresh green tops	yellow or wilted tops, wet
Corn	kernels should be juicy like milk, if in husk—silk should be dark and dry	dry, brittle husks; moist silk; shriveled kernels
Cucumber	smaller, firm; deep green color	puffiness, withered, shriveled, soft, yellowed
Eggplant (aubergine)	heavy, firm, shiny; dark purple and black color	wilted, flabby, soft, shriveled
Fennel (celery-like with a slightly licorice taste)	crisp, firm stalks and bulbs	cracked, yellowed, brown tops
Garlic	dry, unbroken outer covering, firm	soft, spongy bulb or shriveled one
Leeks	young, tender; fresh green tops	yellow or wilted tops, wet
Lima beans	velvety, shiny pods	shriveled, dull spots, yellowed
Mushrooms	clean, firm, dry	soft and moldy
Okra	tender pods that snap easily, less than 4 inches long	dry, dull, shriveled, discolored

Vegetable	Buy	Avoid
Onions	firm, dry, smooth skins	soft, hollow, wet, soggy
Types of Onions:		

Bermuda	—mild and sweet	
Chives	—delicate flavor	
Green (scallions)	—green tops, milder white bulb, stronger	
Maui	—very sweet and juicy	
Purple or red	—robust, great served raw in salads	
Yellow	—strong pungent flavor	
Spanish	—sweet and juicy	
Walla Walla	—very sweet and juicy	
White	—milder	
Vidalia	—very sweet and juicy	

Vegetable	Buy	Avoid
Green onions (scallions)	young, tender; fresh green tops	yellow, wilted tops, wet
Parsley	bright green	yellow (revive wilted in ice water)
Parsnips	smooth, firm; small to medium-size	softness, large and flabby roots
Peas	tender, bright green, velvety pods	swollen pods, dark green, wet and mildewed pods
Peppers (sweet and bell— green, red, yellow, and purple)	firm, thick-fleshed, smooth	soft, pliable, pale, thin-fleshed, surface blemishes

Note: Red and yellow peppers are known as sweet peppers because they are milder than green peppers.

Vegetable	Buy	Avoid
Potatoes	firm, hard, smooth, reasonably clean	discolored, greenish, leathery, very large, soft, sprouting
Scallions (green onions)	young, tender; fresh green tops	yellow or wilted tops, wet
Shallots	firm, dry, well-rounded bulbs	soft, wet
Spinach	crisp, clean leaves, green color	wilted, yellow
Sprouts (radish, alfalfa, bean, and mung)	fresh, sweet fragrance, short, crisp	soggy, brown ends

115

Vegetable	Buy	Avoid
Squash	heavy for size; firm, smooth and glossy	blemishes, soft, dull
Sweet potatoes	smooth, unblemished, firm	cracked, wet, soft, shriveled
Tomatoes	plump, smooth, deep color, firm	blemishes, soft spots
Turnips	smooth, firm; green tops	scars, blemishes
Zucchini	small, firm	wilted, bruised, soft spots, blemishes

Notes: In potatoes, a greenish tinge indicates the presence of solanin, which will make you sick if you eat a lot of it. Peel the green tinge off if you buy potatoes that are greenish. If the entire potato is green, throw it away. A tomato is really a fruit but often thought of as a vegetable! To ripen, place it in a closed bag out of the sun with an apple to speed the ripening time.

SERVING SIZES FOR VEGETABLES

Vegetable	Amount Purchased	Produces	Number of Servings
Asparagus	1 pound	2 cups cooked	3–4
Artichoke	1 pound		3–4
Beans, dried	1 pound	6 cups cooked	5–6
Beans, green	1 pound	4 cups cooked or 2³/₄ cups cut	5–6
Beans, lima	1 pound, unshelled	1 cup cooked	2
Beans, string	¹/₂–³/₄ pound	1¹/₂ cups cooked	2
Beets	1 pound	2 cups cooked	3–4
Broccoli	1 bunch (1¹/₂–2¹/₂ pounds)	2–4 cups cooked	4–6
Brussels sprouts	1 pound	3 cups cooked	4–5
Carrots	1 pound	2 cups cooked or 3 cups shredded	3–4
Cabbage	1 pound	2¹/₂ cups cooked or 4¹/₂ cups shredded	3–4
Cauliflower	1 pound	1¹/₂ cups chopped	2
Celery	1 pound	2 cups	4
Corn	1 Medium ear	¹/₂ cup cut	1
Cucumber	1 pound	2¹/₂ cups	5
Eggplant	1 pound	1³/₄ cups cooked or 3–4 cup chopped	3
Fennel	¹/₃ pound	¹/₃ cup	1
Okra	1 pound	4 cups	1
Onions	1 pound	1¹/₂ to 2 cups cooked	2
Mushrooms	8 ounces	1 cup sliced	4

Vegetable	Amount Purchased	Produces	Number of Servings
Parsnips	1 pound	2½ cups cooked	4–5
Peas	1 pound	1 cup cooked	2
Pepper, green	1 large	1 cup diced	
Potatoes	3 medium	2 cups cubed and cooked or 1¾ cups mashed	2
Rutabagas	1 pound	2⅔ cups diced or 2 cups mashed (cooked)	3–4
Squash	2 pounds	2 cups cooked	3–4
Spinach	1 pound	2 cups cooked	3–4
Sweet potatoes	1 pound	2¾ cups cooked	3–4
Sweet potatoes	3 medium	3 cups sliced	3
Tomatoes	1 pound	2¾ cups cooked	3–4
Turnips	1 pound	3½ cups sliced or 2½ cups cooked	3–4

If you purchase canned vegetables in large quantities at food distributors, the following chart will help determine serving sizes.

SERVING SIZES FOR COMMERCIAL CANS

No. O	=	10–11 ounces	=	1⅓ cups	=	2 servings
No. 1	=	8 ounces	=	1 cup	=	2 servings
No. 1 tall	=	16 ounces	=	2 cups	=	4 servings
No. 303	=	16 ounces	=	2 cups	=	4 servings
No. 2	=	20 ounces	=	2½ cups	=	5 servings
No. 2½	=	29 ounces	=	3½ cups	=	7 servings
No. 10	=	7 pounds	=	13 cups	=	26 servings

Remember: Never purchase canned foods with dents, cracks, leaks, or loose lids or cans that are swollen.

STORING

In general, store all fresh vegetables unwashed in plastic bags in the refrigerator except for the following:

Asparagus: Wrap bottom of stalks with a damp paper towel, place in a plastic bag and refrigerate

Carrots: Cut off the green tops first before storing in the refrigerator

Garlic: Store in a cool, dry place out of the sunlight and do not store in plastic—use a paper bag instead

Onions: Wrap in foil to prevent sprouting and store in a cool, dry place or wrap

117

in old, clean nylon stockings (tie a knot between each onion so they do not touch and then hang them in a cool, dry place)

Potatoes: Store in a cool, dry, well-ventilated place and do not store in plastic (potatoes need air)

Radishes: Cut off the green tops before storing in the refrigerator

Tomatoes: Store in a cool, dry place until ripe and then store in the refrigerator if they are not going to be used immediately. The flavor of a tomato will be better, however, if not stored in the refrigerator

It is best to store vegetables in the crisper section of your refrigerator. The crisper is a confined area and thus has higher humidity than the rest of your refrigerator. The humidity will prevent water loss, which causes vegetables to wilt.

Consult the following chart for the storage life of vegetables.

VEGETABLE STORAGE LIFE

Vegetable	*Shelf Life*
Artichoke	up to 5 days
Asparagus	up to 2 days
Beans, dried	up to 1 year
Beans, snap, green, or string	up to 3 days
Beets	up to 3 days
Broccoli	up to 7 days
Brussels sprouts	up to 3 days
Cabbage	up to 7 days
Carrots (**Note:** cut the green tops off first.)	up to 2 weeks
Cauliflower	up to 4 days
Celery	up to 2 weeks
Chives	up to 5 days
Corn	up to 3 days (in the husks)
Cucumbers	up to 7 days
Eggplant	up to 4 days
Fennel	up to 7 days
Garlic	up to 1 month
Leeks	up to 5 days
Lima beans	up to 2 days
Mushrooms	up to 3 days
Okra	up to 2 days
Onions	up to 1 month
Green onions (scallions)	up to 5 days
Parsley	up to 1 week
Parsnips	up to 3 weeks
Peas	up to 4 days
Peppers	up to 7 days
Potatoes	up to 2 weeks
Scallions (green onions)	up to 5 days

Vegetable	Shelf Life
Shallots	up to 2 months
Spinach	up to 3 days
Sprouts	up to 7 days
Squash	up to 5 days
Sweet potatoes	up to 2 weeks
Tomatoes	if ripe—up to 3 days
	if green—up to 1 week
Turnips	up to 4 days
Zucchini	up to 3 days

VEGETABLE STORAGE TIPS

- To keep celery up to 2 weeks—wash, cut, and drain celery, then place celery in a plastic bag with a paper towel and close the bag tightly.
- Wrap onions in foil to prevent sprouting or wrap them in old, clean, nylon stockings. Tie a knot between each onion so they do not touch and then hang them in a cool, dry place.
- Never refrigerate potatoes. The starch in the potatoes will convert to sugar and the flavor will change as a result. Also store potatoes in paper bags or not in anything. Do not store in plastic because potatoes need air.

Blanching

Fresh vegetables may be frozen but must be blanched first. Blanching sets the colors, seals in the juices, and destroys any bacteria. Wash and prepare vegetables in the way you would like them cooked (whole, sliced, diced, chopped, etc.). Bring a large pot of water to a boil. Add vegetables (blanch a small amount at a time and use a wire basket or cheesecloth to hold the vegetables if possible), bring the water back to a boil, cover the pot, and boil 2 to 3 minutes. Corn will need to boil 7 to 10 minutes. Remove vegetables from the water, place them in a strainer, run cold water over them to stop the cooking, and let them cool. This will takes several minutes. Drain well, dry thoroughly, and wrap well in freezer foil, paper, or plastic wrap.

The following vegetables should not be blanched but frozen accordingly.

Beets: Cook them until tender, peel, slice or leave whole, and wrap with freezer foil, plastic wrap, or paper

Mushrooms: Wash, slice, or leave whole, sauté in butter, and wrap in freezer foil, paper, or plastic wrap and freeze immediately

Onions: Slice, chop, or leave whole and freeze in freezer foil, paper, or plastic wrap (do not cook)

Peppers (green, red, yellow): Wash, chop, or slice, and wrap in freezer foil, paper, or plastic wrap (do not cook)

Potatoes: Wash, cut up, cook until soft, mash and then wrap in freezer foil, plastic wrap, or paper

Pumpkin: Wash, cut up, cook until soft, mash and then wrap in freezer foil, plastic wrap, or paper

Squash (winter): Wash, cut up, cook until soft, mash and then wrap in freezer foil, plastic wrap, or paper

Cooking Frozen Vegetables

To cook frozen vegetables, do not thaw, but cook frozen in salted water until tender. Frozen vegetables will take only half as long to cook as unfrozen vegetables. The only exception to this is corn which should be thawed before cooking.

PREPARING AND COOKING

Following are the basic guidelines to follow when preparing and cooking vegetables.

1. To clean dirty vegetables, use lukewarm salty water. Lift the vegetables out of the water so the dirt remains at the bottom. Do not soak vegetables in water. Most vegetables will need to be washed this way. Mushrooms are an exception.
2. Only cook with enough water to cover the vegetables. If you like, you may add $1/2$ tsp. salt per cup of water.
3. Vegetables may be sliced lengthwise into strips, diced into small cubes, or sliced diagonally into thin or thick julienne strips. It's important to cut the slices into similar sizes so they will cook evenly. A quick way to slice, dice, or julienne vegetables is to use a food processor.
4. Cook vegetables in their skins whenever possible.
5. For maximum color and flavor for green vegetables, leave the lid off the first 5 minutes of cooking. Add a lid for the remainder of the time.
6. Strong vegetables—broccoli, onions, turnips, cauliflower, rutabagas, cabbage, and Brussels sprouts—should be cooked in just enough water to cover without a lid. If the strong vegetables are cut into small pieces, then use a lid.

Following are some "homestyle" ways to prepare and cook various vegetables when you purchase them and want to cook without a recipe.

Artichokes

Cut off an inch from the top of the artichoke. You may also cut off the stem (leaving $1/2$ inch), although some people prefer to peel it before cooking and use it in salads after it has been cooked. Remove any tough bottom leaves. Next, cut off the thorn at the end of each leaf with kitchen scissors. Soak the artichoke in cold salted water (1 tsp. salt per 2 quarts of water) for at least 1 hour. To cook, plunge the artichoke into boiling water (in a non-aluminum or steel pan), bring the water back to a boil, then reduce the heat and simmer uncovered for 5 minutes, next cover for 20 to 35 minutes, depending on the size, or until a leaf pulls away easily. To brighten dull artichokes, add 1 Tbsp. olive oil to the boiling water. To test for doneness, prick the underside of the artichoke with a fork to see if it is tender. Drain the artichokes before serving. To eat, pull off a leaf, dip the wide end into your sauce of choice, and scrape the bottom half of the leaf through your teeth to remove the artichoke meat at the bottom of each leaf. At the very center of the artichoke, under the prickly, grassy-looking fibers, is the heart, considered the most delicious part. Don't eat the grassy part (called the "choke"—it can possibly choke you if eaten), just eat the heart. After eating the leaves, take your fork and knife and remove the choke from the heart (by scraping it off). Cut the artichoke heart, dip, and eat.

Asparagus

Snap off the bottom end. It will break off easily. Throw away the tough bottom part. Wash the spears under cold water to remove all dirt and grit. Stand the asparagus in 2 to 3 inches of cold water until you are ready to cook them. Tie them in bunches with string in order to cook upright. Place asparagus upright in a deep, narrow pot of 2-inches-deep boiling water. Cover and bring the water back to a boil. Cook for 3 to 4 minutes or until tender. You may also cook asparagus flat in a covered skillet, although this is not the preferred way because the bottom half needs to cook longer than the tips. If cutting asparagus into pieces, cook the bottom pieces first and add the tips during the last 5 to 8 minutes. You may plunge them into boiling water for 3 to 4 minutes or steam them for about 4 to 8 minutes, depending on the thickness. Asparagus should be tender when done, although some people prefer them crunchy. Serve with melted butter, mayonnaise, lemon juice, or hollandaise sauce.

Beans, Dried

Dried beans include black-eyed peas, kidney beans, pinto beans, lima beans, black beans, navy beans, garbanzo beans, Great Northern beans, lentils, cannellini beans, fava beans, and split peas. Whatever your bean, the methods for preparing are essentially the same. Place beans in cold water and pick out any pebbles, rocks, or floating pieces. Dried beans must be covered in cold water overnight (or for several hours) in order to rehydrate them, unless you purchase "quick-cooking" beans. If you don't have more than 1 to 2 hours for soaking, place the beans in a pot of cold water, bring it to a boil, remove the pot from the stove, and allow the beans to stand in the pot for at least an hour, preferably two. To cook beans, simmer (try not to boil) them in a pot with plenty of water. For softer beans, cook with a lid. Do not add salt to the water, it toughens the beans. You may add 1 to 2 Tbsp. oil to the water to reduce foaming and boiling over. To test for doneness, you may taste them (should be tender, not hard) or squeeze a bean with your fingers to make sure the core of the bean is no longer hard. Cooked beans must be refrigerated and eaten within 5 days. If you like, you may salt and season beans after they are through cooking, as desired.

Beans (Green, Wax, Snap, and Pole)

Snap off both ends. If there is a string, remove it. Break into 1-to-1¹/₂-inch pieces, or cut into strips, or leave them whole. To cook, place in a large pot of boiling water and simmer over low heat until done. Add a pinch of sugar to the water to enhance the flavor. You may also add a chopped onion or a clove of garlic. Place a lid on the pot if you don't want them crunchy. If you need to add more liquid while the beans are cooking, always add boiling water to keep the beans tender (cold water toughens). Drain and flavor with butter, salt and pepper, and herbs. For low-fat beans, you may cook them in water containing a couple of bouillon cubes or in broth and skip the butter.

For Old-Fashioned Southern Green Beans: Place a piece of uncooked ham, country ham if possible, or a couple of pieces of uncooked bacon, seasoned salt, pepper, chopped onion, and 1 tsp. of sugar in a pot of water. Fill the pot ³/₄ full with water and bring to a boil. Once boiling, reduce the heat to low and simmer for 1 to 2 hours. You will need to add more water during the simmering. Next add your green beans, bring the water to a boil, reduce heat to medium, and cook for 10 to 20 minutes uncovered. Place a lid on the pot, reduce the heat to low, and cook until tender. Let the beans cool in the broth before placing them in the refrigerator. They will taste better the next day. Remember when adding more water to the pot, always use hot water, as cold water will toughen them.

For French-Style Green Beans: Cut the green bean in half lengthwise. Cut each remaining piece in half again, lengthwise. Cook according to directions above, except French-style green beans will cook faster because of their smaller size.

Beets

Cut off all but 2 inches of the green top with a knife or kitchen scissors. Do not cut too close to the flesh or the beets will bleed when cooking. Leave beets whole and boil until tender in salted water in a pot with a lid. Whole young beets will be tender in about ¹/₂ to 1 hour. Older beets will take longer. Drain and run under cold water. The skins and root ends will come off easily when done. Serve with butter, salt and pepper, or herbs such as dill, savory, or thyme. To cook beets quickly, peel and cut into slices or dice. Cook in a covered pot with barely boiling water for about 20 to 30 minutes, or until tender. Beets will discolor other food if cooked together, so always add beets last to a recipe. In addition, beet stains cannot be removed from wood or plastic, so be careful if your countertops are made of these materials.

Bell Peppers

Slice off the end of each pepper and then slide a knife around the inner part to remove the seeds and core. Leave them whole if you wish to stuff or bake them. To bake, parboil the peppers first, then stuff them, if you wish, and place them in a lightly greased container and bake at 350°F. for 25 to 30 minutes. To sauté, heat a small amount of butter, margarine, olive oil, or vegetable oil in a skillet over low heat. Add the chopped peppers and cook for about 5 minutes, or until soft. To parboil, place the peppers in a pot with 1 inch water and ¹/₂ tsp. salt. Bring the water to a boil and simmer for about 5 minutes. Peppers may be stuffed with corn pudding, creamed asparagus, lima beans, and mushrooms. They may also be stuffed with a mixture of 1 cup cooked rice, one 8-ounce can tomato sauce, 2 Tbsp. chopped onion, 1 tsp. salt, ¹/₄ tsp. pepper, and ¹/₂ pound cooked ground beef. This mixture will stuff 4 to 5 peppers.

Broccoli

Cut off the base of the broccoli stems. To cook the stems, you will need to peel the tough outer layer. Next, bring 1 to 2 inches water to boil in a pot. Place the broccoli in the pot and bring the water back to a boil. Reduce the heat to medium and cook the broccoli for 10 to 15 minutes covered. Drain and season with butter, salt, pepper, or lemon juice. Broccoli is done when the stems can be easily pierced with a fork. To ensure even cooking for the stems and florets, insert a knife completely through the stem in 1 or 2 places. If you want lemon juice on your broccoli, add it after the broccoli has cooked. Adding lemon juice or vinegar to the water while cooking broccoli will discolor it.

Brussels Sprouts

Remove the stem ends and any leaves that are brown or discolored. Leave the sprouts whole. Fill a pot with water 1 inch deep, bring to a boil, and add the Brussels sprouts. Bring the water back to a boil, reduce the heat to low-medium, and simmer for 8 to 10 minutes or until tender. Drain and serve with butter, salt, and pepper. You may also season with basil or dill, as you like.

Cabbage

Types of cabbage include red, green, and Savoy. Remove the core and cut the cabbage head into quarters, or shred with a knife. Bring enough water to a boil to cover the cabbage, add the cabbage, bring the water back to a boil, then reduce the heat and simmer (wedges should take 10 to 15 minutes and shredded cabbage 5 to 8 minutes) until tender. You should be able to stick a fork through the cabbage with ease. Season with butter, salt, pepper, caraway seeds, mint, or oregano, or a combination of these. Add 1 Tbsp. vinegar to the water to reduce the odor while cooking.

Carrots

Remove the tops and peel the carrots with a vegetable peeler or scrape with a knife. You may leave carrots whole, slice them lengthwise into strips, or sideways into slices, or dice them. Cover the peeled carrots with a damp towel until ready to cook or the carrots will dehydrate and lose their flavor. You may steam carrots for 5 to 12 minutes, until tender, or boil them in water with a pinch of sugar or a piece of lemon peel. Bring 1 inch of water to boil in a pot, add the carrots, bring the water back to a boil, reduce the heat, cover the pot, and simmer as follows:

Size of Carrot	Boiling Time
large, whole	20–40 minutes
large, sliced	15–20 minutes
small, whole	15–20 minutes
small, sliced	6–10 minutes
strips	10–14 minutes

Use a shorter cooking time for crisper carrots. Drain and serve with butter, salt, and pepper. You may also season with mint, basil, or chives.

Celery

Wash the celery well to remove all sand and grit. Cut the bottom end of the stalk off and remove all strings before cutting up the celery for cooking. Remove all the leaves (unless you are using the celery in stews or soups) and then cut the ribs into 1/2-to-2-inch pieces. When cooking, use only a small amount of water, or the celery will lose its flavor. Add a bouillon cube to the water, bring it to a boil, then add the celery, reduce the heat, and simmer (6 to 9 minutes for small pieces and 15 to 20 minutes for larger pieces) until the celery is tender. You may also steam celery for 7 to 10 minutes. Serve buttered and sprinkled with pepper (celery is naturally high in sodium).

Corn

Cut off the ends of the cornhusks, then remove the husks and scrub the ears under running water to remove all of the corn silk. Fill a pot with water and bring to a boil. Drop the corn into the boiling water, bring the water back to a boil, and boil for 5 to 6 minutes. Do not add salt to the corn while it's cooking, as it will toughen it. Corn really needs no seasoning if it is fresh sweet corn. If you wish, you can add butter, salt, and pepper. Corn may be cut off the cob and then cooked in a double boiler with seasonings (butter, dash of pepper). Cook, covered, over low heat for about 45 minutes, then add a little cream, chopped bell pepper, and cover and cook for another 15 minutes, or until tender.

Cucumber

Make sure your cucumber is firm. Peel and slice it into thick slices or lengthwise into quarters. You may scoop out the seeds if you wish. Place 1 inch of water in a pot and bring it to a boil, place the cucumbers in the pot, cover, and bring the water back to a boil. Reduce the heat and boil for 10 to 15 minutes. Remove the pot from the heat, drain, and season the cucumbers with butter, lemon juice, parsley, dill, or chervil.

Eggplant

Remove the stem ends and rinse well. Peel the eggplant with a knife or vegetable peeler if the skin is tough and then slice eggplant into pieces or strips.

You may also leave the eggplant whole. Bring 1 inch of water to a boil in a pot, add the eggplant, bring the water back to a boil, reduce the heat, and boil for 10 to 15 minutes. You may also sauté eggplant in a skillet with oil or butter for 5 to 10 minutes. Drain and serve with butter, salt, pepper, Parmesan cheese, or tomato sauce. Add the eggplant during the last 15 minutes of cooking if adding to stews or soups because it tends to turn mushy if cooked a long time.

Fennel (Florentine)

This is not the seasoning—the seasoning and vegetable are different. Remove the stalks and any tough or discolored pieces. Cut the fennel bulb in half and remove the core. Slice the bulb into pieces, usually about 1 1/2 inches in size, and cut the stems into smaller pieces. Sauté in a buttered skillet for about 5 minutes, then add 1/2 inch of broth, bring to a simmer, and cook, covered, for 15 to 20 minutes. Drain, and serve with Parmesan cheese sprinkled on top.

Greens

Greens include the **dandelions** and **spinach**, which have a mild taste, and **Swiss chard**, **mustard greens**, and **turnip greens**, which have a strong taste. Always wash greens thoroughly. The water remaining on the greens after washing them is all you need to cook them in because greens are naturally full of water. Place them in a pot on the stove and cook uncovered over low heat for 5 minutes, then cover and cook until done. Tender leaves will take 10 to 15 minutes. Older, more mature leaves will take 20 to 30 minutes. Drain, and add butter, salt, and pepper. In addition, vinegar, lemon juice, or a vinegared pepper sauce are good poured on greens.

Southern-Style Greens: Cook a ham hock (uncooked piece of ham or bacon), 1 tsp. salt, 1/2 tsp. cayenne pepper, and 1 quart water in a pot for 45 to 60 minutes over medium heat. Reduce the heat to low, add greens, cover pot, and slowly cook over low heat until tender.

Leeks

Cut off the green tops plus 2 inches of the white part with a knife or kitchen scissors. Place 1 inch of water in a pot and bring to a boil, then place leeks in the pot, bring the water back to a boil, reduce the heat, and boil them covered for 15 minutes. Drain, and serve with butter, salt, and pepper.

Lima Beans

For fresh lima beans, open the pods and remove the beans. Bring a pot of water to a boil, place the beans in the pot, bring the water back to a boil, reduce the heat, and simmer covered for 20 to 30 minutes, or until tender. Make sure you always have enough water in the pot, since lima beans burn easily. Drain, add a little butter, salt, and pepper. Herbs may also be added. For a change, add a chicken bouillon cube to water while cooking for flavoring.

Mushrooms

Gently wash mushrooms with a soft brush making sure to rub all grit away before draining thoroughly and blotting dry with a paper towel or soft cloth. You do not need to peel mushrooms. **Note:** Some people only wipe mushrooms with a damp cloth to clean. For cultivated mushrooms, trim off the stem ends. For **portobello mushrooms**, cut off the woody part. Completely cut off the stems of **shiitake mushrooms**. You may leave mushrooms whole or you may chop them. If slicing, remember to slice down the middle parallel. Melt butter in a skillet over low heat, add the mushrooms, and cook over low heat about 8 to 10 minutes for whole and 5 to 7 minutes for chopped or sliced. Stir often. Mushrooms are delicious on meats, pastas, or other vegetables.

Okra

Wash okra and cut off stems. Leave okra whole when boiling. It is best to have small, tender okra pods. If they are large, they will take longer to cook. Bring 1 inch of water to a boil, add the okra, bring back to a boil, reduce heat, cover and boil for 10 to 12 minutes, or until tender. Fresh small okra will cook in 7 to 12 minutes. Drain and serve with butter, salt, and pepper. Lemon juice is also good on okra, as are vinegared pepper sauce, French dressing, or chili sauce. Okra may also be dipped in cornmeal and fried in oil in a skillet or it may be sautéed and then cooked with tomatoes. Watch closely when cooking okra because it burns easily.

Onions

Always peel onions before cooking. Cut off both ends of the onion and peel off the outer layers (usually two layers) with your hands or a knife until you reach the "shiny" part. You may peel onions under running water to reduce the burning fumes that cause tears. To help prevent tears when you are chopping or slicing onions, tie a towel very tightly around your face just below your eyes like a bandit. If you are going to slice onion, you may slice first and then peel. Onions may be cooked whole, sliced, or quartered, as you want it. Place 1 inch of water in a pot on the stove and bring it to a boil, add the onions, bring the water back to a boil, reduce the heat, cover, and boil as follows:

Whole, small, white	15–25 minutes
Larger, yellow or white	30–40 minutes
Sliced, 1/4-inch thick	10 minutes

When boiling onions, remove them from the heat, drain, and serve with butter, salt, pepper, basil, etc. To bake, place onion (peeled, whole, and sweet, such as a Vidalia) in a casserole dish. Cut a hole in the top of the onion, place a beef or chicken bouillon cube in the hole, add 1–2 Tbsp. butter to the hole, and cover. Bake at 350°F. for 45 minutes or until tender.

Parsnips

Rinse in cold water, then cut off a slice from the top and the bottom. Peel with a knife or a vegetable peeler, and cut out the center core if it is tough. Then cut it into slices, quarters, or cubes. Place in a pot with water about 1 inch deep and add 1 tsp. sugar. Bring to a boil, reduce heat, and cover. Cook whole parsnips for 20 to 40 minutes, and pieces for 8 to 20 minutes, or until tender. You may also bake parsnips at 350°F. for 30 to 45 minutes. Drain and season with butter, salt, and pepper. You may also mash cooked parsnips and season with salt, pepper, butter, paprika, and a little milk. Beat until fluffy.

Peas

For green peas, shell them when you are ready to cook, not before. To shell, break the pod open and remove the peas. Add 1 tsp. sugar to 1 inch of water in a pot and bring the water to a boil. Add the peas, bring the water back to a boil, reduce heat, and simmer for 8 to 15 minutes. Drain and serve with butter, salt, and pepper. You may also season with mint or basil. **Tip:** Plunge the pea pods into boiling water and boil them until limp. Remove the pods and use the water to cook peas in for a wonderful flavor.

For fresh **black-eyed peas**, shell like a green pea. Place a pot with 1-inch-deep water on the stove, add a piece of uncooked bacon or ham and 1/2 tsp. sugar, and bring to a boil. Add the peas, bring the water back to a boil, reduce heat, and simmer until tender, or about 30 to 40 minutes.

Potatoes

Scrub potatoes well and leave the skins on or use a vegetable peeler or knife to peel. Potatoes will turn brown quickly after peeling so place them in cold water to delay the oxidation. Do not leave the potatoes in the water too long or they will get soggy. For **new potatoes**, scrub and leave whole unless they are large—then cut in two pieces. Place potatoes in a pot with water to cover and bring the water to a boil. Reduce heat to low and simmer covered as follows:

Whole	30–35 minutes
Cut-up	20–25 minutes

Baked potato: Wash well and rub skin with oil. Preheat oven to 350°F. and place potato directly on oven rack. Bake for 1 1/2 hours, or to decrease the baking time, you may increase the oven temperature to 400°F. and bake for 1 hour. (The time may vary depending on the size of the potato.) To steam a potato, wrap it in aluminum foil and bake it at 350°F for 1 hour. If you take a fork and punch a few holes in the potato before you bake it, you will not have a crispy peeling. To make sure potato is done, remove it from the oven and, using a potholder, squeeze the potato gently to make sure it is soft. If the potato feels hard when you gently squeeze it, return the potato to the oven and bake it a little longer.

Mashed potatoes: Peel and cut potatoes into 1-to-1 1/2-inch cubes and place them in a pot of boiling water. Bring the water back to a boil, reduce the heat to low, and simmer covered for 20 to 25 minutes, or until tender (pierce with a fork to test). Drain the water. With an electric mixer, beat the potatoes until mixed. Depending on the amount of potatoes, add $1/4$ to 1 stick of butter and beat some more. Add a $1/4$ to 1 cup of milk and beat until potatoes reach the consistency you like. If they are too thick, add more milk. Season with salt and pepper and serve. If the potatoes are too thin, cook them on low for a few minutes. Remember that mashed potatoes thicken as they cool.

French-fried Potatoes: Peel and cut into strips about $1/2$ inch thick and 2 to 3 inches long. Rinse in cold water and dry on paper towels. Heat vegetable oil in a skillet on medium heat. Add potato strips and fry them, turning often, until they are light brown and crisp. Drain on a bed of paper towels and season with salt, pepper, or seasoning salt.

Pumpkin

Cut a pumpkin in half. Remove the seeds and stringy portions. Cut into smaller pieces, then peel. To boil, place in a pot with water about 1 inch deep and $1/2$ tsp. salt. Bring water to a boil, reduce heat to low, and simmer covered for 25 to 30 minutes, or until tender. Drain, mash, and season with butter, salt, and pepper. To bake pumpkin, place 1 Tbsp. oil or butter in a pan, add pumpkin, and bake at 400°F., covered with aluminum foil, for 1 hour. Season with butter, salt, and pepper.

Rutabaga (sometimes called Yellow Turnip)

Wash well, peel, and cut into pieces, cubes, or strips. Add 1 tsp. sugar to a pan of 1-inch-deep water and bring to a boil. Add rutabagas, reduce heat, and simmer for 25 to 40 minutes, or until tender. If rutabagas are cut up, use a lid on the pot. Drain and season with butter, salt, and pepper.

Spinach

Wash spinach thoroughly to remove all sand and grit. You will have to wash it 3 or 4 times to really clean it well. The best way is to place spinach in a clean sink and fill it with lukewarm water. The spinach will rise to the top, and the grit will sink to the bottom. Lift spinach out and place it in a colander. Clean the sink and repeat the process again. If you add 1 tsp. salt to the water it will kill any bugs or worms hiding in the leaves. Tear off the stems and any wilted leaves. The water remaining on the spinach after its final washing is enough water to cook them in. Steam spinach until it appears wilted (usually 3 to 5 minutes), drain well, and gently press to squeeze it dry. To boil, place in a pot with a small amount of water (if leaves are very wet, do not use any water). Cover and cook on low heat for 3 to 5 minutes if it is young, tender spinach or 20 to 25 minutes for older and thicker leaves. Drain and serve with butter, lemon juice, vinegar, or vinegared pepper sauce.

Squash

Squash is divided into two types: **summer** and **winter**. There are many varieties of each type:

Summer	Winter
White—pattypan (cymlings) or scalloped	Acorn
Yellow—straight-neck or crooked-neck	Green hubbard
Light green—chayote	Tan butternut
Dark green—zucchini	Buttercup
	Banana
	Spaghetti

Cooking Summer Squash: Wash and cut off both ends. (Do not peel summer squash.) You may cook squash whole or slice it lengthwise into strips, sideways into round slices, or dice it into 1/4-inch cubes. To cook, place it in boiling water and simmer until tender. Cubes or slices will take 10 to 15 minutes. Whole squash will take 30 to 60 minutes to cook. When cooking cubed or sliced squash, you may chop up an onion and cook it with the squash. You may bake squash whole by placing it in a covered casserole dish with 1 Tbsp. butter and baking it at 350°F. for 30 to 60 minutes. You may also stuff squash with cheese, butter, and cracker crumbs and then bake.

Cooking Winter Squash: Hard-skinned winter squash such as green hubbard should be scrubbed well. Peel it if you want to, but it is not necessary. Cut the squash into serving-size pieces. Remove all of the seeds and the stringy portion. Bring 1 inch water with 1/2 tsp. salt to a boil, add squash, and simmer for 25 to 30 minutes, or until tender. Serve buttered or with brown sugar and butter. You may also mash squash like potatoes and add milk, ginger, nutmeg, etc.

Sweet Potatoes and Yams

Do not peel. Place them in a pot of boiling water (enough to cover), reduce heat, and simmer covered until tender. When tender, remove skins or cut them up and serve them with butter, salt, and pepper. You may mash sweet potatoes and add butter, granulated or brown sugar, cinnamon, or whatever else you like. In addition, sweet potatoes may be baked. Rub the whole potato skin with vegetable oil and place the potato directly on the oven rack. Bake at 350°F. for 50 to 60 minutes. Serve with butter, salt, and pepper.

Tomatoes

You may leave the skin on tomatoes or remove it, as you prefer. Tomatoes may be cooked whole or cut in quarters or slices. Never add water when cooking a tomato. Place tomatoes in a pan, cover, and cook on low heat for 8 to 10 minutes. To broil tomatoes, place in the oven under the broiling element for 3 to 5 minutes. You may serve them buttered or sprinkled with olive oil and seasoned with basil, dill, or oregano. Green tomatoes are unripened tomatoes that are great to fry or sauté. (**Note:** A tomato is generally considered a fruit).

Turnips

Scrub turnips and peel them. Then cut them into 2-inch pieces, strips, or 1/2-inch cubes. You may also cook them whole. Bring 1 inch water with 1/2 tsp. salt to a boil and add the turnips. Reduce the heat and simmer without a lid for 20 to 30 minutes if the turnips are whole, or simmer with a lid for 15 to 20 minutes if the turnips are cut up. Simmer until tender. Serve with butter, salt, and pepper, or mash adding milk and a dash of nutmeg.

Zucchini

See "Summer Squash."

TIPS FOR PREPARING VEGETABLES

- Refrigerate **onions** before cutting them to avoid tears. You can also peel onions under running water to prevent your eyes from stinging.
- To peel an **onion**, only remove one or two of the outer layers until you reach the shiny part.
- Dampened baking soda will remove the **onion odor** from your hands and cooking utensils.
- To peel **tomatoes** more easily, pierce the tomato with a fork and plunge it into boiling water for a few seconds and then into cold water before peeling.
- Rub the cut edges of an **artichoke** with lemon to prevent discoloration.
- If vegetables are **wilted**, pick off the brown edges, sprinkle or mist the vegetables with water, wrap them in a towel, and place them in the refrigerator for 1 hour.
- To skin a **carrot** easily, drop the carrot into boiling water for a few minutes before you begin to peel.
- Before cooking or serving raw any **leafy vegetables** or **cauliflower**, soak in salted water to kill any bugs.

ADDITIONAL WAYS TO COOK VEGETABLES

Frozen or fresh vegetables may be cooked in a number of additional ways. Canned vegetables have already been cooked, and thus only need to be reheated according to the directions on the can.

Grilling

Cook vegetables on a grill or cook vegetables in a little oil in the oven (*see* "Grilling").

Frying

Cook in oil in a frying pan or electric skillet over high heat. Be sure to cut the vegetables into small pieces of uniform size before frying.

Pressure-Cooking

Using a pressure cooker is a quick way to cook vegetables. Follow the directions that come with your pressure cooker. The vegetables will cook in about half of the normal cooking time, and will taste wonderful.

Roasting

Place vegetables around meat in a roasting pan. They will absorb some of the juices and turn a nice roasted brown as the meat cooks. To place small whole potatoes or turnips in with the meat, you may want to boil them first in water or beef bouillon for 15 minutes (or until barely tender) and then add them an hour before the meat is done.

Sautéing

Heat 1 to 2 Tbsp. olive oil, butter, margarine, or vegetable oil in a skillet over low heat. Add chopped or sliced vegetables and cook for several minutes until tender. Do not cover. Stir occasionally to make sure all sides cook.

Steaming

Place vegetables in a container over boiling water. The vegetable container should be covered with a lid. You may buy small and inexpensive vegetable steamers that fit in your own pots. Remember, steaming takes longer than boiling. To steam in the microwave: Place vegetables in a microwave-proof dish with no more than 1 Tbsp. of water and cover tightly with plastic wrap. Cook on High for 3 to 5 minutes, remove the dish, and pierce the plastic covering with a knife or fork to allow the steam to escape. Be careful when piercing the plastic—the steam will be extremely hot. Keep your face away from the steam. Following is an *approximate* time chart for steaming fresh vegetables.

STEAMING FRESH VEGETABLES

Vegetable	*Approximate Steaming Time*
Asparagus tips	5–10 minutes
Artichokes	25–45 minutes
Beans, lima	30–45 minutes
Beans, green, snap or string	30–60 minutes
Beets	35–60 minutes
Broccoli flowerets	15–25 minutes
Broccoli with stems	15–35 minutes
Brussels sprouts	15–30 minutes

Vegetable	Approximate Steaming Time
Cabbage	10–25 minutes
Carrots, whole (young)	20 minutes
Carrots, sliced (mature)	20–30 minutes
Cauliflower flowerets	15–25 minutes
Cauliflower with stems	10 minutes
Cauliflower, whole	30 minutes
Celery	20–25 minutes
Corn off the cob	15 minutes
Corn on the cob	15 minutes
Eggplant, whole	40 minutes
Greens	20–40 minutes
Leeks	15–35 minutes
Okra	20–40 minutes
Onions	20–45 minutes
Parsnips	35–45 minutes
Peas, green	15–40 minutes
Peppers, green	5 minutes
Potatoes	30–40 minutes
Sweet potatoes	20–30 minutes
Squash—summer	15–20 minutes
Squash—winter	30–40 minutes
Tomatoes	15–25 minutes
Turnips	20–35 minutes

Stewing

Slowly simmer vegetables in water or other liquid in a covered pot over low heat.

Canned Vegetables

This method will help remove the "canned" taste. Drain the liquid from the can into a saucepan, and bring to a simmering boil. Add 1 Tbsp. butter or margarine, plus seasonings (salt, pepper, onion or garlic powder, herbs) and simmer for several minutes. Add the contents of can and cook according to directions. Here are the serving sizes from the various can sizes:

Size of Can	Number of Servings
8 ounces	2
16 ounces	3–4
1 pound, 4 ounces	4–5
1 pound, 13 ounces	6–7

Frozen Vegetables

Do not thaw frozen vegetables before cooking. Follow the directions on the package for cooking. One package, pint-sized, will usually serve 4 (1/2 cup serving each).

Creaming Vegetables

Combine 1 cup of white sauce (*see* "Sauces" chapter) per 2 cups of vegetables. You may combine 2 to 3 vegetables for variety. **Tip:** A quick cream sauce for vegetables can be made by taking a flavored cream cheese (chive, onion, pimiento, etc.) and thinning it with a small amount of milk while heating the cream cheese in a saucepan. Plain yogurt may also be used. Just add chives, pimientos, mushrooms, herbs, and spices.

Sauces

Tomato sauce, hollandaise sauce, sour cream dressing, mushroom sauce, cream sauce, dill sauce, curry sauce, and plain yogurt mixed with herbs and spices all make great sauces for vegetables. For a tasty and quick dish, whip 1/2 pint whipping cream and mix with 1/2 cup mayonnaise; mix into warm vegetables seasoned with salt and pepper; sprinkle vegetables with Parmesan cheese; and bake at 300°F. for 15 to 20 minutes, or until hot. You may also melt a package of seasoned cream cheese into the vegetables (such as cream cheese with chives). Another easy-to-make and delicious sauce is to combine 1/2 cup mayonnaise, 1/2 tsp. grated onion, 1 tsp. mustard, and 1/2 cup cheese; melt the mixture in a saucepan over low heat until thoroughly blended; and pour over vegetables when ready to serve. *See* "Sauces" chapter for additional information.

Scalloped Vegetables

Place sliced or chopped vegetables in a baking dish with a medium white sauce covering them. Sprinkle on a crumb topping (such as crushed crackers or crushed potato chips). Bake at 350°F. for 20 to 25 minutes, or until bubbly.

Au Gratin Vegetables

Add cheese to a medium white sauce (*See* "Sauces" chapter) and mix well. Place vegetables in a baking dish, cover with sauce, and top with cracker crumbs. Bake at 350°F. for 20 minutes, or until bubbly on top.

Vegetable Combinations

Serve vegetables in the following combinations for delicious variety and as a way of using leftover vegetables. You may use your own combination or place them in a sauce if you want to be fancy. The amount of each vegetable is up to you.

Brussels sprouts + small onions + peas + green beans
carrots + sliced onions + lima beans + diced celery
corn + green beans + sliced zucchini + peas
green beans + small onions + lima beans + sliced carrots
parsnips + peas
peas + corn + summer squash + diced celery

summer squash + lima beans + diced zucchini + corn
lima beans + French-style green beans + peas + chopped bell
peppers + a sauce

VEGETABLE TIPS FOR THE KITCHEN KLUTZ

- **While vegetables are cooking**, always add hot water, not cold, when liquid is needed to prevent the vegetables from getting tough.
- **If vegetables are oversalted**, cover pan tightly with a wet cloth for a few minutes. You may also add 1 tsp. vinegar and 1 tsp. sugar. Or, a raw peeled potato placed in the pot will absorb some of the salt; remove the potato before serving the vegetables.
- Cook **spinach** uncovered to preserve the fresh green appearance.
- Soak tightly grown or curled vegetables (**cabbage, cauliflower, Brussels sprouts, artichokes**) in salted water before cooking.
- For **artichokes**, soak for 30 minutes in a quart of water to which 1 Tbsp. vinegar has been added to improve the taste and color.
- For **cauliflower**, place a piece of lemon peel in with it to keep the vegetable white while cooking. Also, cook cauliflower with the head down to prevent "gunk" from settling on the white parts.
- When steaming any of the **strong odor vegetables**, you may place a piece of bread on top of them to absorb the odor.
- When through cooking, pierce **potatoes** with a fork to let the steam escape.
- To quick-bake a **potato** (without using a microwave), boil the potato for 15 minutes in water, oil the skin, then place the potato in the oven and bake until done. Bake at 400°F. for 1 hour, or until soft. The size will affect the cooking time.
- A **potato** wrapped in aluminum foil that is sealed around the potato cooks faster because it steam cooks.
- When cooking **peas, spinach,** and **lima beans,** use milk instead of water to add nutrition and flavor.
- After cooking, run **beets** under cold water, and the peeling will fall off. Do not cool beets before peeling.
- Avoid **overcooking** vegetables so as to retain the most vitamins and minerals.
- To make **mashed potatoes** light and fluffy, add a pinch of baking soda, milk, and butter while whipping.
- To improve the crispiness of **french fries**, let raw potatoes stand in cold water for 30 minutes before frying. Also sprinkle with flour before frying or baking for a golden-brown finish.
- To make **celery** more delicious and crispier, place celery in ice-cold water for 10 minutes (with 1 tsp. sugar per quart of water).
- To remove **vegetable stains** from hands, rub them with a slice of lemon.

- Rather than **shelling peas**, wash the pods well and then boil them until tender. When the pods are through cooking, they will burst open and the peas will sink to the bottom.
- When deciding which **oil** to use, consider the tolerance it has to heat:

  High-heat tolerance: corn oil, peanut oil, soy bean oil, sunflower oil
  Low-heat tolerance: olive oil

- **Cooking oil** may be reused if strained so that leftover food is removed. Remember, though, that the heat tolerance will be lower when oil is reused.

□ □ □ □ □ □

FRUIT

Fruit is found in abundance all year. Most fruit contains little, if any, fat and is rich in vitamins. Cut up a bowl of fresh fruit for a great appetizer, salad, or a healthy dessert. Fruit, which may be baked or broiled, is also an excellent accompaniment to meat or a delightful garnish on your plate. Take advantage of the different varieties available within each family of fruit.

When purchasing fruit, be sure to check the buying chart as well as the directions for storing fruit in this chapter. Correct storage is crucial for maximizing fruit's taste, as well as its storage life.

Dried fruit is delicious and often overlooked. It is tasty stewed and served for breakfast. Some of the wonderful summer fruits may be frozen and then used in the middle of winter. It's fun to be able to serve peaches that you have frozen previously during the summer in a cobbler or over ice cream in the middle of the winter.

BUYING CHART FOR FRUIT

Note: Most fruits are available all year. The available times listed below are the peak seasons for the various fruits. In general, fruits are more plentiful and less expensive during these times.

Fruit	Peak Season	Look For	Avoid
Apples		firm, good color, smooth	bruises, soft spots, skin breaks
Some Varieties:		Good for:	
Baldwin	November–April	eating raw, cooking	
Cortland	October–November	eating raw, cooking	
Crispin	October–November	eating raw, cooking	
Delicious (Red)	October–May	eating raw	
Delicious (Golden)	October–May	eating raw, cooking	
Gala	January–May	eating raw	
Granny Smith	January–May	eating raw, cooking	
Gravenstein	July–September	cooking	
Grimes (Golden)	September–January	eating raw, cooking	

Fruit	Peak Season	Look For	Avoid
McIntosh	September–January	eating raw, cooking	
Newtown Pippin	October–November	cooking	
Northern Spy	October–November	cooking	
Rhode Island Greening	October–November	eating raw	
Apricots	July, August	plump, golden orange, juicy, small	firm, mushy, greenish
Avocado	summer	shake to hear the seed rattle	mushy, skin breaks
Banana	all year	plump, firm (not hard), yellow	grayish color, large brown spots
Blackberries	May–August	juicy, firm, full-colored, plump (with caps may mean underripe)	bruised, leaky, mold, in wet container
Blueberries	May–September	firm, juicy, full-colored, plump	bruised, mold, in wet container, leaky
Cantaloupe	May–September	should "give" slightly when pressed; fragrant; cream-colored; webbing should stand out	soft spots
Casaba melon	July–November	should "give" slightly when pressed; no odor	soft spots, green
Cherries	June–August	glossy, bright, large, deep red, plump	light color, sticky
Crenshaw melon	August–September	no odor, will yield slightly on stem end when pressed	green, odor
Coconut	September–December	heavy for its size, fibrous and hard shell	light in size
Cranberries	September–December	firm, plump, small, bright red	soft, shriveled
Currants	midsummer	small, bright red	large
Dates	August–October	brown, soft, plump, smooth skin	hard, shriveled, moldy
Figs	June–November	soft, plump	sour odor
Gooseberries	April–August	ripe, good color	soft, shriveled

Fruit	Peak Season	Look For	Avoid
Grapefruit	January–May	firm, heavy for size (**Note:** colored spots do not affect the fruit), shiny	puffiness, soft spots, dents
Grapes		green stems, plump, unblem- ished, good color	wrinkled, soft, sticky
Calmeria	October–February		
Concord	August–November		
Emperor	September–February		
Exotic	June–August		
Flame	June–October		
Perlette	May–July		
Ribier	August–January		
Ruby	August–January		
Tokay	September–October		

Types of grapes by color:

Red: Cardinal, Catawba, Delaware, Emperor, Red Malaga, Tokay, Flame (seedless), Ruby (seedless)

Black: Concord, Ribier, Malagas, Exotic

Deep Blue: northeastern Concord

Green or White: Almeria, Calmeria, Muscadine, Niagara, Thompson (seedless), Perlette (seedless)

Honeydew	July–October	velvety and creamy rind, slightly gives on end (**Note:** Freckles signal a high sugar content)	white rind
Kumquats	November–February	firm, heavy, small, orange color	soft, light, green
Lemons and Limes	all year	heavy for size, firm, smooth, shiny; light-colored are more tart	soft, poor color, thick skin
Loganberries	June and July	firm, plump, full-colored, juicy	leaky, mold, in wet container
Mangoes	May–August	greenish color with some yellow and red	grayish color, black spots
Nectarines	June–September	yellow-orange, firm, heavy, should "give" when pressed, softening along the "seam"	bruised, green-ish, small

138

Fruit	Peak Season	Look For	Avoid
Oranges		firm, heavy, thin-skinned	poor color, soft spots
Valencias (California)	May–November		
Valencias (Florida)	February–May		
Navel	November–May		
Hamlins	October–February		
Parson Browns	October–February		
Papayas	May–June and October–December	half-yellow, medium size	greenish color, hard
Peaches	June–September	firm, softening along the indentation, heavy	greenish color, hard, dull, wrinkled, blemished, brown spots
Pears			
Anjou	October–April	firm, unbruised, soft at the stem	soft, blemishes
Bartlett	August–November		
Bosc	September–January		
Comice	October–February		
Winter Nelis	December–June		
Kieffer	September–November		
Persimmons	October–December	plump, green cap, deep orange or red color	shriveled
Pineapple	March–June	large, firm, heavy, fragrant, dark green leaves	soft spots, rotted bottom
Plums	July–August	yield to pressure, colorful, plump	bruised
Pomegranates	September–November	pink or bright red rind	dry
Prunes	September–November	yield to pressure, colorful, blue-black, smooth	bruised
Raspberries	April–July	juicy, firm, full-colored, plump (with cap may mean under-ripe)	leaky, in wet container, mold
Rhubarb (really a vegetable)	January–June	crisp and firm stalk, rosy	soft, limp
Strawberries	April–August	plump, juicy, full-colored, firm (without caps may mean too ripe)	leaky, in wet container, mold

Fruit	Peak Season	Look For	Avoid
Tangelos	November–February	heavy for size, firm, thin-skinned	light in size, soft
Tangerines	November–January	heavy for size, dark, orange color	shriveled, blemishes
Tomatoes	all year (peak—summer)	plump, deep color, firm, smooth	soft spots, blemishes
Watermelon	May–September	dull rind, firm, smooth (cut should be juicy, red, dark seeds)	white streaks, white under-side

SERVING SIZES FOR FRUIT

Fruit	Measurement
1 pound **apples**	= 3 medium apples or 3 cups sliced
1 large **apple**	= 3 cups diced or 1½ cups sauce
1 pound dried **apricots**	= 5 cups cooked
1 pound fresh **apricots**	= 3 cups sliced or 8–12 apricots
1 medium **avocado**	= 2 cups cubed
1 pound **avocado**	= 2½ cups sliced or 2 medium-sized avocados
1 ripe, medium **banana**	= ⅓ cup mashed
1 pound **bananas**	= 3 medium = 2½ cups sliced = 1¾ cups mashed
1 sliced **banana**	= ⅔ cup
3 mashed **bananas**	= 1 cup
1 pint **blackberries**	= 2 cups
1 pint **blueberries**	= 2½ cups
1 average **cantaloupe**	= 3½ cups diced or 50 melon balls
1 pound **cherries**	= 75–80 cherries or 2½ cups pitted or 3 cups stemmed
1 pound **coconut**	= 2½ cups fresh shredded or 5½ cup canned shredded
1 pound **cranberries**	= 4 cups or 4 cups sauce
1 pound **dates**	= 2¼ cups whole
1 pound **figs**	= 2¾ cups whole
½ pound **candied fruits**	= 1½ cups
1 medium **grapefruit**	= 1⅓ cups fruit or ¾ cup juice
1 pound **grapes**	= 2 cups halved
1 medium **lemon**	= 2–3 Tbsp. of juice or 2 Tbsp. grated rind
1 dozen **lemons**	= 2½ cups juice
Juice of 1 **lime**	= ¼ cup
1 **mango**	= ¾–1 cup flesh
1 medium **orange**	= ⅓ cup juice or 2–3 Tbsp. grated rind
1 dozen medium **oranges**	= 3–5 cups juice

Fruit	Measurement
1 pound fresh **peaches**	= 2½-3 cups, peeled, sliced, seeded, or 4-6 peaches
3-4 medium **peaches**	= 1½ cups purée
1 bushel **peaches**	= 18–24 quarts of canned peaches
1 pound of **pears**	= 3–5 pears or 2½ cups cooked
2 pounds **pineapple**	= 2½ cups diced
1 pound **plums**	= 12–20 plums or 2 cups cooked
1 pound **prunes**	= 2⅓ cups whole
15 ounce package **raisins**	= 3 cups
1 pint **raspberries**	= 2 cups
1 pound **rhubarb**	= 4–8 stalks or 3½ cups diced or 2 cups cooked
1 quart **strawberries**	= 4 cups sliced
5 pounds **watermelon**	= 3 portions

STORING

Fresh fruit should be stored in the refrigerator according to the following recommendations.

STORAGE CHART FOR FRESH FRUIT

Fruit	Manner of Storage	Storage Life
Apples	at room temperature or in the refrigerator	1–2 weeks
Apricots	refrigerator in a plastic bag	up to 3 days
Avocado	if ripe: refrigerator	2 days in the refrigerator
	if green: ripen at room temperature in a dark place or in a brown paper bag or bury in a bag of flour	
Banana	at room temperature, uncovered	up to 7 days
Blackberries	covered in the refrigerator	up to 3 days
Blueberries	covered in the refrigerator	up to 3 days
Cantaloupe	ripen at room temperature, then refrigerate and eat soon	up to 2 days in the refrigerator
Casaba	at room temperature until ripe, then in the refrigerator	up to 2 days in the refrigerator
Cherries	refrigerator	up to 3 days
Coconut (fresh)	refrigerator in a plastic bag or container with a lid	up to 4 days
Cranberries	refrigerator	up to 2 weeks
Crenshaw	ripen at room temperature, then refrigerate	up to 2 days in the refrigerator
Dates	well-wrapped in the refrigerator	up to 2 weeks
Figs	at room temperature or in the refrigerator	up to 1–2 days

Fruit	Manner of Storage	Storage Life
Gooseberries	covered in the refrigerator	up to 3 days
Grapefruit	at room temperature or in the refrigerator	up to 2 weeks
Grapes	refrigerator	up to 1 week
Honeydew	at room temperature until ripe, then in the refrigerator	up to 2 days in the refrigerator
Kumquats	at room temperature or in the refrigerator	up to 1 week
Lemons and Limes	well-wrapped in plastic in the refrigerator	lemons—up to 3 weeks limes—up to 4 weeks
Mangoes	at room temperature until very soft, then in the refrigerator	up to 5 days in the refrigerator
Nectarines	refrigerator	up to 1 week
Oranges	at room temperature or refrigerator	up to 3 weeks
Papayas	ripen at room temperature and then store in the refrigerator	up to 2 days in the refrigerator
Peaches	at room temperature until soft, then in the refrigerator	up to 4 days in the refrigerator
Pears	at room temperature until ripe then in the refrigerator (pears are ripe when the stem comes off easily—ripen in a paper bag)	up to 2–3 days in the refrigerator
Persimmons	at room temperature until ripe, then refrigerator	up to 2 days in the refrigerator
Pineapple	at room temperature or in the refrigerator	up to 3 days
Plums	at room temperature or in the refrigerator	up to 3 days in the refrigerator
Pomegranates	refrigerator	up to 3 days
Prunes	at room temperature or in the refrigerator	up to 4 days in the refrigerator
Raspberries	covered in the refrigerator	up to 3 days
Rhubarb	loosely wrapped in plastic in the refrigerator	up to 2–3 days
Strawberries	covered in the refrigerator	up to 3 days
Tangelos	at room temperature or in the refrigerator	up to 1 week
Tangerines	refrigerator	up to 1 week
Tomatoes	if ripe, in a cool, dry place (do not refrigerate) To ripen, place in a closed paper bag out of the sunlight; to shorten ripening time, add an apple to the bag	up to 2 days
Watermelon	if uncut, at room temperature if cut, in the refrigerator	up to 3–4 days in the refrigerator

Notes: If you are unsure how to store fruit, see how it is stored at the grocery store! Also, coconut will become moldy if stored incorrectly. Fresh uncut coconut should be stored in the refrigerator up to 4 days. Freshly cut coconut should be stored in the refrigerator in a plastic bag or covered plastic container up to 4 days. Dried, toasted coconut should be stored in a jar in a cool place but not in the refrigerator.

To Freeze Fruit

Fresh fruit may be frozen "as is" in freezer bags, foil, plastic wrap, or paper and will keep up to 6 months in the freezer. Fruit may also be frozen any of the following four ways:

1. **In a container with nothing added:** Peel, slice, or prepare fruit in the manner you want it stored, place in a freezer container, tightly seal, and place in the freezer. If you are not peeling the fruit, be sure to wash it well, drain, and dry thoroughly. If you are freezing peeled fruit such as apples, pears, bananas, or other fruit that discolors, you will need to gently mix fruit with ascorbic acid or a commercial preparation (bought at the grocery store) to keep fruit from changing color. Lemon juice, lime juice, and pineapple juice may also be used to prevent discoloration, but they will affect the flavor a little.
2. **In a container with granulated sugar added:** Peel, slice, or prepare fruit in the manner you want it stored, place it in a bowl, and gently stir fruit with 1/2–3/4 cup sugar per quart of fruit. Let the mixture sit for 10 minutes or more (during which the sugar should dissolve on the fruit). Place sugared fruit in a freezer container, tightly seal, and place in freezer.
3. **In a container with sugar syrup:** Prepare one of the following sugar syrups to pour over the fruit:

- Lightly sweet sugar syrup—2 cups sugar per 4 cups water (will make 5 cups syrup)
- Medium sweet sugar syrup—3 cups sugar per 4 cups water (will make 5 1/2 cups syrup)
- Very sweet sugar syrup—4 3/4 cups sugar per 4 cups water (will make 6 1/2 cups syrup)
- Ultrasweet sugar syrup—7 cups sugar per 4 cups water (will make 7 1/2 cups syrup)

To make syrup: Heat water and sugar in a pot over medium heat. Stir constantly until the sugar is dissolved, then refrigerate until cool. Once cold, add 1/2 tsp. ascorbic acid or a store-bought preservative to keep the fruit from changing color. Mix the ascorbic acid with 1/4 cup cold water per 4 cups sugar syrup. After making syrup, place fruit in a freezer container, cover completely with the syrup, and place in the freezer.

4. **In a container with fruit juice or water:** Place whole fruit in a freezer container, cover with water, and place in the freezer. You may also cover the fruit with fruit juice or crush fruit and pack it in its own juice.

Remember to leave ¹/₂ inch of space in both pint and quart freezer containers to allow for expansion when packing fruit for freezer storage.

DRIED FRUIT

Dried fruits may be stored in an airtight container in a cool, dry place for up to 1 year and may be used dried or baked. Follow the directions on the package for cooking or you may cook dried fruit as follows:

Bring water (enough to cover the fruit) to a boil in a pot. Add fruit and bring water back to a boil. Then cook according to the recommendations below. Remember to add more boiling water to the fruit if necessary.

COOKING DRIED FRUIT

Fruit	Boiling Time
Apples	40 minutes
Apricots	40 minutes
Figs	25–30 minutes
Peaches	50 minutes
Pears	40 minutes
Prunes	45–50 minutes
Raisins	10 minutes
Prunes and raisins mixed	40–50 minutes

If you want, you may add sugar to the stewing fruit, but do not add it until the last 5 minutes of cooking because sugar easily toughens fruit. To soften hard-dried fruit, place in the microwave in a covered glass dish with 1 tsp. water. Cook on High for 15 to 45 seconds.

Raisins

Raisins are naturally or artificially dried grapes. Types of raisins include golden seedless, muscat, natural seedless, sultanas, and zante currants. **Golden seedless** are made from the Thompson seedless grape and are semi-tart. They are treated with sulphur dioxide to prevent darkening and are golden in color. **Muscat** raisins are made from the Muscat grape and are sun-dried. They are very dark and large, as well as very sweet. **Natural seedless** raisins, which have a sweet taste, are made from the Thompson seedless grape and are the most common commercially sold raisin. They also are sun-dried and dark brown. **Sultanas** are sun-dried from the Sultana grape and have a tart taste. **Zante currants** are made from the Black Corinth grape. They are sun-dried, very small, dark brown, and tart. Zante currants are mainly used in baking.

Store raisins in a tightly sealed plastic bag in a cool, dry place for up to 6 months. You may also freeze raisins in a freezer container for up to 1 year. If raisins stick together, place them in a strainer and spray with hot water. Try soaking raisins in sherry or orange juice overnight for a plump, great-tasting raisin.

FRUIT TIPS FOR THE KITCHEN KLUTZ

- To ripen an **avocado**, bury it in a bag of flour or place it in a brown paper bag until ripe.
- To determine if a **pineapple** is ripe, thump the fruit with your thumb and middle finger. Then thump the inside of your wrist. If the sound is similar, the fruit is ripe! Also, the stem should twist off easily and the pineapple should smell very sweet.
- To ripen **tomatoes** and **bananas**, place them in a closed paper bag out of the sunlight. To shorten the ripening time, add an apple to the bag.
- To determine the ripeness of **watermelon**, look at the stem:
    - a shrunken, discolored, and attached stem = ripe melon
    - a fresh and green stem = an unripe melon
    - an absent stem = too ripe melon
- Milk or ice water prevent **peaches** from turning dark.
- **Peaches** and **plums** are divided into two types:
    - Clingstones—good for preserves, canning, and cooking
    - Freestones—good all-around, the flesh separates easily from the pit (seed)
    - **Note:** The red part around the pit or seed is bitter and should always be removed before cooking peaches or plums.
- To open a **coconut:** Use an icepick or a screwdriver and pierce the "eyes." Drain the milk (the liquid inside the coconut). Place the coconut in an oven at 350°F. for 20 to 30 minutes. Remove, break into large pieces with a hammer, and peel.
- **Coconut** will grate more easily if frozen first. To color grated coconut, place 1 tsp. water and a few drops of food coloring in a jar. Mix together, add the coconut, and shake.
- Place **lemons** in hot water for 15 minutes before squeezing, or roll firmly between your hands to yield twice as much juice.
- To remove the white membrane from **oranges** easily, soak oranges in boiling water for 5 minutes before peeling.
- To skin **peaches** and **tomatoes**, place them in boiling water for a few minutes and then in cold water.
- To prevent **blueberries** from changing color when cooking with them, substitute baking powder for baking soda, and milk for buttermilk.
- When chopping **dates** and **figs** in a food processor, add a few drops of lemon juice to prevent the fruit from sticking.
- To ripen **bananas** quickly, peel them and place them in an oven at 350°F. for 10 minutes.
- To sweeten **berries**, add 1 Tbsp. granulated sugar per cup of berries, gently stir together, and let stand for 30 to 45 minutes.
- To remove **berry stains** from your hands, rub them with lemon wedges or lemon juice.
- To prevent discoloration of peeled surfaces from **pears, avocados, apples**, or **bananas**, sprinkle with a little lemon juice or pineapple juice.

□ □ □ □ □ □

PASTAS & GRAINS

Pastas and grains are delightful, easy to make, somewhat economical, and healthy staples that should be found in every kitchen cabinet. Once you learn how to cook pasta and rice, you will find yourself making it often.

Pasta is not only easy but quick. With so many quick sauces to prepare, as well as those that can be purchased, you can have a meal fixed in minutes. In fact, if you are using a store-bought pasta sauce, often the longest part of cooking pasta is waiting for the water to boil. In this chapter you will find a description of some of the more popular pastas available for purchase, as well as the approximate length of time they take to cook. Just follow the directions, and you will become a pasta pro in no time.

Rice complements most vegetables and meat so it is a great food to serve with a meal. There are many varieties of rice available as well as a great number of recipes containing rice. Learn to cook rice so it is not gummy. It's easy to do—just follow some of the directions and tips found in this chapter.

For a special touch when having guests for dinner, fix a rice mold. It will definitely bring compliments to the cook.

Risotto, or "Italian rice," is quickly gaining popularity. In this chapter are various methods for making it. Try it—you'll be hooked on this delicious specialty rice.

PASTA

Pasta can be made from scratch or store-bought either fresh or dried. Fresh pasta is made with eggs and all-purpose flour. Dried pastas are generally made with flour, usually from the inner part of the wheat grain, and water, although some are made with eggs and flour. Toppings and sauces can be made from anything pleasing to the palate.

SERVING SIZES FOR PASTA

Type	Amount	Serving Size	
Spaghetti, uncooked	8 ounces	4 cups cooked	= 4 servings
Egg noodles, uncooked	8 ounces	4 cups cooked	= 4 servings

Type	Amount	Serving Size	
Macaroni, uncooked	8 ounces	4 cups cooked	= 4 servings
Macaroni, uncooked	4 ounces	2½ cups cooked	= 2–3 servings
Noodles, uncooked	4 ounces	2 cups cooked	= 2 servings
Dried pasta	1 ounce	½ cup cooked	= 1 small serving
Fresh pasta	1 pound	8 cups cooked	= 6–8 servings

Note: Allow 6–8 ounces per serving if pasta is the main dish.

STORING

Dried manufactured pasta will keep for 1 year in an airtight container at room temperature. Fresh pasta may be stored for 1 week in the refrigerator, or frozen for 3 months. Do not thaw frozen pasta—add it directly to the boiling water when cooking. Filled, uncooked fresh pasta will store for 2 to 7 days in the refrigerator, depending on the filling. Cooked pasta will only keep for about 1 to 2 days in the refrigerator.

METHODS OF COOKING

Pasta should be cooked to be tender and chewy ("al dente"). To cook, fill a large pot with 4 quarts of water for every pound of pasta cooked, or 1¼ cups water for every ounce of pasta cooked. Make sure that there is enough water so the pasta is completely covered once it's added. To prevent the noodles from sticking to each other and to help prevent the water from boiling over, add 2 Tbsp. oil, lemon juice, or lime juice to the water. Bring water to a boil over high heat. The water should be *fully* boiling before adding the pasta. Once the water is boiling well, add pasta to the pot. Don't break fettuccini, spaghetti, or any other long noodles to fit them in the pot. Instead, gently add them and as the submerged part softens, you will be able to move the pasta around to fit all in the pot. Boil the pasta uncovered. The package in which the pasta came should tell you how long you will need to boil it or you can refer to the time chart on the following page. It's a good idea to set a timer for the minimum length of time required, then begin testing the pasta for doneness when the timer goes off. In general, cooking fresh pasta takes approximately 2 to 5 minutes to cook, depending on the size and shape. Dried pasta usually needs 8 to 15 minutes to cook. Stir the pasta occasionally while the water is boiling to prevent the noodles from sticking together.

Taste for doneness. Pasta should be "al dente," or firm to the bite—not too hard or too soft. After cooking, place the pasta in a colander to drain, then serve.

It's best to begin cooking the sauce first—especially if you are making it from scratch—because as soon as the pasta is done, it needs to be added to the sauce. If the pasta is cooked before the sauce is ready, drain the pasta, place it in a bowl, and cover it with hot water. The pasta can be kept this way up to 15 minutes. To add a homemade taste to store-bought tomato sauces, sauté chopped onion, minced garlic, and chopped bell pepper in 2 Tbsp. oil for 5 to 8 minutes, or until soft, add the sauce, and simmer over low heat to let the flavors blend.

If serving pasta without a sauce, after draining the pasta, place it back in the pot, add a little butter, margarine, or olive oil, and toss well to coat the pasta. Parmesan cheese or chopped parsley may be sprinkled on top before serving.

COMMON PASTAS AND COOKING TIMES

There are numerous pastas with various shapes and tastes. Below are some that are popular and easy to find at your grocery store.

Fresh pasta will take 2 to 5 minutes to cook. Watch closely!

Type of Pasta	Looks Like	Approximate Cooking Time for Dried
Bucatini	hollow rods, similar to spaghetti	12–14 minutes
Cannelloni	large tubes usually stuffed	8–10 minutes
Cappelletti	small round hats, similar to tortellini	8–10 minutes
Cappelli d'angelo ("angel hair")	long, thin strands	8–10 minutes
Conchiglie	seashells	8–10 minutes
Farfalle	bow ties or butterflies	10–12 minutes
Fettuccini	narrow ribbons	6–8 minutes
Fusilli	spirals	10–12 minutes
Gemelli	two short strands that are twisted around each other	10–12 minutes
Gnocchi	seashells with a ridged surface	8–10 minutes
Lasagna	wide strips—usually 2 to 3 inches wide	10–20 minutes
Lumache	snail shells	8–10 minutes
Linguine	thick, narrow strips that look like spaghetti	6–8 minutes
Macaroni	very small, short, curved tubes	8–10 minutes
Manicotti	large tubes usually stuffed	7–9 minutes
Pappardelle	flat strips that are about 1 1/4 inches wide	6–8 minutes
Penne	short, narrow tubes cut at an angle to resemble "quills" or pen nibs	10–12 minutes
Radiatore	tiny radiators, rectangular-shaped	8–10 minutes
Ravioli	small squares stuffed with some sort of filling	7–9 minutes
Rotelle	tiny wheels	8–10 minutes
Rotini	small corkscrews	8–10 minutes
Rigatoni	medium-sized tubes with a ridged surface	10–12 minutes
Spaghetti	long, thin, round strands	10–12 minutes
Tagliatelle	wide ribbons	6–8 minutes
Tortellini	small squares usually stuffed with some sort of filling, similar to ravioli but usually folded in half	10–12 minutes
Vermicelli	very thin strands	6–8 minutes
Ziti	short and long tubes	10–12 minutes

SERVING

Serve pasta in a flat bowl or on a flat plate with a rim. Because pasta cools quickly, heat the bowl or plate before serving. You may heat the bowl in any of the following three ways: place the dish in the microwave on High for 45 seconds if the dish is microwave-safe, place it in an oven at 250°F. for 10 minutes, or place in a clean dishwasher on the "drying" cycle.

To determine which sauce to use, apply the following rule: the shorter the pasta, the thicker the sauce. The longer the pasta, the thinner the sauce. There are three ways to serve pasta with sauce:

1. Add drained cooked pasta to the sauce in the pan for 2 minutes to "join" the two and toss together over low heat (the Italian way). **Tip:** Add lots of grated Parmesan to the pot and let it simmer with the sauce and pasta before serving.
2. Place pasta in a bowl or on the dinner plate and spoon the sauce on top of the pasta.
3. Place sauce in a bowl and place the pasta on top.

PASTA TIPS FOR THE KITCHEN KLUTZ

- To test if pasta is ready after cooking, pull a piece from the boiling water and fling it at a vertical surface. If the pasta is done, it will stick to the surface.
- For the most delicious pasta, use only fresh Parmesan and freshly ground black pepper and mix the Parmesan with the pasta before adding the sauce.
- If cooking noodles for a casserole, reduce the cooking time of the pasta by 1/3 since the noodles will continue to cook in the casserole.
- You do not need to rinse cooked pasta when preparing a hot dish. You do need to rinse cooked pasta when preparing it for a cold salad.

RICE AND RISOTTO

There are at least 7,000 varieties of rice. They are categorized as either long, short, or medium grain. Short grains are rounded, fat, very starchy, and, when cooked, they will be moist and tend to stick together. Long grains are long and thin and dry when cooked. Medium grains are in between long and short, and the following types of grains or grain products can be bought in most food stores:

Arborio is an Italian rice that is short-grained and usually used to make risotto.

Basmati is a long-grain rice with a nutty flavor from northern India and Pakistan. It is very aromatic and doubles in length when cooked. Basmati must be washed before cooking.

Brown rice is a whole-grain rice with some bran. It has a nutty flavor and takes longer to cook as well as more water than converted rice.

Converted rice is a processed or parboiled rice with a bland flavor. Converted rice takes less time to cook and uses less water than brown rice.

Couscous is a North African grain product made from semolina into tiny flour-coated pellets that cook quickly.

Instant or precooked rice has been cooked and dried before packaging. It cooks much faster and is available in both brown and converted rice.

Regular rice has no hull or germ and very little bran. It comes in long and short grains and has a bland flavor.

Texmati rice is a cross between Basmati and Texas long-grain rice. It is similar to Basmati rice.

White rice is brown rice that has had the bran layers and hull removed.

Wild rice is actually a water grass rather than a grain. It has a nutty flavor and is long-grained.

SERVING SIZES

Allow 1 cup cooked rice per serving. One cup of uncooked rice will produce 3 cups cooked rice. One pound of uncooked rice equals $2^{1}/_{4}$ cups uncooked rice and will yield 8 cups cooked rice. You can look on the package to determine how much you need to buy or consult the following chart.

RICE EQUIVALENTS CHART

Rice	Uncooked	Cooked
Brown	1 cup uncooked = 4 cups cooked	
Converted	1 cup uncooked = $3^{1}/_{2}$ cups cooked	
Regular	1 cup uncooked = 3 cups cooked	
Instant	1 cup uncooked = 2 cups cooked	

STORING

Uncooked rice, excluding brown rice, should be stored in a cool, dry place in an airtight container for up to 6 months. Brown rice should be stored in the refrigerator. Cooked rice should be covered and stored in the refrigerator for up to 7 days or in the freezer for 6 to 8 months.

METHODS OF COOKING

There are several ways to cook rice. For best results, follow the directions on the particular package. When cooking rice, you generally do the following: Bring 2 cups water and 1 tsp. butter to boil in a very heavy saucepan. Flavors may be added to the water before cooking, or substitute beef or chicken broth for the water. You may also add basil, celery seeds, dill, oregano, rosemary, or thyme. Slowly add 1 cup rice, cover tightly, and simmer on low heat for 20 minutes. Do not lift the lid while the rice is cooking. Fluff it with a fork before serving.

If cooking long-grain rice, combine 1 cup long-grain converted rice, 1/2 tsp. salt, and 1 1/2 cups cold water in a very heavy saucepan. Bring the ingredients to a boil, cover tightly, and turn down heat to low and cook for 25 minutes. Again, do not lift the lid while the rice is cooking.

For a foolproof way to cook converted white rice, place 1 cup rice in a heavy pan with 2 cups water. Add 1 tsp. butter or margarine. Turn the burner to high and bring to a full boil. Put a lid on the pan and turn the heat *off*. The rice will cook perfectly. Do not remove the lid for 25 minutes. Fluff rice with a fork and serve.

To keep rice hot after cooking, you can do either of the following. You can keep the rice covered in a pan, and then place it in the oven on low heat. If the rice is dry, add a small amount of liquid to keep it from sticking. You may also place the rice in the top of a double boiler or rice steamer and keep the burner on low heat.

To reheat cooked rice, place it in a double boiler or rice steamer and cook on low heat. In addition, you may place the rice in a very heavy pan and add 1 Tbsp. water for every 2 cups of rice. Cover with a tight lid and cook on very low heat for about 5 to 8 minutes, or until hot.

Following is a list of food items that can be added after cooking rice for quick and delicious variations.

- chopped green onions or chives
- sautéed mushroom slices
- raisins and a dash of curry
- grated cheese
- slivered, toasted almonds
- cooked bacon
- pimientos or olives
- chopped green peppers
- chopped parsley
- peas

A quick way to make rice look special is to take 1 cup uncooked white converted rice and place it in a casserole dish. Pour 1 can French onion soup and

1 can beef broth over the rice. Cover and bake at 350°F. for 45 to 60 minutes, or until no liquid is left.

Rice Rings

Rice rings are a fancy way to serve rice. You may place the rice ring on a platter with your meat or other vegetables in the center. If you are serving chicken à la king or shrimp créole, place the topping in the center of the rice mold.

To make a rice ring with white rice, grease a ring mold well with vegetable shortening or nonstick cooking spray. Add ½ stick melted butter to *cooked* rice and press the rice into the mold. Place the mold in a pan of hot water (make sure the water does not get in the rice) and heat uncovered in the oven at 350°F. for 10 to 15 minutes. To unmold, place a platter on the top of the mold and invert the two. The rice should easily unmold.

To make a rice ring with wild rice, after cooking 1 cup wild rice, add ½ stick butter, 1 cup sautéed chopped onions, 1 cup sautéed sliced mushrooms, and ¼ cup sherry (optional). Place the rice mixture in a well-greased ring mold. Place the mold in a pan of hot water (make sure no water gets in the rice) and bake uncovered at 350°F. for 15-20 minutes.

SERVING SIZES FOR RICE MOLDS

8½" × 2¼" ring mold = 4½ cups rice = 8–10 servings
9¼" × 2¾" ring mold = 8 cups   = 14–16 servings

RICE TIPS FOR THE KITCHEN KLUTZ

- To prevent rice from sticking, add 1 tsp. oil or butter to the water.
- Always use a pot with a tight-fitting lid.
- To keep rice from becoming "gummy," do not stir rice after it comes to a boil.
- To make rice whiter, add 1 tsp. lemon juice to the water while cooking.
- To make rice fluffy after you've cooked it, stir rice with a fork. Make sure no moisture remains—be sure to stir the bottom of the pot. If there is any moisture, cook on low heat a minute or two more.
- Substitute chicken or beef broth for water when cooking rice.

RISOTTO (ITALIAN RICE)

Risotto is a creamy dish made with short-grained Italian rice, broth, butter, and cheese. To this mixture can be added a variety of vegetables, poultry, meat, fish, herbs, and spices. Arborio is the most common variety of short-grained Italian rice used in making risotto.

Methods of Cooking

The rice should be cooked until it is tender but still firm in the center. In general, follow the directions on the package of rice. Stock should be added evenly during the first 18 minutes of the slow, steady simmering. The rice will absorb the stock and thicken. If the rice starts to lose its creaminess or becomes too dry, add more stock.

To Cook Risotto on the Stove: Place beef or chicken stock in a pot set over low-medium heat. Melt 1/2 stick butter in a large iron skillet. Add 1 cup long-grain rice or 1 cup short-grain (Arborio) rice and cook over medium heat, stirring constantly, until the butter is absorbed by the rice and the rice looks opaque. Next pour in 1 cup hot beef or chicken stock, still stirring constantly. After the rice has absorbed all the stock, add another 1/2 cup hot stock. Continue to cook, stirring constantly, until all of the stock is absorbed. Then add another 1/2 cup hot stock. Stir well, and simmer, covered, until all stock is absorbed.

To Prepare Risotto in the Microwave: Place 1 cup long- or short-grain rice in a microwave-safe dish and add 1/2 stick butter. Cook uncovered on High for 1 minute. Add 1 1/2 cups beef or chicken stock and cook uncovered on High for 6 minutes. Stir. Cook another 6 minutes uncovered on High. Stir. Add 1/2 cup stock and microwave for 6 more minutes uncovered on High. Stir and let stand for 5 minutes before serving. **Note:** Risotto will be drier if prepared in the microwave.

RISOTTO TIPS FOR THE KITCHEN KLUTZ

- If you are making a recipe that uses a lot of Parmesan cheese, you may want to use salt-free chicken stock.
- You may substitute broth for stock but you will need to dilute the broth by substituting water for half of the amount of stock called for in the recipe, and use broth for the other half.
- Serve risotto immediately because it thickens quickly as it cools. (Warm your bowls first in the microwave on High for 45 seconds or in the dishwasher on the "dry" cycle.)

SOUPS & SALADS

Soups and salads offer almost unlimited combinations. Some soups contain meat or seafood, some contain vegetables, some consist of only stock, while others are primarily cheese. Likewise, many soups are a combination of foods. Soups are versatile and may be served hot or cold, as an appetizer, entrée, or a snack. Many areas of the United States are famous for a particular soup—New England clam chowder, Manhattan clam chowder, Brunswick stew, and Louisiana or Mississippi seafood gumbo, for example. You may serve soups in bowls, cups, mugs, or even hollowed-out bread.

Soup and salad is a wonderful meal. Salads can be made with fruit, vegetables, meat, and seafood. They can be green, congealed, or frozen. There are endless possibilities for variety when serving soups and salads.

SOUPS

There are many different kinds of soup. **Bisque** is a cream-based soup usually made with shellfish or fish and seasonings, sometimes with tomatoes. **Bouillon** is a seasoned, concentrated, brown stock that has been clarified. Brown stock is liquid that is made from meat, bones, and fat; an exception is bouillon made from clams. **Broth** is a clear liquid that is produced from simmering any type of meat or vegetable in water. **Chowder** is a thick soup made with cream, fat, and vegetables added to a fish or meat base and then stewed. **Clear soups** include bouillon, broth, or stock made from vegetables and meat with bones. **Consommé** is a clarified, double-strength brown stock usually made from two or more meats such as beef, chicken, or veal. **Cream soups** are made by adding milk and butter or cream to a vegetable base. *(Never boil cream soups.)* You can thicken cream soups with cream of wheat, flour, or tapioca. **Jellied soups** are made with the gelatin from cooking bones, or with packaged unflavored gelatin. **Stew** is usually a combination of meat and vegetables simmered over low heat.

Notes About Stock

Stock is the liquid in which fish, meat, poultry, or vegetables have been cooked. The different types of stock include:

- Beef, brown—made from meat, bones, and the fat of beef
- Fish—made from fish and their bones
- White—made from chicken or veal
- Vegetable—made from vegetables

Recipes will often call for stock as an ingredient. For quick stock, you may use commercial canned broth, consommé, or cubes of beef, chicken, or vegetable bouillon that have been dissolved in a cup of hot water. For another quick stock, buy chicken stock seasoning (in the spice section of the grocery store), which, when added to boiling water, produces chicken stock.

For homemade stock, you may use the following recipe.

Beef Stock Ingredients

2½ lbs. beef bones or 4 lbs. beef shank (from butcher)
3 onions, sliced
3 celery stalks, sliced
3 carrots, sliced
3 sprigs parsley
½ tsp. dried thyme
1 bay leaf
2 Tbsp. cooking oil
16 cups cold water
10 peppercorns
1½ tsp. salt

Preheat the oven to 450°F. In a large pan, add 2 Tbsp. cooking oil and the shank or bones cut into chunks. Bake in the oven to brown, stirring occasionally. After baking for 10 minutes, add the sliced onion, celery, and carrots to the pan and brown them. After the vegetables have browned, transfer the contents of the pan to a large stockpot. Add 1 cup boiling water to the pan and scrape up all of the browned pieces from the pan, and add to the pot. Add the parsley, thyme, bay leaf, peppercorns, and 16 cups cold water to the pot. Slowly bring the water to a boil over medium heat. Once the mixture begins boiling, reduce the heat to low and simmer for 4 to 5 hours. Watch the mixture carefully during the first 45 minutes and skim off any fat that rises to the surface. You may cover the pot for part of the simmering time, if you wish. After stock has simmered for 4 to 5 hours, strain the liquid through a strainer and let it cool uncovered.

If you are careful in making stock, you should not have to clarify it. If you need to remove any of the cloudiness from the stock, then fully cool stock, and add 1 slightly beaten egg white mixed with 2 tsp. water and 1 crumpled eggshell per quart of stock. Stir well and bring the stock to a boil. Stirring constantly, boil for 2 minutes. Reduce heat to low and let sit for 20 minutes. Strain through a fine strainer.

To store stock: After cooking and/or clarifying stock, let it cool uncovered at room temperature. Store tightly covered in the refrigerator for up to 3 or 4 days. While stock is in the refrigerator, a layer of fat will rise to the surface. Do not remove this layer of fat until you are ready to use the stock. You may also freeze stock in a freezer container for up to 6 months. When ready to use refrigerated or frozen stock, always heat it first to the boiling point. You may freeze stock in an ice cube tray and use as many "stock cubes" as you need.

CHOOSING WHICH SOUP TO SERVE

As a first course, choose a soup that will stimulate the appetite as well as complement your entrée. For example, choose a light soup to serve before a very seasoned entrée. Never serve a cream soup with a creamy entrée. Serve soup bowls on a plate to protect the table from spills and for a place to lay the soup spoon when finished eating. Doilies may be placed under the bowl to prevent the bowl from slipping on the plate.

Add any of the following as garnishes for soup:

Bacon	Cheese	Curry powder	Parsley
Basil	Chili powder	Lemon rind/slice	Parmesan Cheese
Broccoli	Chives	Mushrooms	Scallions
Carrots	Croûtons	Nuts	Sour cream (dollop)
Celery	Eggs (chopped hard-cooked)	Onion	Yogurt (dollop)

From Fisherman's Wharf in San Francisco comes a great presentation for serving soup—take a rounded bread or a large roll and hollow it to make a bowl. Brush the inside with olive oil and toast it at 350°F. for 10 minutes. Pour the soup in the bread bowl to serve. Other natural soup bowls for serving include hollowed-out pumpkins or cabbages.

You may also use wine to complement soup. For consommé, chicken, and vegetable soups, add chablis. For onion soup, add sherry, and for beef or minestrone soups, add claret or burgundy.

HOW MUCH SOUP TO SERVE

Plan on 1 quart for 4 servings of soup as a first course (1 cup per serving).

Plan on 2 quarts for 4 servings of soup as a main course (2 cups per serving).

SOUP TIPS FOR THE KITCHEN KLUTZ

- Chill bowls for serving cold soup, and warm bowls for serving hot soup.
- Cover soup when cooking it to blend the flavors better.
- Always cool soups uncovered.
- Remember that cold soups need more seasoning than hot soups since the heat intensifies the flavor of ingredients.
- Make soup a day ahead if possible since soups usually have a better flavor on the second day.
- Salt and pepper soup toward the end of cooking because the seasoning flavors will intensify the longer the soup is cooked.
- Spruce up canned soup with a dash of sherry, vermouth, lemon juice, or a dash of red pepper sauce.
- If soup is too salty, add a peeled raw potato, boil the soup for a little while, and remove the potato. You may also add 1 tsp. sugar after cooling the soup and then reheat before serving.
- To remove fat from soup or stock, allow the soup to cool in the refrigerator, then remove the congealed fat with a spoon. You may also lay a paper towel on top of the soup, and remove the towel after it is saturated. Another way is to drop in a leaf of lettuce to absorb the grease.
- Quick soup: Purée leftover vegetables in a blender and add milk and seasonings. Serve hot or cold.
- If soup curdles (becomes lumpy), place it in a food processor and beat until smooth.
- To thicken soup, add flour, tapioca, cream of wheat, tomato sauce, or tomato paste.

SALADS

DIFFERENT TYPES OF SALAD GREENS

While **Boston** and **iceberg** lettuces are used most often, try some of the following greens to add color, taste, texture, and variety to your salads, as well as your sandwiches.

Arugula is a small, narrow, dark green leaf with a peppery taste. It is also called **rocket** or **roquette**.

Bibb lettuce is succulent and has medium to dark green leaves. It has a mild taste.

Boston (or Butterhead) lettuce consists of delicate leaves with an oily, buttery texture. The outside leaves are light green, and the inside are light yellow. Boston lettuce is very perishable, so it should be used as soon as possible.

Chicory has a prickly texture, bitter flavor, and curly fringed red leaves. It is also called **curly endive**.

Cabbage is available in green, red, curly, Chinese, and savory types. It is crisp and delicious in coleslaw.

Endive (also called **Belgian endive**) is a strongly flavored green used often in Italian cooking. It looks like an unshucked ear of corn. Because of its strong flavor, it often mixes well with blander lettuces.

Escarole has pale, large, broad leaves that are slightly ruffled and slightly bitter tasting.

Iceberg lettuce comes as a compact, round, smooth head with medium green leaves on the outside and pale green leaves on the inside. Iceberg adds crunch to salads and does not wilt easily.

Kyona is a green in the mustard family that has a peppery taste and comes from Japan.

Leaf lettuce has no head and has ragged ruffly edges.

Mustard greens are a variety of Chinese cabbage that is light green with a white stalk. They have a pleasant taste.

Radicchio looks like a small red cabbage and is bitter, so use it sparingly. It is nice as a garnish.

Romaine lettuce consists of an elongated head of stiff leaves that are medium to dark green. It is usually preferred for Caesar salads.

Spinach has tart and tangy leaves.

Sprouts may be alfalfa, radish, or bean. **Alfalfa** are wispy green shoots. **Radish sprouts** have a strong flavor. **Bean sprouts** are tender and pale.

Swiss chard has dark green leaves and is similar to spinach. Swiss chard has a white thick stem.

Watercress has small, dark, green glossy leaves with a pungent and peppery flavor.

BUYING

In general, when buying salad greens, avoid ones with withered, yellow, or brown leaves, since this indicates that the greens are old. Lettuce should feel heavy for its size, which indicates a high water content. Choose a firm head for salads and a loose head for use on sandwiches or as "cups" for salads. Leafy lettuce should have a firm core and pale green leaves. Spinach should have small, dark, tender leaves. Endive, chicory, and escarole have tender inside leaves and a few dark, tough, outer leaves. Remember, 1 pound generally will yield 5 to 6 cups of cut-up leaves. If serving a green salad as an appetizer, allow 1 to 2 cup of greens per serving, and 3 to 4 cups if serving as the main dish.

STORING

Lettuce is very perishable because it has a high water content. Greens may be stored up to 7 days in the refrigerator, depending on their freshness when purchased. Always wash and dry greens before storing. Store greens in a tightly sealed plastic bag (vegetable bags if possible) or in a covered container in the refrigerator (in the crisper drawer). Remove any leaves that have turned brown, so they do not affect the taste of the other greens. Always store mint, watercress, and parsley separately.

PREPARING

Prepare salad greens in advance to save time, and always wash well. The grit may not be visible, but you can still taste it. To clean, remove the stems and core with a knife. Hold the greens under running water or plunge them into a sink full of water and gently swirl them around to remove any grit or dirt. Drain with a salad spinner or wire basket, if possible, and place on paper towels for further drying.

Wash spinach and mustard greens thoroughly to remove all sand and grit. You will have to wash these 3 or 4 times to really clean them well. Place greens in a clean sink, fill with lukewarm water, and the greens will rise to the top, while the grit will sink to the bottom. Lift greens out and place in a colander. Clean the sink and repeat the process again. If you add 1 tsp. salt to the water it will kill any bugs or worms. Tear off the stems and any wilted leaves before using.

If you are not ready to use the greens after washing, dry them and then place them in plastic bags or a covered container with paper towels and store in the refrigerator.

SERVING

When preparing a salad, you may tear lettuce into bite-sized pieces with your fingers, or cut it up using a knife or scissors. Always make sure salad greens are in bite-size pieces when serving a salad. Always apply the salad dressing at serving time, not before. For the perfect oil and vinegar dressing, combine 1 part vinegar with 2 parts of olive oil or any other oil you prefer (*see* "Salad Dressings".)

WHAT TO ADD TO A SALAD

Anchovies
Artichoke hearts
Avocado
Apples
Bacon (crisp and
  crumbled)
Beets (cooked, cut in
  cubes or slices)
Carrots
Cauliflower
Celery

Cheese (grated, cubed,
  crumbled)
Chives
Croûtons
Coconut
Corn chips
Cucumber
  (slices)
Eggs (hard-cooked,
  shredded, or
  chopped)

Flowers (daisy petals,
  dandelions, pansies,
  chamomile)
Grapefruit
Grapes
Jicama
Leeks
Meat (in strips
  or cubes)
Mushrooms (sliced,
  pieces)

Nuts (halves,
slivered)
Olives (stuffed, sliced,
grated)
Onion (rings,
slices)
Oranges (especially
mandarin)
Pears
Peppers
Pickles
Pineapple (rings or
chunks)

Potatoes (canned shoe-
string)
Radishes
Raisins
Sausage (slices)
Scallions (chopped or
slivered)
Seafood (shrimp, lob-
ster, crab pieces)
Sesame seeds
Sprouts (store in water
in the refrigerator for
up to 1 week)

Strawberries (sliced or
whole)
Sunflower seeds
Peas
Tangerines
Tomatoes (sliced
vertically for
firmer slices or
quartered or
cherry tomatoes
whole)
Zucchini (chopped or
sliced)

SALAD DRESSINGS

Salad dressings are used to enhance and highlight salad ingredients. Remove dressings from the refrigerator about 30 minutes before serving so they are at room temperature when used. Shake dressing well before using to make sure all of the ingredients are mixed thoroughly. Add dressing to greens right before serving so they will not become soggy. Add fresh herbs or garlic to store-bought dressings for a homemade taste. To thicken French dressing, stir an ice cube in it right before serving. In addition, place a clove of garlic in the bottle of French dressing for some zest.

Homemade mayonnaise is delicious, easy to make, and a great base for many salad dressings. Keep it covered in the refrigerator for up to 7 days. To make, mix 1/2 tsp. dry mustard, 1/2 tsp. sugar, and 1/2 tsp. salt in a bowl. Add 2 chilled or cold egg yolks and 1 Tbsp. fresh lemon juice or vinegar. Mix together well. Add 1 cup of *chilled* salad oil very slowly while beating the mixture with an electric beater on high speed. As the mixture thickens, add another Tbsp. vinegar or lemon juice and a dash (1/16 tsp.) cayenne pepper or 1/2 tsp. paprika. Beat mixture until stiff. Refrigerate. Make sure you use fresh eggs. To thin, add lemon juice.

Remember: add the chilled oil slowly. This is the key to delicious homemade mayonnaise. You may substitute 1 whole egg for the 2 egg yolks. If the mayonnaise curdles, place an egg yolk in a clean bowl and beat it. Slowly add the curdled mayonnaise spoonful by spoonful while beating the additional egg yolk.

Using mayonnaise as a base, you may prepare the following salad dressings by mixing the following combinations together:

Basil—1/2 cup mayonnaise + 1/4 cup diced fresh tomatoes + 1 1/2 Tbsp. fresh basil
Bleu Cheese—1/2 cup mayonnaise + 1/2 cup French dressing + 1/4 cup crumbled bleu cheese
Cucumber—1/2 cup mayonnaise + 1/4 cup cucumber (minced) + 1/2 tsp. chives

Curry—1/2 cup mayonnaise + 1 tsp. curry powder + 1 Tbsp. parsley

Garlic—1/2 cup mayonnaise + 6–8 cloves of minced garlic

Russian—1/2 cup mayonnaise + 1 Tbsp. minced celery + 1 Tbsp. sweet pickles or sweet pickle relish + 1 Tbsp. chili sauce + 2 tsp. ketchup + 1 Tbsp. minced green pepper

Low-fat Tips: You may use plain yogurt in place of mayonnaise in the salad dressing recipes listed above for a low fat dressing. A low fat dressing is 1 cup plain yogurt mixed with 2 Tbsp. lemon juice and some minced onion and 1 Tbsp. ketchup and/or pickle relish.

Olive Oil can be combined with many other ingredients to make delicious salad dressings. Olive oil is the oil extracted (pressed) from olives.The taste of olive oil depends on many factors: the variety and quality of the olive, the country of origin, the climate, the soil, the manner in which the olive is picked, the storage conditions, and the way the oil is extracted. Cloudiness or residue at the bottom of the bottle, which sometimes results from a certain type of extraction, is not harmful. Olive oil is graded according to its acidity/sharpness. *Extra-virgin* (which is the oil first extracted and the most expensive) has the least amount of acidity, with less than 1%, and *virgin* has the most, with a maximum of 3%. Store olive oil in a cool, dark place. Do not store in the refrigerator, as the cold will cause the oil to congeal. Olive oil should last at least 1 year after opening. A fine olive oil will not turn rancid. Remember not to tightly seal the lid when closing—olive oil needs to breathe. You can smell olive oil to determine if it's rancid—the odor will be musty.

Vinegar is available in many different flavors and may be mixed with oil to make tasty oil-and-vinegar dressings. The standard recipe for oil-and-vinegar dressing is:

1 part vinegar + 2 parts of oil (any type)

To make **vinaigrette dressings**, combine the oil, vinegar, and any other ingredients you prefer in a bottle, add an ice cube, and shake well. Remove the ice cube after shaking. You may also blend the ingredients in a blender (without the ice cube). The following may be added to oil-and-vinegar dressings for extra zest:

1–2 tsp. chopped herbs	2–3 tsp. mustard (any type)
a crushed clove of garlic	1/2 avocado (mashed)
crumbled bleu cheese	dash of salt and pepper

Another way to spice up your oil and vinegar dressing is to use a flavored vinegar. Not only are they available commercially, but they are easy to make with rosemary, basil, oregano, and thyme. To make a **Lemon Thyme and Rosemary Vinegar**, place 1 sprig each of rosemary and lemon thyme, 4 whole black peppercorns, and 5 small grapes in a 16-ounce bottle, and fill with white wine vinegar. To make an **Oregano and Sweet Basil Vinegar**, place 1 sprig each of oregano and sweet basil and 4 whole black peppercorns in a 16 oz. bottle, and fill with red wine vinegar.

NOT JUST A SALAD

In addition to the traditional salad composed primarily of salad greens, there are numerous other salads such as chicken, tuna, fruit, vegetable, frozen, bean, or congealed salads.

Bean Salad

You may take any canned beans, wash and drain well, and mix them with a dressing and any other ingredients (such as chopped onion, green peppers, olives, celery, or pimientos). An easy bean salad to make is to combine the following in a bowl: 1 medium size can of *drained* green peas, green beans and kidney beans, corn, or yellow wax beans (for a total of 3 cans of vegetables) + 1 cup chopped green pepper + 3/4 cup of chopped celery + a small jar of chopped, drained pimientos. Mix together a marinade of 1/2 cup salad oil, 1/2 tsp. salt, 1/8 tsp. pepper, 1/2 cup sugar, and 1/2 cup wine vinegar. Boil the marinade for 1 minute and pour it over the vegetables. Refrigerate the salad in a covered container for 6 to 8 hours before serving.

Chicken Salad

An easy yet delicious salad to make is to combine 2 cups cooked chopped chicken + 1 cup diced celery + 1 cup mayonnaise + salt and pepper to taste. You may add other ingredients if you wish, such as halved grapes or toasted almonds, to the chicken salad.

Chicken salad is delicious served on a cantaloupe slice or in a pineapple half. Also, you may serve it on an avocado half or stuffed in a tomato. To serve in a tomato, peel and slice the tomato down 5 or 6 places from the top to within 1/2 inch of the bottom to form an "open flower." Gently spread the wedges apart and fill. Another great way to serve chicken salad is to place it on an English muffin, warm it in the oven, add a slice of Cheddar cheese to cover, and melt the cheese. Serve warm. (You need to warm the chicken salad before placing the cheese on top if you want the chicken salad warm.) You may also place chicken salad in a casserole dish, sprinkle crushed potato chips on top, and bake at 350°F. until bubbly.

Gelatin (Congealed) Salad

There are many delicious salads made with fruit gelatin and fruit, as well as with vegetables. You may take a box of fruit gelatin, add canned or fresh fruit, and then congeal. Remember never add fresh pineapple to a congealed salad because it will prevent the salad from jelling. Use canned pineapple instead. Save fruit juices and use them as part of the liquid when making congealed salads. You may also use cola or lemon-lime carbonated beverages for 1 cup of the liquid for a different taste. For a congealed vegetable salad, try using lemon gelatin, unflavored gelatin, tomato juice, and vegetables.

A basic congealed salad is made as follows: Prepare 1 package of fruit-flavored gelatin according to the directions on the box. Place it in the refrigerator and when it begins to set, remove it from the refrigerator and add $1^1/_2$ to $2^1/_2$ cups well-drained fruit, vegetables, or seafood (such as shrimp). If adding fruit, use fruit juice for $^1/_2$ of the liquid when preparing the gelatin. If adding vegetables, add 2 Tbsp. lemon juice when preparing the gelatin. Pour into molds or a square pan and refrigerate until set. Unmold or cut into squares and serve. To unmold, dip the mold in warm water, being careful not to let any water in the salad. Then take a knife or spatula and run it around the edge of the mold, place your plate face-down on the mold, and invert the mold and plate. The mold should lift off easily from the salad. You may then serve congealed salad on a lettuce leaf and top it with a dollop of mayonnaise or dressing if you wish.

Fruit Salad

When preparing fruit salad, you may use either canned or fresh fruit. Serve fruit salad in a chilled bowl or on a lettuce leaf. Fruit salad is delicious when served with a poppy seed dressing or cottage cheese.

Several easy fruit salads to make are:

- Cut-up balls of watermelon, cantaloupe, honeydew, grapes (halved), pineapple (chopped), and banana slices
- Pear halves or pineapple slices topped with a dollop of mayonnaise and grated cheese
- Peach or pear halves topped with cottage cheese

Waldorf Salad and Mandarin Orange Salad

A Waldorf salad consists of diced apples, diced celery, and chopped nuts (optional) mixed with mayonnaise and thinned with cream or lemon juice. You may also add raisins. An unusual and easy fruit salad is to combine 1 cup of each of the following: mandarin oranges, pineapple chunks, shredded coconut, miniature marshmallows, and sour cream. Refrigerate the mixture for 8 hours and then serve.

Meat and Seafood Salads

Meat salads can be made with shrimp, crabmeat, ham, turkey, chicken, or salmon. Try serving a meat salad such as chicken salad or crabmeat salad hot by baking it at 350°F. until it bubbles. Add crushed potato chips or cracker crumbs on top before baking.

Pasta Salad

Be sure to cook pasta and then rinse with cold water before adding to your salad. Pasta may be mixed with fresh vegetables, meat, salt, pepper, other seasonings, and dressing. Pasta salad will taste best if you let it marinate several hours in the refrigerator before serving. Use store-bought Italian dressing over pasta when you're in a hurry—it works great!

Potato Salad

Use new potatoes for potato salad if you want the potatoes to hold their shape, and Idaho (or similar) potatoes if you want the salad to be sort of creamy. Add dressing to potato salad while the potatoes are hot—they will absorb the flavor better. Add a homemade touch to store-bought potato salad by adding chopped dill, sweet pickles, basil, or cilantro.

For a quick potato salad, scrub 2 pounds of red potatoes. Place them in a pot and cover with water. Cook over medium heat until tender—you should be able to pierce them with a fork easily. Mix together 1 cup mayonnaise, 1/4 cup chives, 1 Tbsp. dried dill, 1 Tbsp. dried parsley, and 1 Tbsp. Dijon mustard. After the potatoes have cooked, you may peel them if you wish or leave the skin on. Dice them in 1/2-to-1-inch cubes and blend with the mayonnaise mixture. Refrigerate 1 hour before serving, or keep in the refrigerator for several days—it will taste better as it ages. Remember that if you use fresh herbs instead of dried, use 3 Tbsp. fresh instead of 1 Tbsp. dried. You may make this in any proportion you wish, or omit any ingredients. The recipe is very flexible.

Tuna Salad

An easy yet delicious salad to make is to combine 2 cups canned tuna + 1 cup diced celery + 1 cup mayonnaise + salt and pepper to taste. You may add other ingredients, if you wish, such as minced sweet pickles or pickle relish and chopped hard-cooked eggs to tuna salad. Serve tuna salad on an avocado half or in a tomato.

Vegetable Salad

Vegetable salads may be made from any assortment of vegetables. Some quick, easy, and tasty variations include:

• Grated raw carrots, crushed pineapple or pineapple chunks, and raisins, mixed with mayonnaise or plain yogurt. Mix and chill before serving.
• Sliced cucumbers and onions mixed with half oil, half vinegar, salt and pepper—marinated for several hours in the refrigerator before serving. You may add 1 Tbsp. parsley and 1 Tbsp. dill.
• Tomatoes stuffed with cottage cheese that has been seasoned with chopped cucumbers, chives, shredded carrots, or bell peppers.
• Asparagus and sliced tomatoes sprinkled with Parmesan cheese.

- Cooked lima beans mixed with green onions, mushrooms, oregano, and sprinkled with oil and vinegar.
- Marinate vegetables of any type in a store-bought Italian dressing. Use cherry tomatoes if you want tomatoes in your salad, they will hold up better with the other vegetables.
- Make a marinade of $2/3$ cup salad oil, $1/4$ cup tarragon vinegar, $1/4$ cup chopped parsley, 1 minced clove garlic, $1/2$ tsp. dried thyme, and $1/4$ cup chopped onion. Place 6 tomatoes that have been peeled and quartered in the marinade. Chill together for 4 to 6 hours. Drain tomatoes and serve on lettuce leaves.

SALAD TIPS FOR THE KITCHEN KLUTZ

- Add tomatoes last to a salad; the juice will thin the salad dressing.
- To make croûtons, trim the crust from bread, cut the bread into $1/2$-inch cubes, sauté in melted butter until golden-brown, add garlic if desired, or toss cubes in melted butter and brown in an oven at 300°F.
- Remember when serving salads as appetizers, they should whet the appetite without filling up the stomach.
- For a luxurious garnish, add caviar to your salad.
- If you are making a salad for a crowd and don't have a large bowl for mixing or storing the greens, use the vegetable keeper from your refrigerator.
- For a no-fail, looks-great, tastes-great salad, mix Boston, Bibb, and red leaf lettuce.
- Make a delicious salad seasoning by combining 1 Tbsp. salt, 1 tsp. pepper, 1 Tbsp. marjoram, 1 Tbsp. basil, 1 Tbsp. dried chives, 1 Tbsp. celery seed, 2 Tbsp. parsley flakes, and 1 Tbsp. dillweed. Store mixture, which will make $1/2$ cup, in an airtight container.
- For a great Italian seasoning for salad, mix together 1 Tbsp. thyme, 1 Tbsp. basil, 1 Tbsp. savory, 1 Tbsp. oregano, 1 Tbsp. dried marjoram, 1 Tbsp. sage, 2 crushed bay leaves, and 1 crushed dried red chili pepper.
- Chill salad plates or bowls in the refrigerator or freezer (make sure they are thoroughly dry) before using, to help greens stay crisp longer.

DESSERTS

Everyone has a favorite dessert. You may serve fruit and cheese, cookies, or a wonderful rich concoction. No matter what you serve, dessert is the finale of your meal. A good dessert can make an average meal a memorable one, so don't skimp when making your choice. It doesn't have to be fancy, just pleasant to the eye and taste. In this chapter you will find many types of desserts as well as helpful tips. A chart of dessert terms is also included to help you decide what to serve.

CHOOSING A DESSERT TO SERVE

Choose a light dessert to accompany a heavy meal. Examples of light desserts are custard, fruit desserts, frozen desserts, or gelatin desserts. Alternately, if your meal is light, choose a rich, heavy dessert to accompany it. Examples of heavy desserts are tortes, pastries, a cake such as cheesecake, and pies. In addition, be careful not to repeat the flavor, color, or texture of other foods served during the meal—for example, do not serve pecan pie if you have served a salad with pecans; instead, use a different nut in your salad or serve a different pie.

CAKE

There are many excellent cake mixes so don't hesitate to use them or store-bought frostings. Check your grocery shelf and choose one to your liking. Be sure to read the cake mix label before leaving the supermarket in case you need to purchase additional ingredients for the mix such as eggs, milk, or oil. If you are ambitious and would like to bake a cake from scratch, make sure all the ingredients are at room temperature and always preheat your oven. You should only use the type of flour called for in the recipe—it makes a difference in the finished product. Some cake recipes use cake flour while others use all-purpose flour. If you need to substitute all-purpose flour for cake flour, use 1 cup less 2 Tbsp. of all-purpose flour for each cup of cake flour. When mixing ingredients together, mix the dry ingredients with a spoon before adding them to the cake mixture. Then slowly mix the dry ingredients into the mixture only until they "disappear" and all lumps are gone. *When a recipe says to add the flour and liquid alternately, always start with the dry ingredients and end with the dry ingredients.* Cream butter well to prevent a rough-textured cake. In addition, add all spices and vanilla when creaming the sugar and butter so that the flavors will be better absorbed. Before adding raisins, berries, or nuts, coat them with some of the flour from the recipe in order to prevent them from settling to the bottom during the baking. After mixing the ingredients, be careful not to overbeat; it will make the cake flat and heavy.

To prevent cakes from sticking to the pan, grease the pan (both bottom and sides) with shortening (use your fingers or a paper towel to grease). Then lightly dust the pan with flour, making sure the sides are covered. An empty salt shaker filled with flour works great. If you are baking a chocolate cake, use cocoa instead of flour. Turn the greased and dusted pan over, hold it over the sink, and tap the bottom of the pan. The excess flour will fall into the sink. Then pour the batter in. When pouring batter for a layer cake, use a measuring cup and add equal amounts of batter to each pan.

Always use the pan size called for in your recipe to produce a nice shape and rounded top. Using too small a pan will cause the cake to lose its shape and cook over the edges of the pan. Using too large a pan will produce a flat cake with pale color. If you do not know the size of your cake pan, measure it from one inside to the other. Use fingernail polish to record the dimensions on the underside of the pan. Use the following chart if you need to substitute the required pan size:

$8^{1}/_{2} \times 4^{1}/_{2} \times 2^{1}/_{2}$-inch loaf pan = two $5^{1}/_{2} \times 3^{1}/_{4} \times 2^{1}/_{4}$-inch pans
$8 \times 4 \times 3$-inch loaf pan = $8 \times 8 \times 2$-inch square pan
10-inch tube pan = two $9 \times 5 \times 3$-inch loaf pans
$9 \times 3^{1}/_{2}$-inch tube pan = two 9-inch layer cake pans
$13 \times 9 \times 2$-inch pan = two 8-inch or 9-inch round or square pans
9-inch round pan = one 8-inch square pan
$13 \times 9 \times 2$-inch rectangular pan = two 9-inch layer cake pans
$12 \times 8 \times 2$-inch rectangular pan = two 8-inch layer cake pans

Use shiny pans for baking a cake, because they reflect the heat and cause a delicate browning. Straight-sided pans produce a better texture. Remember to reduce the oven temperature 25°F. when you're using a glass pan.

To test for doneness, insert a toothpick, uncooked spaghetti noodle, or broomstraw into the cake and remove. If it comes out clean, the cake is done. In addition, the cake should spring back when lightly touched. Another sign that a cake is ready is that it will shrink from the sides of the pan. If the cake is not done, bake it for a few minutes more and test again. If a cake overbakes and is too dry, moisten the cake by punching holes in the cake with a toothpick and pouring in a mixture of $^{1}/_{2}$ cup sugar and 1 cup water that has been cooked into a syrup (you may substitute fruit juice for the water). To make this syrup, heat water and sugar in a heavy saucepan over medium heat until the sugar is dissolved.

After removing from the oven, place the cake pan on a wet towel. Wait until the pan is cool, and the cake will come out of the pan easily. Another way to remove the cake from the pan is to let the cake sit in the pan for 10 minutes. Then take a flat knife and run the knife around the edge of the pan to loosen the edges, being careful not to cut the cake. Place a cake rack on top of the cake pan and invert the pan and rack. Lift up the pan, and the cake will remain on the rack to cool. Place powdered sugar on the cake plate before you place the cake on it. This will help keep the cake from sticking.

Allow to cool before storing or cutting. When cutting cake, use a serrated knife. To cut fresh cake easily, run the knife under very hot water first.

For Angel Food, Chiffon, and Sponge Cakes: Use ungreased cake pans unless the recipe states otherwise. Make sure your pans are clean and completely grease-free. Egg whites beat much better at room temperature. Always gently fold in egg whites. **To fold in egg whites:** Place egg white mixture on top of the mixture you are folding them into. Then gently take your spoon or rubber spatula and move it to the bottom of the bowl and back up to the top so that some of the bottom mixture is on top. Stir the mixture in a vertical fashion (up and over) until the egg white and the other mixture are blended. Do not over-do this step—stir and blend sparingly.

To test for doneness, angel food cake will leave no finger imprint when touched. Chiffon and sponge cakes will spring back when you touch them with your finger. Angel food, chiffon, and sponge cakes must be cooled in the pan to prevent shrinking. To cool this type of cake, remove the cake from the oven, invert it, and let it hang upside down for 1 hour or until it is cold. A great way to do this is to invert the cake pan and place the center opening/tube of the cake pan on the neck of a bottle such as a wine or glass soda bottle or a funnel. Let the cake pan hang suspended until cool. To remove the cake from the pan after it cools, go around the edges of the cake pan with a knife or spatula to make sure the cake is not sticking. Then invert the cake pan onto a cake rack. The pan should come off easily. You may then frost the cake.

Cheesecake

Cheesecake is made with cheese, eggs, sugar, and such flavorings as almond, vanilla, raspberry, and lemon. This type of dessert must be cooked on low heat in the oven to reduce shrinking and should always be cooled in the oven to room temperature and then refrigerated to enhance the flavor and texture. Cheesecake may be refrigerated up to 3 days or frozen for up to 1 month.

Cupcakes

A cupcake recipe containing 2¼ cups of flour will make 18 to 24 cupcakes. Bake cupcakes in muffin pans. After preparing the batter, line the pans with paper fluted cups (found in the baking section of the grocery) or you may grease and flour the muffin pan. Fill individual cupcake pans only ½ to ⅔ full with batter. A 350°F. oven is usually the best temperature for baking cupcakes, but if you are using a store-bought mix, follow the box directions. Let the cupcakes cool in the pan for 5 minutes before removing them. Allow cupcakes to cool *completely* before icing. Instead of icing cupcakes a nice alternative is to sprinkle them with powdered sugar.

When Frosting (Icing) and Filling a Cake

Frosting and filling for a cake may either be made or purchased. The following measurements will help you determine how much frosting and filling you will need:

Two 8-inch layer pans will use 1½ cups frosting
Two 9-inch layer pans will use 2 cups frosting
A 8-inch or 9-inch layer cake will use ¾ cup filling

If you are making frosting or filling, there are several tricks to keep in mind. Always sift confectioners' sugar when adding it to a butter frosting in order to make it smooth. Some frostings and fillings are cooked, while others are not cooked. If the cooked frosting is too thin, place it in a double boiler over low heat, (making sure the water in the bottom pan is not touching the bottom of the top part of the double boiler), and beat the frosting until it thickens. If cooked frosting is too thick, gradually beat in a few drops of water. If uncooked frosting is too thin, add sifted confectioners' sugar and beat the mixture. If too thick, gradually beat in a few drops of milk or water. For tinted frosting, use a few drops of food coloring. To tint sugar or coconut, place a few drops of food coloring in a jar with the sugar or coconut, cover with a lid, and shake.

It's best to wait until a cake thoroughly cools before adding the frosting and filling. Uncooked frosting made with butter may be spread on warm cakes although the frosting may melt some. Cooked frosting should only be spread on thoroughly cooled cakes.

Before frosting a cake, brush off any excess crumbs with a pastry brush. If the cake is crooked, use a sharp serrated knife and trim to make it even before frosting. When you are ready to frost the cake, frost the sides first and then the top. When frosting a layer cake, make sure the two flat sides are facing each other in the middle. If you frost the bottom layer so that the round part is on top, when you add the top layer it will slide off. If a layer begins to slide, use toothpicks to hold the layers together. To make swirls in the frosting, use a tablespoon or spatula. To make a butter frosting glossy, frequently dip the utensil you are using in hot water to spread the frosting better. Likewise, if frosting on a cake gets messed up, dip a knife blade in hot water and spread over frosting. If frosting made in a double boiler loses its gloss while you are frosting the cake, beat it again.

When using a filling, cool the cake first. Spread the bottom layer of the cake with the filling and wait a few minutes. Then add the top layer.

In addition to decorating cakes and cupcakes with frosting, you may also add gumdrops, crushed candy (such as peppermint), nuts, chocolate chips, tinted sugar, or coconut. For chocolate curls, which are a great garnish for frosting, take a vegetable peeler or sharp knife and scrape it over the chocolate bar to produce curls.

COOKIES

There are six different types of cookies. To make **bar and square cookies** the dough is baked in a pan and the size of the cookie is determined when the baked dough is cut. **Drop cookies** are made by dropping the cookie dough from a teaspoon on to the cookie sheet. **Molded cookies** are made by rolling or molding the dough by hand and then placing them on a cookie sheet. **Rolled cookies** are made by rolling the dough out with a rolling pin, cutting the dough into shapes with cookie cutters, and then placing them on a cookie sheet. To make **roll and slice cookies**, roll the dough into a log shape, refrigerate it, then slice and place the cookies on a cookie sheet. **Pressed cookies** are made when the dough is put in a cookie press and then placed directly on the cookie sheet to form shapes.

When baking cookies, always make sure your ingredients are at room temperature before you begin and remember to preheat your oven. A wooden spoon is best for stirring your ingredients together. Be careful not to overmix cookie dough or bake cookies too long. Before rolling out cookie dough, chill it in the refrigerator for 10 minutes. When rolling out cookie dough, do not use too much flour. You may use powdered sugar instead of flour to prevent toughness.

Cookies really should be baked on cookie sheets. When a recipe calls for a greased cookie sheet, lightly spread solid vegetable shortening over the surface or spray with nonstick cooking spray. In between oven batches, wipe the cookie sheet with a paper towel so that no crumbs are left and then lightly regrease if necessary. Use baking sheets without sides so the cookies will bake evenly and quickly. Make sure they are cool before placing cookie dough on them. Two cookie sheets are best when making cookies—one goes in the oven while the other cookie sheet is cooling. Always use shiny cookie sheets, never dark ones. Dark ones tend to make cookies brown on the bottom. If a cookie sheet is only partially full, place a cake or pie pan on the empty part while the cookies are baking; this will help the baking to be even. If your cookies are getting

---

COOKIE TIPS FOR THE KITCHEN KLUTZ

- For baking bar cookies, be sure to use the correct size pan for bar cookies. If the pan is too small, the cookies will be cakelike. If the pan is too large, the cookies will be dry.
- For baking rolled cookies, first dip the cookie cutters in water to keep the dough from sticking to them.
- To top uncooked cookies with a sprinkling of sugar, place the cookies on the cookie sheet, sprinkle the sugar on, and then take the back of a spoon or spatula and barely press the sugar into the cookies.
- To restore crispness to soft cookies, place them in an oven at 300°F. for 3 to 5 minutes.
- To mail cookies, you may pack popped popcorn around them to help prevent breaking.

too brown on the bottom, turn the cookie sheet over and place the cookies on the bottom side of the cookie sheet to cook. When baking cookies, use shiny pans to reflect the heat for a delicate crust.

Storing Cookies

To maintain freshness, store cookies in a container with a lid. For crisp cookies, store with a tight lid. For soft, chewy cookies, store with a loose lid. To keep cookies soft, place a slice of bread in the cookie jar. If crisp cookies become soft, place them in a 300°F. oven for 3 to 5 minutes. Most cookies will freeze well. Be sure to wrap them well with freezer paper or foil before freezing. Frozen baked cookies should be thawed in the wrapper for 10 to 20 minutes at room temperature. Frozen cookie dough should be thawed in the wrapper in the refrigerator for at least 1 hour.

PIES

Pies may be fruit, cream, custard, chiffon, ice cream, frozen, meringue, or made into tarts. **Fruit pies** are made with fresh or canned fruit. The fruit is placed in an unbaked pie shell and then baked in the oven. Types of fruit pies include apple, cherry, strawberry, blueberry, and blackberry. **Cream pies** are made with milk, eggs, butter, sugar, sometimes cornstarch, and flavorings such as vanilla, lemon, or almond extract and the filling is cooked on the stove. The hot mixture is then poured into a baked pie shell and usually topped with meringue or sweetened whipped cream. Types of cream pies include chocolate, banana, coconut, and lemon. **Custard pies** are usually made with custard that is baked in the oven in an unbaked pie crust. Sometimes the custard and the pie shell are baked separately and then placed together. Types of custard pies include chess, pecan, and pumpkin. A **chiffon pie** is very light and airy. It is usually made with unflavored gelatin and refrigerated until ready to serve. A **frozen pie** is made with fruit, whipped cream, egg whites, and flavorings. An **ice cream pie** is made by placing softened ice cream in a pie crust and then freezing it. It is often served with chocolate, butterscotch, or caramel sauce and topped with whipped cream and nuts. You may also add the sauce before you freeze the pie, but never place whipped cream on the pie until you are ready to serve it. A **meringue pie** is a cream pie with meringue (egg whites) on top. **Tarts** are simply small pies and may be any of the above types.

Be sure to use the correct pie pan with your recipe. A pie pan with a 9-inch diameter will produce 6 to 8 servings. A pie pan with a 10-inch diameter will produce 8 to 10 servings. The first item to consider when baking a pie is the type of crust used. You may purchase various types of pie crust at the store or make your own. When using store-bought refrigerated or frozen pie crust, brush it with milk and sprinkle with granulated sugar before baking to improve its flavor. Basic crust dough contains flour, shortening, salt, and water. You may also make crust out of cookies such as vanilla wafers, chocolate wafers, graham crackers, zwieback, or gingersnaps. Cookie pie crusts are made with cookie crumbs, butter and sugar.

If making pie dough (see how to on p. 173), remember to handle it as little as possible in order to have a flaky crust. Chill the dough first (covered in the refrigerator) and it will be much easier to roll. You may roll dough out on a lightly floured, smooth, clean countertop using a floured rolling pin. If the dough sticks to the counter, you may need to add more flour, but be careful because using too much flour will make dough tough. You may also roll out the dough using a pastry cloth and stocking (purchased at a kitchenware store) that fits over your rolling pin or by using two sheets of wax paper or aluminum foil between which you place the dough.

Roll the pie dough out about $1/8$ inch thick. If the dough breaks, pinch it back together and continue rolling. Make the circle 1 inch larger than the edge of the pan. When placing the dough in the pie pan, be careful not to let any air get between the pan and the crust and remember not to stretch the dough because it will shrink when you bake it. If you break the dough, just patch it with more dough. Trim off the excess dough with scissors or a knife, leaving about $1/2$ inch of dough hanging over the edge of the pan.

For a single-crust pie, fold the edge under and pinch or flute the edge with your thumb and forefinger. For a double-crust pie, place the filling in the pie crust and place the second circle of dough on top. Seal the top pastry to the bottom pastry by pressing the dough together with your fingers and pinch or flute the edge. You must then take a knife and make slits in the top of the pastry to allow the steam to escape while baking. You may also cut strips of pastry, about $1/2$ inch wide, and make a lattice design on top of a two-crust pie. This may be done using a knife or pastry wheel (which may be purchased at a kitchenware store). When through, press the lattice strips into the edge of the bottom pastry to seal. For a variation of the lattice design, use cookie cutters and cut shapes out of the dough and place them on top of the pie. For instance, you can cut a lemon shape to place on a lemon pie or an apple shape for an apple pie.

With fruit and custard pies, the pie crust and pie filling are baked together. Do not prick the pie crust bottom and sides when baking the crust and filling together. In order to prevent a soggy crust, brush the bottom surface of the crust with slightly beaten egg whites before adding the filling. For a golden-brown crust, take 1 egg yolk and beat it with 2 Tbsp. water. Using a pastry brush, brush this mixture over the pie crust before baking. This is enough egg mixture to cover a double-crust (top and bottom) pie. To glaze the top of a pie crust before baking, brush it lightly with a beaten egg yolk, milk, or ice water. You may also sprinkle the crust with water and then with sugar or brush it lightly with currant jelly. Right before baking a pie, insert straws or macaroni into the top of the pie crust to allow steam to escape during baking and to prevent juices from running over the top.

The pie crust is baked by itself for a cream, chiffon, frozen, or ice cream pie. When baking only the pie crust, always preheat the oven and use the lower rack in the oven. Prick the bottom and sides of the pie crust with a fork every 2 to 3 inches to allow the steam to escape. Bake uncovered at 450°F. for 12 to 15 minutes, or until lightly browned. Another way to bake an empty pie crust is to prick the bottom and sides with a fork, line the shell with aluminum foil, fill it with dried beans, and bake it for 5 minutes at 450°F. Then take the pastry shell out of the oven and remove the dried beans and aluminum foil. Bake the pastry shell for another 5 minutes, or until the shell is golden-brown. Baking with the dried beans will prevent the crust from bubbling up. Bake purchased refrigerated pie dough the same way as homemade pie crust. Frozen ready-made pie shells purchased from a store may need to be baked for several minutes longer.

Uncooked and unrolled pie dough may be well wrapped and stored in the refrigerator up to 4 days or in the freezer for up to 3 months. Store well-wrapped baked pie shells in the freezer up to 6 weeks. Storing baked pie crust in the refrigerator makes the shell soggy. You may store it wrapped in the refrigerator for 1 to 2 days but you will need to reheat it in the oven to recrisp it.

If you are baking an apple pie and are using eating apples rather than baking apples, add 1 Tbsp. lemon juice. For a quick streusel topping, mix together 1/2 cup. flour, 1/2 cup packed brown sugar, 1/2 tsp. cinnamon, and 4 Tbsp. (1/2 stick) butter. Crumble over the pie and bake as you would with a pastry crust.

To Make Pie Crust

There are three different types of pie crust that can be made. You can make a pastry that must be rolled out, cut, and placed in the pie pan or you can make a crust that does not have to be rolled out but simply pressed into the pan. The third type is a crust made with some type of crumbs.

To make a pastry pie crust—one that must be rolled out—mix 2 cups of sifted all-purpose flour and 1 tsp. salt in a bowl. Cut 2/3 cup shortening into the flour mixture using a pastry blender or two knives. Do this until the mixture looks like peas or smaller. **Tip:** For a tender crust, cut shortening in until there are small pieces; for a flaky crust, cut the shortening in until there are large pieces. Then sprinkle 6 to 8 Tbsp. water over the mixture, 1 tablespoon at a time, and mix it all together using a fork. Do this step quickly and lightly. The water is used to help form the dough into a smooth ball. You do not want the dough wet. After adding the water, lightly flour the surface you will use for rolling the dough and then roll the dough out. This recipe makes enough dough for a double-crust pie or 10 to 12 tart shells. Pie pastry may be wrapped well and stored in the freezer for 3 months.

To make a no-roll pie crust, sift 1 1/2 cups flour, 1 1/2 tsp. sugar, and 1 tsp. salt into a 9-inch pie pan. Mix together 1/2 cup vegetable oil and 2 Tbsp. cold milk. Pour this mixture over the dry ingredients and with a fork, mix together. Then press this mixture around the sides and bottom of the pan with your fingers. Flute the edge.

To prepare a crumb crust, mix together 1 1/3 cups of any kind of cookie crumbs, 3 Tbsp. sugar, and 1/3 cup melted butter. Press mixture into the pie pan and bake at 350°F. for about 10 minutes, or until brown.

Meringue Pies

For a delicious meringue topping use the directions that follow.
You will need the following ingredients, depending on the size of your pie:

8-inch pie	9-inch pie
2 egg whites	3 egg whites
1/4 tsp. cream of tartar	1/4 tsp. cream of tartar
4 Tbsp. sugar	6 Tbsp. sugar
1/4 tsp. vanilla	1/2 tsp. vanilla

Separate whites from yolk when eggs are cold. Make sure whites are at room temperature to yield more volume. Beat the whites and cream of tartar until frothy. Use a copper or stainless-steel bowl if possible because whites darken in aluminum bowls. Gradually add the sugar, a little at a time, while beating. Continue beating until stiff, glossy, and well mixed. The sugar will dissolve. Add vanilla (or substitute 1/2 Tbsp. lemon juice if baking a lemon pie) and beat. Do not underbeat your meringue. When you lift the beaters out of the meringue, the peaks that form should be stiff and should not fall over. Once the meringue is whipped, spread it evenly with a spoon over the hot pie filling. Make sure you seal the edge of the meringue to the pie crust because you do not want any spaces between the two in order to keep the meringue from shrinking when baking. If you desire, you may make swirls and peaks in the meringue. Bake the meringue at 400°F. (in a preheated oven) for 8 to 10 minutes. Watch your pie and make sure the meringue does not burn. The meringue should be barely brown. After browning, allow the meringue to cool slowly away from air blowing on it to prevent shrinking and falling.

Additional Tips for Making Meringue

• Sunny, dry weather is best for making meringue. High humidity causes limp meringue.
• **Tip:** To cut a meringue pie, rub butter on both sides of the knife or place the knife in water first before slicing.

Storing Pies

Uncooked pies may be frozen for up to 3 months. Be sure to wrap them well with freezer paper or foil. You may bake frozen pies according to the recipe directions and add 20 to 30 minutes extra to allow for the frozen pie. If you don't have a recipe to follow, bake the frozen pie uncovered at 425°F. for 15 minutes then lower the oven temperature to 350°F. and bake until ready. Uncooked chiffon, fruit, meringue, and custard pies need to be frozen, thawed, and baked as follows: **Chiffon pie** must be covered well with freezer paper or foil and may be frozen without whipped cream on top for 2 to 3 months. When ready to serve, unwrap the pie, thaw in the refrigerator for 1 to 2 hours and serve. **Custard pies** do not freeze well (pumpkin pies are the exception). If you really need to freeze a custard pie, freeze it well wrapped without any whipped cream for 2 to 3 months. When ready to serve, unwrap the pie and thaw it at

DESSERT TIPS FOR THE KITCHEN KLUTZ

- Add garnishes that echo the flavor of the dessert—for example, nuts, fruits, or chocolate curls.
- For cupcakes, instead of using muffin pan liners, place flat-bottomed ice cream cones in the muffin pan and fill halfway with batter.
- Before frosting a layer cake, place wax paper strips on the outside of the plate or dish and place the cake on top. After frosting pull out the wax paper for a clean dish.
- Place a doily on top of a cake and sprinkle powdered sugar over the doily. Carefully remove the doily. Do not apply the sugar until the cake has cooled.
- Drizzle a chocolate mixture of a 1-ounce square of melted unsweetened chocolate and $1/2$ tsp. oil for an icicle pattern effect on cakes and desserts.
- For fruit pies, cut the shape of the fruit out of the dough and place these on top of the pie in place of the top crust.
- Take an orange, lemon, honeydew, or canteloupe and slice off the top. Remove the fruit and trim the bottom so the fruit will stand steady. Trim a zigzag pattern around the top or leave the rim straight. Fill the fruit cup with sherbet, ices, or fresh fruit covered with liqueur.
- Add colored sugar or grated coconut on top of cakes, cookies, pies, cupcakes, etc. To color grated coconut or sugar, place 1 tsp. of water and a few drops of food coloring in a jar. Add the coconut or sugar and shake the jar well.
- When making angel food cake from a mix, add 1 tsp. almond extract for better flavor.

room temperature for 1 to 2 hours. Another way to freeze a cream pie is to freeze the filling separately from the pie crust, then thaw the filling when ready to serve and pour into a baked pie crust. **Fruit pies** should be covered well with freezer paper or foil and frozen up to 2 to 3 months. When ready to serve, remove from the freezer, unwrap, and bake frozen at 425°F. for 45 to 60 minutes. **Meringue pies** must be frozen without the meringue topping. When ready to serve, place the meringue on the frozen pie and bake uncovered at 350°F. for 20 to 25 minutes. Let the pie sit at least 45 minutes before serving. **Frozen and ice cream pies** may be frozen for up to 1 month.

Cooked pies may be stored in the refrigerator in a container or covered with plastic wrap or foil but should be eaten as soon as possible. Cooked pie crust becomes soggy when pies are stored too long. Cream pies should be eaten within a day of baking. If you really need to freeze a cream pie, you may freeze it well wrapped without any whipped cream for 2 to 3 months. When ready to serve, remove from the freezer and bake frozen according to the recipe directions.

Tip: Store meringue pie with plastic wrap that has been rubbed with butter or vegetable oil to prevent the plastic from sticking to the meringue.

Cooked pies may also be frozen for up to 4 to 6 months. Pies need to be well wrapped with freezer foil or paper. *Cream and custard cooked pies should not be frozen.* To reheat a frozen pie, defrost the pie unwrapped and bake uncovered at 425°F. for 15 to 20 minutes.

USING CHOCOLATE IN DESSERTS

Chocolate is classified as one of the following: cocoa powder, milk chocolate, semisweet/bitter chocolate (also called dark chocolate), sweet chocolate, and unsweetened chocolate (also called cooking, baking, bitter, or pure chocolate). Store unused chocolate in an airtight container in a cool, dry place. Do not store chocolate in the refrigerator because it will get moist and ultimately moldy. Chop chocolate into even-size pieces before melting so it will melt evenly. You may also grind chocolate in a food processor before melting.

There are four ways to melt chocolate. One method is to heat 3 cups of water to boiling in the bottom of a double boiler or in a large saucepan. Place the chopped or ground chocolate in the top part of the double boiler or in a dry metal bowl. Place the boiler top or bowl over the boiling water and begin stirring the chocolate. When the chocolate is about 75% melted, remove it from the heat and continue to stir until completely melted. **Tip:** Place a large piece of wax paper in the top of the double boiler and place the chocolate on top of the wax paper. The chocolate will melt and come off easily when you pour it into your bowl.

Another way to melt chocolate is to place chopped or ground chocolate in a heatproof bowl and pour hot (not boiling) liquid that is called for in your recipe, over the chocolate. Let this mixture stand for 5 minutes and then stir the mixture until the chocolate is dissolved. A third way to melt chocolate is to chop it into *even* pieces and place in a microwave-safe bowl. Microwave uncovered on Medium power for 30 seconds. Remove the bowl and stir. Return the bowl to the microwave and continue to microwave on Medium power for 15-second intervals (stirring after each 15 seconds) until the chocolate is fully melted. The fourth and easiest way to melt chocolate is to wrap the chocolate in foil and bake at 300°F. for 10 minutes.

If a recipe calls for melting butter and chocolate, melt the butter first and then place the chocolate in the pan to keep the chocolate from sticking. Melt the chocolate slowly over low heat because it burns easily. The temperature should never rise above 110°F. Milk chocolate and sweet chocolate will melt between 86°F. and 96°F., and unsweetened and semisweet chocolates will melt at 96°F. When melting chocolate occasionally a gray film will form on the top. This is the cocoa butter rising to the top as the temperature changes from hot to cold. You may still use the chocolate; the flavor and taste are not affected. If melted chocolate becomes lumpy, stir in 1 Tbsp. solid vegetable shortening for every 3 ounces of chocolate. Stir until the chocolate is creamy. Do not use butter or oil! Use chocolate at room temperature.

HELPFUL CHART OF DESSERT TERMS FOR THE KITCHEN KLUTZ

Dessert Terms	Description
À la mode	Topped with ice cream
Au lait	Made with milk
Bavarian	Made with a gelatin-cream base
Bombe	Two or more mixtures that are frozen and packed into a mold
Bonbon	Dipped into fondant
Caramel	Burnt sugar syrup used
Charlotte	Made by lining a dish with ladyfingers, cake, or bread and then filling the dish with custard, fruit, or whipped cream
Cobbler	Deep-dish fruit pie with a pastry or crumb top
Custard	Baked mixture of milk, eggs, sugar, and flavorings, if desired; types include baked, boiled, and frozen
Eclair	Finger-shaped pastry filled with custard or whipped cream; often with icing on top
Fondant	Candy made from sugar syrup kneaded to creaminess
Ice	Frozen dessert of fruit juice, sugar, and water
Kisses	Very small dessert meringues
Macaroons	Tiny cakes made with sugar, almonds, and egg whites
Marzipan	Mixture of sugar and almond paste that is shaped into miniature fruits or other shapes
Meringue	A mixture of egg whites and sugar that is stiffly beaten and used as a topping
Mocha	A mix of coffee and chocolate flavors
Mousse	A dessert made with sugar, egg whites, cream, and flavorings that is light, airy, and smooth; chilled and served cold
Parfait	A mixture of any of the following: ice cream, custard, fruit, and sauce, which are layered in a tall stemmed glass and topped with whipped cream
Petit four	Tiny tea cake with frosting
Sherbet	Frozen mixture of fruit juice, sugar, milk and egg whites
Soufflé	A cream sauce containing egg whites, sugar, and flavorings; can be fruit, nuts, liqueurs, etc.; cold soufflés contain unflavored gelatin for consistency (see Eggs)
Torte	Baked pastry mixture of eggs, sugar, and nuts/bread crumbs that is filled with jam or fruit and covered with filling and/or frosting

MORE DESSERT TIPS FOR THE KITCHEN KLUTZ

- If you need to **mix by hand,** count 150 strokes per minute in place of electric beating time.
- When a recipe says **add flour and liquid alternately**, you always start with the dry ingredients and end with the dry ingredients (flour mixture)—example: flour, liquid, flour.
- To keep **raisins, nuts, or fruits** from sinking to the bottom of the batter, lightly dust them with flour from the recipe before adding them to the recipe.
- Use **unsalted butter** in recipes when baking.
- To measure **molasses or corn syrup,** lightly grease the measuring cup.
- **Eggs** are used in baking to help solidify the liquids. Always use size "large" eggs in recipes unless otherwise specified.
- Double the amount of **vanilla extract** for better taste.
- Unfilled **pastry puffs** can be crisped by baking them in a preheated oven at 325°F. for 5 minutes.
- Individual **meringue shells** can be dried in a 225°F. oven for 15 to 25 minutes. Fill them with ice cream or custard for a delicious dessert.
- To **toast nuts:** Spread nuts in a shallow pan and bake in a 350°F. oven for 6 to 14 minutes, or microwave on High for 4 to 8 minutes, stirring frequently.
- To **toast coconut:** Spread shredded coconut in a shallow pan and bake at 350°F. for 6 to 14 minutes, stirring often until golden-brown, or microwave at Medium-High heat for 5 to 10 minutes, stirring frequently.
- To **blanch almonds:** Place almonds in a pan and pour boiling water over them. Let the almonds stay covered with the boiling water for 1 minute, drain, run cold water over them, and rub the skins off.
- For **slivered nuts:** Blanch nuts and then while the nuts are warm, cut them into slivers using a sharp knife.
- To **stuff dates:** Remove the seed, place whatever you want in the dates, such as nuts, marshmallows, cream cheese, etc., then roll in granulated sugar. You may add 1 tsp. of cinnamon or other spices to each ½ cup sugar if you desire.
- To **cut dates:** always use scissors, dipping them in water first.
- To **frost grapes:** Dip them in slightly beaten egg whites and then in granulated sugar; place on a rack to "set." Then refrigerate the grapes until ready to use.
- To **cut marshmallows** easily: Use scissors that have been rubbed with butter.
- Use only **cane or beet sugar** for baking. Blended sugar will make cookies spread and candy sticky.

□ □ □ □ □ □

SNACKS

Snacks may be store-bought or homemade, fresh or dried fruit, raw vegetables, chips and dip, crackers and cheese, pretzels . . . the list is endless. Although you probably have favorites, this chapter has a selection of quick-and-easy snacks or appetizers you may fix for friends, family, or yourself.

Many may be prepared a day ahead and served as an appetizer while you finish cooking your meal. Others are great to have on hand in case someone drops by to visit. Keep the ingredients for your favorite snacks and appetizers on hand so they can be put together quickly.

QUICK-AND-EASY SNACKS TO MAKE

Grilled cheese sandwich: Place ¹/₂ to 1 Tbsp. butter in a skillet and melt on low. Place a slice of bread in the skillet and add a slice of cheese on top of the bread. Butter another piece of bread and place its unbuttered side on top of the cheese in the skillet. Cook over low heat a few minutes, then turn the sandwich over. Cook until both sides are light brown and cheese has melted. Cut into 4 squares for a snack.

Cheese toast: Preheat the oven to "Broil." Place a slice of bread on a cookie sheet and place it in the oven. Watch and remove when lightly browned. Turn bread over and place a slice of cheese on top. Place the bread back in the oven and broil until the cheese melts. Remove and serve.

Gorp: Mix together 1 or 2 cups of any of the following: plain M & Ms, peanuts, raisins, chocolate chips, butterscotch chips, shredded coconut, granola cereal, chinese noodles, sunflower seeds, salted mixed nuts, and raisins.

Bubbly Brie: Top Brie with preserves and nuts, such as apricot preserves and almonds. Bake at 350°F. until bubbly. Serve with crackers, apples, and grapes.

Colleen's in a Hurry: Top cream cheese with one of the following: pepper jelly, steak sauce, chutney, or a can of smoked oysters, or spread a thin layer of prepared horseradish on top and cover it with store-bought red chili or cocktail sauce. Serve with any type of crackers.

Fast Guacamole: Buy store-bought guacamole, add some lemon juice, 2 tsp. chopped onion, and a fresh *chopped* avocado for a homemade touch, and serve with tortilla chips. (To make homemade guacamole, mix together 3 peeled and chopped avocados, 1 small chopped tomato, 1 tsp. salt, 2 tsp. chopped onion, 2 tsp. lemon juice, 1 tsp. mayonnaise, and a dash of red pepper sauce.)

Fancy Popcorn: Add garlic salt and Parmesan cheese to melted butter and pour over popcorn or add small cubes of cheese after popping and mix together.

Cheesy Chips: Sprinkle plain potato chips with Parmesan cheese and lightly broil them in the oven. Watch chips closely since they can burn easily.

The Klutz's Favorite: Mix together 1/4 cup brown sugar, 1 Tbsp. brandy or Amaretto, and 1/4 cup almonds. Spread this on top of a wheel (14 oz.) of Brie cheese and bake at 325°F. until the topping is bubbly. Serve with crackers and fruit.

Yummy Cheese Spread: Mix 2 cups grated sharp Cheddar cheese, 3/4 cup mayonnaise, 1/16 tsp. (dash of) garlic powder, and 1/2 cup chopped onion together. Bake mixture at 350°F. until bubbly and serve with crackers, corn chips, or tortilla chips. You may also make this and serve it cold with strawberry preserves on top. Serve with wholewheat crackers.

The Klutz's Delight: Dip pretzel sticks in pepper jelly.

Veggies (Crûdités): Cut broccoli, carrots, celery, cucumbers, cauliflower, and green peppers into bite-size pieces or strips, sprinkle lightly with onion or garlic salt, and serve with a dip.

Artichoke Dip: Mix a 14-ounce can of artichoke hearts that have been drained and chopped with 1 cup mayonnaise, 1 cup grated Parmesan cheese, and 1/4 to 1/2 tsp. garlic powder. Place in a small casserole dish and bake at 350°F. until bubbly, about 15 minutes. Serve with crackers.

Cashew Chews: Melt 1 package chocolate chips (6 ounces) and 2 packages butterscotch chips (12 ounces) in the top of a double boiler. When they are melted, stir in 1 small can Chinese chow mein noodles and 1/2 cup cashew nuts. Drop by teaspoon onto wax paper and cool. Store them in an airtight container.

Surprise Dip: Mix together one 8-ounce package cream cheese and one jar marshmallow creme. Dip apples or fruit in it. You may use low-fat cream cheese and low-fat marshmallow creme to reduce fat content.

Heather's Stuffed Pickles: Take 2 large dill pickles, cut off each end, and scoop out the seedy pulp. Fill each pickle with your favorite cheese spread, and chill for 2 hours. Cut into slices and serve. Two pickles should yield about 24 slices.

Stuffed Mushrooms: Fill the cap part of large mushrooms with canned deviled ham. Place on a baking sheet and broil for 5 minutes. Serve hot with toothpicks.

Peanut Delight: Spread 1 to 2 cups of salted peanuts on a baking sheet, and bake at 350°F. for a few minutes. Remove and toss with 1 cup of raisins.

Sweet Peanuts: Place 2 cups raw shelled peanuts, 1 cup granulated sugar, and 1/2 cup water in a large skillet. Cook over medium heat, stirring constantly until the water evaporates completely. Spread evenly on a piece of aluminum foil and let cool before serving.

Easy Easy Dip: Mix together 1/2 pint store-bought French onion dip, 1 small can deviled ham, and 4 to 5 drops Worcestershire sauce. Serve with chips.

Olive Elation: Take large olives, stuffed with pimientos, and spread softened cream cheese around each. Then roll in chopped pecans and refrigerate until ready to eat. These may be made 2 days before serving.

Hot Clam Dip: Melt the following over low heat: an 8-ounce package cream cheese, an 8-ounce can minced clams (drained), and 1 Tbsp. Worcestershire sauce. Serve hot with potato or corn chips.

Beer Cheese: Mix the following ingredients together with an electric mixer: 1 lb. Cheddar cheese (shredded), 1 lb. Swiss cheese, 1 minced clove garlic, 1 Tbsp. dry mustard, 2 tsp. Worcestershire sauce, and 1 cup beer. Serve with crackers. Store in a jar in the refrigerator; this will keep for 2 to 3 weeks.

□ □ □ □ □ □

SEASONINGS

Herbs, spices, and sauces will make whatever you are cooking taste better, so become familiar with all of the seasonings. It's easy to get in the habit of only using a few of your favorites, but you will be pleasantly surprised when you try others. Remember to use seasonings sparingly. They should enhance the flavor of food rather than smother it. To taste a flavor, place one-half of a teaspoon or less in a cup of hot water, smell, and taste. Keep in mind the seasonings will actually taste milder in the food.

POPULAR HERBS AND SPICES

Allspice is a dried berry from the West Indies. It is a separate spice, in spite of its name, and it has a flavor that tastes like a combination of cinnamon, cloves, and nutmeg. It is a sweet yet sort of sharp spice. Allspice comes whole or ground. Whole allspice is used in fish dishes, pickling, and soups. Ground is used in beef, breads, cakes, carrots, cookies, eggs, ham, lamb, and puddings.

Angelica is an herb that is native to Europe. The candied green stalks are used in decorating pastries and the roots are sometimes used in liqueurs. The leaves have a musky smell and may be used in vegetables and salads.

Anise is an herb belonging to the parsley family. It has a licorice-like flavor and greenish-brown seeds. Whole anise is good in cheese dishes, coffee cakes, shellfish, sweetbreads. Ground anise is good in cakes, cookies, fruit recipes, poultry, veal.

Basil is an herb from western Europe belonging to the mint family. It has a spicy, robust, and distinct flavor and is very aromatic. It sometimes is referred to as "sweet basil" and is available either dried or fresh. Basil is used in many Italian dishes. Use basil in bean dishes, cheese dishes, pastas, eggplant, eggs, lamb, meats, spaghetti, peas, tomato dishes.

Bay leaf is the leaf from the laurel tree originating from the eastern Mediterranean, usually Turkey. It is very strong in flavor with a woodsy odor. Bay leaves from California are very strong. Bay leaf may be used while cooking the entire recipe and then removed at the end. It is available as a whole leaf or crushed. If you are using bay leaves to season soups or sauces, you will only need 1/4 to 1/2 a bay leaf, which should be removed at the end of cooking unless you use the crushed. Use bay leaves in beef, bouillon, carrots, chicken, liver, soups, stews, and veal.

Beau monde seasoning is a blend of several basic seasonings such as salt, onion, and celery seed. Use as an all-purpose seasoning or at the table in cheese dishes, meats, and seafood.

Bee balm has a fresh lemony flavor. It can be used to garnish food such as soups, etc. It is easy to grow because it does well in the sun or shade.

Bouquet garni is a combination of fresh or dried herbs, usually consisting of bay leaf, thyme, and parsley, or any herb you like. The herbs may be purchased fresh and dried in a jar or you may make your own by tying them together with a string or in cheesecloth and placing the bouquet in your pot only during cooking. Remove when through cooking. Bouquet garni is great in sauces, soups, spaghetti, stews, and vegetables.

- *Basic bouquet garni:* bay leaf, parsley, thyme
- *Bouquet garni for beef:* bay leaf, basil, clove, parsley, chives
- *Bouquet garni for pork or lamb:* celery, parsley, rosemary, dill, thyme
- *Bouquet garni for veal:* lemon rind, parsley, thyme

Caraway seeds are spicy dark brown seeds from Holland that have a tangy taste. Caraway seeds are used in rye bread. They may be purchased whole or crushed; crushed are best added to salads and vegetable dishes. Use in bread, cabbage, cakes, cheese dishes, beans, cookies, marinades, sauerkraut, stews, soups, and turnips.

Cayenne pepper is made from the dried pods and seeds of chilis or red peppers. It is pungent and should be used sparingly. Use in chicken, chili, eggs, meat, sauces, sausages, and seafood.

Cardamom seeds are the blackish-brown seeds from small green pods that have an exotic flavor similar to ginger and lemon. Next to saffron they are the second most expensive spice and are used in Scandinavian and Spanish cooking. May be used whole in barbecue sauces, breads, ham, pickling, and soups; use ground in cakes, cookies, and soups.

Celery leaves are the fresh leaves on a celery stalk. They are very good chopped and used in soups, stews, and salads. If using dried celery leaves, use sparingly since they are strong.

Celery seed is a small seedlike fruit that is from a certain type of celery. It has a strong celery flavor. It is good used in cheese dishes, eggs, fish, pot roasts, potato and other vegetable salads, seafood, stews, and vegetables.

Chervil is an herb that has a delicate, sort of peppery flavor. It is a relative of parsley, which it also resembles. Use with carrots, chicken, eggs, fish, peas, salad dressing, and tomato dishes.

Chili powder is a blend of dried chilis and spices including cayenne pepper. It is used in many Spanish and Mexican dishes. Use in bean dishes, chili, cocktail sauce, egg dishes, pot roasts, and stews.

Chives are an herb in the onion family. It is a wonderful all-purpose herb with a delicate onion flavor. Chives should be used fresh whenever possible and should be green in color. Chop and use in cheese dishes, chicken, eggs, fish, meat, salads, sauces, soups, vegetables, sour cream, or cream cheese.

Cinnamon comes from the sweet, hot, spicy bark of the laurel tree. It is used ground or in long sticks. Use ground in beverages, cakes, cookies, fruit dishes, ice cream, lamb, pork, ham, sweet potatoes, and french toast. Use cinnamon sticks in drinks such as apple cider or mulled wine.

Cloves are the unopened dried flower buds, nail-shaped, from the clove tree, which originated in Zanzibar. May be used ground or whole. Use ground in bread, cookies, mincemeat, pickles, preserves, soups, stews, sweet potatoes. To use whole, press them in a ham before baking or an orange and hang for a nice odor. You may also use whole in pickling, pork, and hot drinks.

Cilantro, also called Chinese parsley, is made from the leaves of the coriander plant. It has a perfumed sweet taste. It is commonly used in Chinese, Indian, and Mexican dishes.

Coriander, like cilantro, is from the coriander plant but has a different taste and use despite their similar origin. Whole coriander seeds are used in pickling and vegetables. Ground coriander seeds are used in baked goods such as gingerbread, curries, soups, and stews.

Cream of tartar is the residue left behind when squeezing grapes for wine or grape juice. It is used in beating egg whites, making frostings, and in baking soda.

Cumin is a member of the parsley family and has a nutty flavor. It is used in many Mexican and Oriental dishes as well as Indian chutneys. Use sparingly. Whole or ground can be used in cabbage, cheese dishes, meats, soups, sausages, and vegetables.

Curry powder is a blend of several spices with a very distinct flavor and may range from mild to hot. It is yellow in color and is one of the oldest seasonings. It is used often in Indian and Middle Eastern dishes. Remember to always purchase good-quality curry; the quality will affect the taste. Most curry powder contains allspice, cardamom seed, cayenne pepper, cinnamon, coriander seeds, cumin, ginger, mustard seed, nutmeg, black and red pepper, saffron, and turmeric. Use in cheese dishes, chicken, eggs, fish, lamb, meats, and vegetables.

Dill originated in India but is now grown in most herb gardens since it is easy to grow. It has a tart lemon flavor that is good with fish and vegetables. Dill comes in fresh, dried (called dillweed), or in small seeds. Dill is used in many Scandinavian and Russian dishes. Chop fresh dill and use in fish, salads, with cucumbers and vegetables. Use dried dill like fresh but use less of it. Use dill seed in pickling, eggs, and lamb.

Duxelles are mushrooms used for seasoning that have been minced and sautéed in butter until all of the liquid is gone. Duxelles may be refrigerated or frozen as long as they are placed in an airtight container. Use in stuffings and vegetable dishes.

Fennel comes in seeds and leaves and has a licorice-like flavor. Fennel is used in Italian and Swedish dishes. Use whole seeds in cheese dishes, eggs, apple pie, and cakes. Use the leaves and bulb in fish, salads, soup, and vegetables.

Filé Powder comes from Louisiana and is made from dried sassafras leaves. It has a root-beerish, woodsy flavor and is added to Créole dishes and gumbos after cooking and prior to serving because it not only flavors but also helps thicken the mixture.

Fines herbes is a combination of three to five herbs that are chopped or minced and added at the end of cooking. The basic ingredients are equal amounts of chives, parsley or chervil or chives, parsley, tarragon or thyme. The combination may also include basil or savory. Use fines herbes in butter, chicken, eggs, sauces, soups, stews, and steaks.

Garlic is a hardy plant that has a bulb with a strong onion-like smell. The bulb contains many individual pieces which are called cloves. Be sure to note if a recipe calls for a "bulb" or a "clove." When a clove has not been peeled, it has a mild flavor. When chopped or minced, it has a medium-garlic flavor. A mashed clove has the strongest flavor. Garlic comes fresh, dried in powder, or as a salt. You may also buy fresh garlic in a jar that is minced or chopped. Garlic is used often in Italian, Mediterranean, and French food. If you like garlic, you may use it in bread, fish, chicken, beef, lamb, salad dressings, eggs, soups, stews, pastas, vegetables, or anything else you like.

Ginger is the irregularly shaped root of an Asian herb that is grown in many tropical climates. It has a sharp, sweet, pungent flavor and is used often in Chinese cooking. The root will keep in the refrigerator for 7 days and also freezes well. If you keep it in the freezer, cut off the amount you need and place the root back in the freezer. Ginger may be purchased crystallized, in pieces, or ground. Ginger may also be bought preserved and dried. Use crystallized ginger in desserts and ground ginger in canned fruit, chicken, gingerbread, pumpkin pie or bread, pot roast, and steak. Use pieces of fresh ginger in chutneys, pickling, or stewed dried fruits.

Horseradish is a long root that is from a coarse herb plant. It has a sharp, pepper-like flavor and may be purchased fresh or in a jar as a condiment. If you buy horseradish in a jar, you will find it in the refrigerated section of the grocery store. Both the white or red types are good. If you buy fresh horseradish, grate it and use it to flavor dips, sauces, and salad dressings. You may also place grated horseradish in a jar, add a dash of salt, and cover with vinegar. Refrigerate the jar and you will have your own horseradish to use in cooking.

Juniper berries are the fruit of a wild shrub from Europe. They have a wonderful and unusual flavor (they are used in making Gin). Use in fish, game, marinades, and sauces.

Mace is a spice made from the middle layer of the nutmeg shell which protects the nutmeg kernel. It is similar to nutmeg in taste but stronger and may be ground fresh or dried. Use in cakes, gingerbreads, sauces, and sausage.

Marjoram is a pungent, spicy herb from France and Chile that is a member of the mint family. It is available in powdered, crushed, whole dried leaves or fresh. Use in cheese dishes, eggs, chicken, fish, lamb, meat, salad dressings, stews, veal, and vegetables.

Mint is a delicious, cool, clean, fresh-flavored herb similar to spearmint or peppermint. It is easy to grow in your backyard. There are over 30 types of mint, including apple mint, ginger mint, and spearmint. Their fresh leaves add a fresh flavor to beverages, fish, fruits, jellies, lamb, veal, sauces, and vegetables.

Monosodium Glutamate (also known as MSG) is a white crystalline seasoning used to intensify flavors in food. It is a concentrated form of sodium and should not be used if you are watching the sodium content in food.

Mustard is a spice that comes from crushing and grinding mustard seeds. It is available as dry mustard and prepared mustard. Mustard has a sharp and spicy flavor and ranges from mild to extra strong. (Powdered mustard is very strong.) Use ground dry mustard in beef, biscuits, cheese dishes, chicken, dips, ham, pickles, pork, salad dressing, veal and vegetables. Prepared mustard is often used on sandwiches, in sauces, or meatloaf.

Nutmeg is an all-purpose spice that is the dried seed or nut from the nutmeg tree and has a mellow, spicy flavor. It is available whole or ground. (You may grate whole nutmeg using the small part of your grater or a nutmeg grater.) Use nutmeg in breads, cabbage, cakes, cauliflower, custard, eggnog, fruit recipes, greens, puddings, sauces, and soups.

Oregano (Wild Marjoram) is a strong flavored herb originally from Italy and Mexico. Oregano's flavor is between sage and marjoram. The herb is available fresh or dried but is also easy to grow. Oregano is used in Italian, Mexican, and Spanish dishes. Use dried oregano with caution because it is stronger than fresh. Use oregano in beef, cheese dishes, hamburgers, chili, spaghetti, sauces, lamb, meatloaf, onions, omelets, potatoes, pork, shrimp, and veal.

Paprika, a member of the pepper family, comes from the dried pods of large, sweet red peppers. Hungarian paprika is excellent. Paprika is available mild to hot. Use it to add color, to garnish, or for flavor.

Parsley is an all-purpose fine herb that is sweet yet spicy. Parsley is available fresh or dried. Since it is easy to grow, as well as available in the produce section of the grocery store, use fresh parsley whenever possible. Curly-leaf parsley has a milder flavor than the flat plain leaf parsley. Parsley is great to use as a garnish as well as in chicken, eggs, fish, beef, salads, soups, pasta, and stews.

Pepper is the world's most popular spice and originates from an Indonesian plant. The plant is a climbing shrub that produces a green berry the size of a green pea. The berry is picked as it is beginning to turn red, then dried until it turns black. This is the **black pepper** that you eat and use. It comes whole or ground. Be sure to crush slightly whole peppercorns when using them in a recipe. Other types of pepper include: **White pepper** is made from the ripened berries of the same shrub. The hulls are removed and the berries are ground. White pepper is a milder pepper than black pepper. It's great to use when you don't want pepper to show in your food. The subtle flavor is nice in many dishes. **Green peppercorns** are made from the under-ripened berries of the same shrub. They are not as hot as black pepper. **Cayenne pepper** is a hot red pepper from the fruit or pods of a type of capsicum plant (see "Cayenne pepper" previously). It is dried and ground and is very hot-tasting. (Paprika is made from another type of shrub in the capsicum family that is milder.) **Red pepper flakes** are from dried red peppers and are hot. They should be used sparingly. **Small hot peppers** are dried and may be either green or red. Use gloves when handling them because they can burn your skin. Do not place your fingers near your eyes. When chopping, remove the seeds and remember to use them sparingly because they are hot-tasting. **Hot red pepper sauces** are a mixture of hot red peppers, salt, seasonings and vinegar. They are great used in soups, stews, vegetables, or eggs. The best one is from Louisiana.

Pickling spice is a mixture of whole spices purchased in a jar or can at the grocery store to be used in making pickles. It usually contains some of the following spices: allspice, bay leaves, cinnamon, cloves, coriander, dill seed, ginger, mustard seed, or pepper.

Pimientos are sweet red peppers that have been preserved in oil. They are good served with cheese dishes, eggs, or vegetables or used as a garnish.

Poppy seeds are from Holland and come from a plant in the poppy family that produces tiny blue-black seeds that have a nutty flavor. Use in bread, cookies, cakes, noodles, pork, and salad dressings.

Poultry seasoning is a blend of sage, black pepper, onion, celery seed, thyme, and marjoram used for flavoring any type of poultry—chicken, turkey, duck, dove, etc.

Rosemary is a strong lemon-type flavored herb whose leaves resemble pine needles. Rosemary is used in many French dishes and comes dried or fresh. Use it in beef, chicken, deviled eggs, fish, fruit, potatoes, lamb, and veal.

Rosewater is used in Middle Eastern dishes and is produced from roses distilled with water.

Saffron comes from the stamen of the autumn crocus blossom and is pleasantly bitter in flavor. It is the world's most expensive spice because it takes about 70,000 hand-picked autumn crocus blossoms to produce 1 pound of saffron threads. Saffron is a beautiful golden color and is used in French, Italian, and Spanish dishes. It is available in powder form and thread form and should be used sparingly. **Remember:** A little goes a long way! Also, always buy a good brand. Use saffron in breads, egg dishes, rice, and meats.

Sage is a very pungent herb that is available in over 500 varieties. It is easily grown and comes as dried leaves, ground, or fresh. Sage is widely used in poultry stuffings. Use also in sharp cheese spreads, fish, game, poultry dishes, stuffings, soups, and sauces.

Salt is a mineral that helps bring out the flavor of food. Taste food before adding salt because many foods, like celery, already contain salt naturally. Salt comes uniodized or iodized (has iodine).

Seasoned salt is a must in your kitchen. It is a combination of salt, sugar, and spices such as paprika. Seasoned salt also usually contains onion and garlic. It may be used in place of salt in a recipe but be careful because it has its own distinct flavor. To make seasoned salt, combine 1 cup salt, 1 tsp. garlic powder, 1 tsp. chili powder, 1 tsp. onion powder, 1 tsp. red pepper, $1/2$ tsp. sugar (optional), and $1 1/2$ tsp. black pepper.

Savory is an herb belonging to the mint family that comes from France and Spain. There are two varieties of savory—summer and winter. Summer savory is a delicate, all-purpose herb, while winter savory is a strong-flavored herb. Both are available dried or fresh and are easy to grow in an herb garden. Use in bean salads, egg dishes, fish, meats, poultry, shellfish, stuffings, and vegetables.

Scallions (also called spring onions) are young green onions that are picked before they develop a bulb. They have a mild onion taste and are wonderful as a garnish in soups and salads.

Sesame (benne) is an herb that produces a nutty-tasting seed (**sesame seed**) from the flowers. The sesame seeds produce an oil (**sesame oil**) that is also used in cooking, especially Chinese dishes. Use sesame seeds in breads, cookies, rolls, salads, and soups.

Shallots are similar to onions but the bulbs grow in clusters, like garlic. The taste of shallots is stronger than an onion but not as biting. Use in salads, sauces, soups, and meats.

Sorrel is a plant belonging to the buckwheat family with leaves shaped like an arrow. Sorrel has a sourlike flavor. Cut the leaves in strips and use them in salads, sauces, and soups.

Soy sauce is made from soy beans and also contains salt, sugar, wheat, and yeast. It is used in Oriental cooking as well as in many marinade recipes.

Tarragon is an herb that is easily grown in an herb garden. It has a delicate and slightly licorice-lemon flavor. It is used to flavor vinegar and is available dried or fresh. Use sparingly in dressings, fish, marinades, poultry, salads, salad dressings, sauces, soups, and veal.

Thyme is a strong fragrant herb with a minty type flavor that is produced from an oil in the leaves. Thyme is easily grown and is used dry, fresh, or ground. Use sparingly in breads, cheese dishes, chowder, fish, pork, salad dressings, stews, stuffings, and veal.

Turmeric is the root of a plant from Southern Asia and is available ground or fresh. Turmeric has a rich, sweet, sort of spicy flavor and is an ingredient in curry powder. It provides a yellow color to foods and while it may be used in place of saffron, the flavor is different. Use in beef, condiments, eggs, lamb, pickles, and sauces.

Worcestershire sauce is a strong, spicy sauce first made in Worcestershire, England. It is great on meats and in sauces. Use sparingly.

Vanilla is a sweet delicious flavor that comes from the pods of an orchid native to Central America and is used to flavor. **Vanilla extract** is a liquid extracted from the pods with alcohol and is widely used in baking cookies, cakes, pies, egg custards, ice cream, fruit dishes, and many desserts.

STORING HERBS AND SPICES

Dried herb and spices usually only have a shelf life of 6 months, so purchase them in small quantities. Old herbs and spices can ruin your recipes, so mark the purchase date on the container and be sure to check them frequently for freshness! Dried herbs and spices keep freshest if stored in glass containers. Store herbs and spices away from heat (below 80°F.), moisture, and light. Make sure lids are tightly closed. If spices have lost their aroma, discard them and purchase new. Refrigerate paprika, cayenne pepper, and chili powder to maintain freshness longer.

Fresh herbs should be wrapped in damp paper towels and stored in the refrigerator for up to 5 days. The ambitious kitchen klutz may want to dry fresh herbs—it's not that difficult.

To dry fresh herbs for Leaves: Pick them in the morning, making sure no dew is on the plant. Choose plants that are beginning to bloom and pick off the nicest stalks, free of yellow or decaying leaves. Rinse and spread them on a tray that is covered with cheesecloth or paper. Place the tray in a warm, dry, sun-filled spot (an attic with a window can be a great place). Turn herbs over daily. This drying process should take 3 to 4 days. Another way to dry herbs is to tie the stems in bunches and hang them upside down in a warm room on a clothes line. Make sure you place newspapers underneath to catch any leaves or seeds. After drying, crush only the leaves and place them in a jar with a secure lid.

To *dry fresh herbs for seeds*: Let the herbs flower and then cut. Dry the same way for drying leaves, making sure there is no moisture. Then rub the flower heads between your hands and the seeds will fall out. Place seeds in an airtight jar.

To *freeze fresh herbs*: Fresh herbs such as basil, chives, fennel, marjoram, sage, tarragon, and thyme are good for freezing. When cutting, make sure you have a nice-size stem. Wash in cold water and place on paper towels to dry. Tie stems together with string or thread and dip herbs in a pot of boiling water for 1 minute. Then dip herbs in a pot of ice water for 2 minutes. Rinse with cold water and drain. Place in freezer bags and label. Thaw herbs when ready to use. Remember not to refreeze herbs that have been thawed.

Seasoning a Cast-Iron Skillet

When you purchase a new cast-iron skillet, you will need to "season" it so that food will cook in it without sticking. First, wash the skillet with soap and water. Rinse and dry it well. Then rub vegetable oil all over the skillet. Place the skillet in a preheated 250°F. oven for 3 hours. Remove the skillet, wipe out any grease with a paper towel, and allow to cool. The skillet is now ready to use.

After using your skillet, rinse it out with water and dry thoroughly. If you absolutely must, you may use a mild soap. However, never use a scouring pad on your skillet, and never place your skillet in a dishwasher. If you have to scrub your skillet, you will need to reseason it.

HERB AND SPICE TIPS FOR THE KITCHEN KLUTZ

- Buy good-quality spices and herbs.
- To determine if you like a certain spice or herb, take 1/2 cup hot water and 1/4 tsp. ground or 1/2 tsp. flaked herbs or spices and let it sit for 1 hour. Then taste. Remember that in food, the herb or spice will taste milder.
- Try grinding whole spices such as nutmeg or pepper just before using for the freshest flavor.
- Always measure spices carefully before adding them to a recipe.
- Do not double or triple the measurements for herbs and spices when doubling or tripling the recipe. When doubling, use 1 1/2 times the amount of the recipe. When tripling, use 2 times the amount in the recipe.
- When adding dried herbs to a recipe, crumble them for more potency.
- Use herbs and spices to enhance, not disguise, the flavor of food.
- Cooking herbs and spices too long will cause bitterness and loss of flavor. Thus, do not add herbs and spices until the last 15 minutes of cooking with the following exceptions. Bay leaves should be used throughout and removed at the end. Some recipes call for adding herbs and spices early. Salad dressings and marinades may require more time to absorb the flavoring.
- If substituting dried herbs for fresh herbs in a recipe, only use 1/3 the amount of fresh herbs. *Dried herbs are stronger than fresh herbs.*
- It's better to use too little than too much because herbs and spices can overwhelm food.
- If you overseason, you may do the following:

  1. If too sweet—add 1/2 to 1 tsp. lemon juice or wine vinegar.
  2. If too salty—add a quartered or whole, peeled raw potato and simmer for 15 minutes and then remove the potato. If still too salty, add 1/4 to 2 tsp. brown sugar.
  3. Use a strainer and pour mixture through the strainer to separate out the herbs and spices.

- Remember to taste as you season!

SAUCES

Sauces are the extra touch to any meal—the icing on the cake. They not only contribute moisture, color, and taste but visually and deliciously enhance the dish to which they are added. There are countless variations of the basic sauces: tomato, pepper, béchamel, cranberry, hollandaise, béarnaise, and gravy.

In this chapter you will find basic sauces that are quick and easy to make. There are also some that take longer to prepare but are well worth the extra effort. Sauces may be used with meat, vegetables, salads, pasta, and desserts. They are vital to being a good cook, so try them!

Remember that most sauces contain ingredients that burn easily. To prevent burning, always cook sauce over low heat and stir constantly.

To add a smooth texture to any sauce, whisk in 1 to 2 Tbsp. butter or whipping cream right before serving. If your gravy or sauce is too thin, make a smooth paste of water and flour or cornstarch using the following proportions:

> 1 Tbsp. flour + 1 cup liquid (thin paste)
> 2 Tbsp. flour + 1 cup liquid (medium paste)
> 3 Tbsp. flour + 1 cup liquid (thick paste)

Use the thin paste if your sauce is somewhat thin, the medium paste if your sauce is thin, and the thick paste if your sauce is very thin. Make sure the liquid is very hot when you add the flour or it will be lumpy in your sauce. Stir this paste into your gravy or sauce and bring it to a boil, stirring constantly. When it becomes thick, remove it from the heat and serve.

SOME BASIC SAUCES

Cream Sauce

Every cook should know how to make a basic cream sauce. This recipe will make 1 cup. Here are the ingredients.

Thin Cream Sauce	Medium Cream Sauce	Thick Cream Sauce
1 Tbsp. butter	2 Tbsp. butter	4 Tbsp. butter
1 Tbsp. flour	2 Tbsp. flour	4 Tbsp. flour
1/4 tsp. salt	1/4 tsp. salt	1/4 tsp. salt
1 cup milk	1 cup milk	1 cup milk

In a heavy saucepan or on the top of a double boiler, melt the butter. Slowly blend in the flour and salt and cook over low heat until it's bubbly and smooth. Remove from the heat. Slowly stir in the milk. Place the pan back on the burner over low heat and cook, stirring constantly until mixture comes to a boil. Boil for 1 minute. For a richer sauce, use half milk and half cream or half-and-half. You may also add a dash of white pepper if you wish.

A thin sauce is delicious over vegetables or in soup. The medium sauce is great over vegetables or meat or scalloped dishes. Thick sauce is nice with soufflés or croquettes. To the cream sauce you may add one of the following:

- 1/4 tsp. dry mustard and 1/2 cup of diced sharp Cheddar cheese (serve over vegetables)
- 2 chopped hard-cooked eggs, 1 tsp. chopped chives or onion (serve with fish)
- a dash of nutmeg and 1/2 tsp. dried dill (serve on meat or fish)
- 2 tsp. chopped onions and 1 cup mushroom slices or pieces that have been sautéed in butter (serve on vegetables or meat)
- 1 tsp. curry powder
- toasted almonds

Velouté or Velvet Sauce

A velouté sauce is a French white sauce used as a base for many other sauces such as béchamel. It may be served with croquettes and fish. A basic velouté sauce can be made as follows:

Melt 2 Tbsp. butter in a heavy saucepan or double boiler over low heat. Slowly blend in 2 Tbsp. flour and cook until smooth and bubbly. Remove pan from heat. Slowly stir in 1 cup of chicken broth. Place the pan on the stove and bring sauce to a boil. Then boil on low heat for 1 minute and add 1/8 tsp. salt and 1/8 tsp. white pepper. This will make 1 cup.

You may add to this sauce just as you would add to a basic cream sauce. To make **béchamel sauce**, add 1/2 cup cream, 1/2 tsp. salt, 1/8 tsp. pepper, 1/4 tsp. paprika, and 1/4 tsp. parsley.

Brown Sauce

Melt 2 Tbsp. butter in a heavy saucepan or double boiler over low heat. Add 1 Tbsp. minced onion and 1/2 bay leaf. Cook until the butter is brown, stirring constantly. Slowly stir in 2 Tbsp. flour and cook until bubbly, still stirring constantly. After the flour is added, the mixture should be a deep brown color. Remove from the heat. Slowly stir in 1 cup beef bouillon or stock and place back over the heat. Cook until thick and smooth. Remove the bay leaf when done. Add salt and pepper to taste, or add sautéed mushrooms, and serve. This will make 1 cup of sauce.

Hollandaise Sauce

In a small, heavy saucepan, place ½ stick (4 Tbsp.) butter, 1 Tbsp. fresh lemon juice, and 2 slightly beaten egg yolks. Cook over very low heat, stirring constantly until the butter is completely melted. Add another ½ stick butter and continue to stir constantly over low heat until the butter melts and the sauce thickens. Remove from the heat and serve either hot or cold on vegetables or fish. This will make approximately ¾ cup.

If you wish, you may add a dash of cayenne pepper. Other ingredients you may add after cooking the sauce are 2 Tbsp. chopped cucumber or 2 Tbsp. orange juice.

Remember the key to making hollandaise sauce is to cook it on very low heat and stir it constantly. If your sauce curdles or separates, add 1 Tbsp. cream to the sauce and beat. Store leftover sauce in the refrigerator. To reheat, place sauce in a heavy saucepan on very low heat and stir constantly. To make **béarnaise sauce**, add the following to Hollandaise sauce: 1 Tbsp. minced parsley, 2 tsp. tarragon, 2 tsp. tarragon vinegar, and 1 Tbsp. chopped chives.

Gravy

Mix 2 Tbsp. flour and 2 Tbsp. fat (oil, bacon grease, butter, or pan drippings) in a heavy saucepan or iron skillet. Turn the burner on low and stir constantly until mixture is bubbly and medium brown in color. Take the skillet off the burner and slowly stir in 1 cup hot liquid (meat stock or bouillon). Place the skillet back on the burner over low heat and bring the mixture to a boil, stirring constantly. Then boil for 1 minute, still stirring constantly. Once cooked, remove the pan from the burner. This mixture is called a **roux** and is used as the basis for gravy, gumbo, and soups.

For a thick gravy, use 3 Tbsp. fat and 3 Tbsp. flour to 1 cup hot liquid. For a thin gravy, use 1 Tbsp. fat and 1 Tbsp. flour to 1 cup hot liquid. You may add mushrooms and a dash of Worcestershire sauce if you like. You may use milk for half the liquid to make chicken gravy. For stock, you may use the liquid you cook the meat in, canned stock, or a bouillon cube dissolved in 1 cup of water.

For a quick gravy, add 1 cup broth, cream, or wine to the liquid remaining in the pan after you cook fat from meat and then stir over low heat.

Cajun Roux

A cajun roux is a blend of flour and fat cooked in a heavy pot or iron skillet over slow heat until the mixture becomes brown; it is used in gumbo, stews, and gravies. Always use a heavy pot and add only hot water to a roux or it will curdle. To make a cajun roux, mix 2 Tbsp. flour and 2 Tbsp. fat (from chicken, roast, turkey or butter or oil) in a heavy pot. Turn the heat on low and begin stirring constantly to make sure the flour and fat do not stick to the pot. A roux must brown slowly. After it turns a dark brown, turn off the heat but continue stirring. Slowly add 1 cup hot water to stop the cooking and prevent the roux from burning. If you wish, you may add 1 cup chopped onion in place of, or in addition to, the water. The roux is ready to be added to whatever you are cooking, such as gumbo or stew.

Tartar Sauce

Tartar sauce is easy to make. Mix together the following ingredients: 1 cup mayonnaise + 2 Tbsp. chopped sweet pickles + 1 or 2 Tbsp. chopped onion + 1 Tbsp. chopped parsley. If you wish, you may also add chopped green olives or pimientos.

Low-Fat Sauce

Mix together a can of light evaporated milk, 1 package dried onion soup mix, and 1 Tbsp. cornstarch. Cook over low heat until the mixture begins to thicken. Then add any of the following: chopped onion, minced garlic, and herbs. Mix well. Remove from the heat and add 1 cup plain yogurt or 1 cup nonfat sour cream. This sauce can be used for vegetables, with meat, or poured over pasta.

QUICK SAUCES FOR . . .

Beef

- Whip 1/2 cup whipping cream and mix with 2 or 3 Tbsp. horseradish and 2 Tbsp. lemon juice and a dash of salt.
- Melt 1/2 cup butter in a saucepan over low heat. Add 1 Tbsp. dry mustard, 1 Tbsp. Worcestershire sauce, and 4 Tbsp. lemon juice. Stir over low heat until thoroughly blended.

Chicken

- Melt 1 cup currant jelly with 1 cup orange juice and 1 Tbsp. regular prepared mustard.
- Heat 6 ounces of sour cream, 1/3 cup of sherry, 1 can of cream of mushroom soup, 1 cup of chicken broth.

Desserts

- Heat 1 cup of currant jelly in a heavy saucepan over low heat and add 1 cup of drained Bing cherries or raspberries (frozen, thawed, and drained) or any fresh berries. Heat and serve.
- Heat fruit preserves (such as strawberry) in a heavy saucepan over low heat.
- Heat honey and add toasted nuts.

Fish

- *See* "Tartar Sauce" above.
- Use a mix of 1 cup mayonnaise and 2 Tbsp. dried dill.
- Clarified butter, melted butter, parsley, lemon juice, and toasted almonds (or any nut) all may be poured over fish.

Lamb

- Use pepper jelly.
- Melt 1 cup currant jelly with 2 chopped mint leaves and 2 Tbsp. orange juice.
- Melt 1 cup currant jelly with 1 cup orange juice and 1 Tbsp. regular prepared mustard.
- Melt 1/2 cup currant jelly then add 1/2 cup ketchup and 1/2 cup sherry

Pork

- Melt 1 cup apple or currant jelly, then add 1 Tbsp. soy sauce and 2 Tbsp. sherry. Cook, stirring constantly, for several minutes over medium heat.
- Melt 2 Tbsp. butter, then add 2 Tbsp. flour and mix. Remove this from the heat and slowly add 2 cups apple juice or apple cider and 1/2 cup raisins. Place mixture back on the burner and cook over low heat. Bring to a boil and cook for about 1 minute, or until mixture thickens. Remove from the heat and serve.

Vegetables

- Whip 1 pint whipping cream, then add 1 cup of mayonnaise and mix well.
- Mix cream cheese with a little milk and heat in a saucepan over low heat (use flavored cream cheese, if you like).
- Combine sour cream, milk, mayonnaise, fresh lemon juice, and white pepper and pour over vegetables.
- Melt processed cheese with a little milk for an easy cheese sauce.

SAUCE TIPS FOR THE KITCHEN KLUTZ

- Sauces and gravies are best served right after you make them.
- Stir sauces and gravies well while cooking and/or adding ingredients.
- To prevent overseasoning, add salt and pepper when the sauce is almost ready.
- If you substitute cornstarch or arrowroot for flour in a recipe for a sauce or gravy, only use half of the amount of the flour called for in the recipe.
- Use a wire whisk or wooden spoon when stirring.
- Any sauce or gravy containing cornstarch or arrowroot will become thin if you overcook them.

- Mix 1 cup sour cream, $1/2$ cup mayonnaise, 2 tsp. lemon juice, and 2 tsp. horseradish.
- Melt 2 Tbsp. butter, the juice of 1 fresh lemon, and any of the following: 1 tsp. of either celery or caraway seeds, $1/2$ tsp. garlic salt, $1/4$ tsp. rosemary or marjoram.
- Melt in a saucepan over low heat until thoroughly blended: $1/2$ cup mayonnaise, $1/2$ tsp. grated onion, 1 tsp. mustard, and $1/2$ cup grated cheese.

EASY TIME-SAVING COOKING METHODS

With a busy and hectic schedule, grilling and microwaving are both easy and time-saving ways of cooking. Microwaving actually cooks food faster, and grilling takes less time for clean up after you have eaten. In this chapter, you will find instructions and tips for grilling as well as useful information for microwaving successfully.

GRILLING

Grilling is lots of fun when having friends for dinner because it enables you to cook and visit at the same time. You should keep a bowl of "nibbles" nearby because grilling creates such a tantalizing aroma, you will become famished before the meal is even prepared. The taste of meat and vegetables that have been grilled is unique and can be enjoyed by all. The fat automatically drains through the grills and the smoke rises, giving a wonderful flavor to the food being grilled, and a low-fat alternative to frying or sautéing.

Since grilling is a method of cooking food by direct heat, any meat or vegetable that can be broiled can be grilled. Grills may be uncovered, covered, or portable and may be operated with electricity, gas, or charcoal. If using an electric or gas grill, read the directions for operating the grill in your owner's manual. The following is information for using a charcoal grill.

PREPARING A CHARCOAL GRILL

First you need to plan what to use as fuel for the fire. You may use either briquettes or charcoal. **Briquettes**—wood scraps that have been burned and then the ashes have been mixed with certain substances to increase their burning life—do not get as hot as **charcoal**—wood chunks that are carbonized slowly to which no chemicals are added. Charcoal is available in many "flavors," such as mesquite, hickory, apple, and elder. Mesquite flavoring is great for beef, pork, lamb, poultry, and shellfish. Hickory tastes great with pork, while apple and elder are great with pork or chicken. Arrange the charcoal pieces in a pyramid-shaped mound in the center of the fire base. They will heat faster this way.

After preparing the fuel for the fire, you are ready to light it. You may use either lighter fluid or an electric charcoal lighter. Always be very careful when using **lighter fluid**. Do not use gasoline or kerosene—they may explode. Soak the charcoal with lighter fluid, wait 1 to 2 minutes for the fluid to soak in, and then ignite the coals with a long match. To use an **electric charcoal lighter**, plug it in near the grill and leave it for 8 minutes in the coals until they are red-hot.

Allow the charcoal or briquettes to burn for 30 minutes before adding the meat or vegetables. Charcoal and briquettes are ready when there is a layer of white ash across the coals and they have a dull red glow. Another way to know if the fire is ready is to hold your hand extended above the coals at approximately the same height you will be grilling. If you can hold your hand for:

• over 4 seconds, the fire is not hot enough
• 3 to 4 seconds, the fire is medium hot to hot
• 2 seconds, the fire is very hot
• 0 to 1 seconds, the fire is too hot to cook

Sprinkle any flavor chips over the hot coals before placing the food on the grill.

Tip: Soak flavor chunks/chips in water and then drain before burning for maximum flavor.

GRILLING THE MEAT

After the coals are ready for cooking, you will need to arrange them with tongs according to the food you are cooking:

Steaks, burgers, chops, fillets need direct heat, so spread the coals evenly over the fire base to produce even heat. You need to leave 1 inch of space between each coal to avoid a flame-up. Place the meat directly over the coals and grill uncovered.

Ribs, roasts, chicken, turkey, fish need indirect heat, so move the coals into a ring around the perimeter. In the center of the coals, place a disposable foil drip pan. You can make a drip pan with aluminum foil if you don't have one. Take a piece of aluminum foil that is about twice the length of your grill, fold it in half, and fold all four edges up about 1 1/2 to 2 inches to form a "pan." The drip pan will catch any drippings and thus reduce flame-ups, which could burn the meat. Place the meat on the grill so that it is over the drip pan (not the coals) and cover the grill.

Marinating is only necessary for less tender cuts of meat such as flank, round, or London broil. Thin cuts of meat dry out quickly, so if you are not marinating the meat, rub a small amount of olive oil on both sides of the cut. A marinade on chicken, pork, as well as beef can be delicious. If you need a quick marinade for chicken, use a store-bought Italian dressing. Use a brush to add marinade during grilling. **Tip:** If you don't have a brush, use the leafy end of a piece of celery.

GRILLING CHART

Type of Meat	Serving Size	Distance from Coals	Approximate Grilling Time
Chicken	1 broiler = 3–4 servings	8 inches	60 minutes—turn occasionally
	2 split pieces = 1 serving	8 inches	6–10 minutes per side
Fish	1/4–1/2 pound fish fillet	8 inches	4 minutes per side (until fish flakes)
Hamburgers	1–2 patties	5 inches	4 minutes per side
Hotdogs	2 wieners	5 inches	4 minutes per side
Lamb Kebabs	1/4 pound cut into 1 1/2-inch cubes	8 inches	25–30 minutes—turn occasionally
Ribs	1 strip per 2–3 servings	12 inches	45 minutes—turn occasionally
Steaks	1/2 pound	2–3 inches	for 1-inch-thick cuts, minutes per side: rare—5 medium—6 well done—8 for 2-inch-thick cuts, minutes per side: rare—15 medium—18 well done—20

Meat will continue to cook after you remove it from the grill so it's best to remove it a minute early.

ADDITIONAL GRILLING KNOW-HOW

Grilling Beef

Make sure the beef has been out of the refrigerator for 1 hour before grilling. You may marinate beef overnight, or 4 to 6 hours before grilling. Steaks that have been marinated will definitely be tender. Use the same marinade for basting during grilling. To make a delicious marinade for beef, melt 1/2 cup butter in a saucepan over low heat. Add 1 Tbsp. dry mustard, 1 Tbsp. Worcestershire sauce, and 4 Tbsp. lemon juice. Cook over low heat until thoroughly blended.

Grilling Chicken

Always grill chicken in its skin to keep the meat moist and tender. If you don't want to eat the skin, remove it after the chicken is through grilling. Always use a drip pan under the chicken to prevent flame-ups. Cook chicken 5 to 10 minutes before adding barbecue sauce. Add the sauce and grill slowly. Chicken will take 45 to 60 minutes, depending on the size of the pieces; pieces will cook faster than whole chicken.

Grilling Fish

Spray the grill with cooking spray so the fish does not stick. The best fish for grilling are those with a firmer flesh such as catfish, halibut, mahi-mahi, salmon, swordfish, and tuna. Use a fish basket to grill flakier fish such as haddock or orange roughy. You may also place fish on a piece of heavy duty aluminum foil and place any of the following on top of the fish: a slice of onion, bell pepper, lemon, or artichoke hearts. Then top with butter, salt and pepper, and fold the foil so it is sealed. Place foil on grill and turn it with tongs so that the fish cooks evenly. Cook 15 to 30 minutes, depending on the thickness of the fish. If marinating fish, place the fish in marinade, cover, and place in the refrigerator for 30 minutes. Also apply marinade while the fish is grilling. The following herbs are delicious with grilled fish: dill, fennel, oregano, and thyme. If using fresh herbs, soak them in water and then add them directly to the coals. Another way to season fish is to rub a little olive or vegetable oil on the fish, and sprinkle with your choice of seasoning. Sprinkle Cajun/Créole seasoning on the fish while it's grilling for a taste similar to "blackened" fish. If serving grilled fish, prepare it last. It cooks quickly and cools quickly. Shrimp is good placed in kebabs and grilled. Baste shrimp with soy sauce for a delicious flavor.

Grilling Spareribs

Marinate spareribs for at least 4 hours, turning occasionally in the marinade. Drain and use the same marinade for basting. If the ribs don't have much fat, oil them lightly or use nonstick cooking spray on the grill. Turn them often and baste, but don't baste during the last 15 mintues of cooking, unless you want a lot of sauce on the ribs. They will be messier to eat with more sauce. If you don't have a special sauce for basting the ribs, use vinegar.

Grilling Vegetables

Onions are delicious grilled. Take a large onion, peel it, and cut a piece out of the center. Fill the hole with butter, brown sugar, salt and pepper, or with butter and a beef bouillon cube. Lightly rub the onion with oil and place it on a large piece of heavy-duty aluminum foil. Wrap the foil around the onion and seal it airtight. Place the onion on the edge of the grill and cook for approximately 15 minutes. You may turn the onion over during cooking. Allow one large onion per serving.

Tomatoes can also be stuffed like an onion or filled with butter, basil, salt and pepper, and cooked the same way. Allow 1 tomato per serving.

Corn can be cooked on the grill, in the husk, but the silk should be removed first. Pull the husk back gently, remove the silk, then pull the husk back over the corn cob. Soak the corn for 10 minutes in water, then place each ear on a piece of heavy-duty aluminum foil with a pat of butter. Wrap the corn tightly and place it on the grill, turning frequently, for about 15 to 20 minutes.

Carrots, eggplant, and **potatoes** can be cooked on the grill in a piece of heavy duty aluminum foil. Be sure to close the aluminum foil tightly before grilling. You may place anything on top of the vegetables that you like.

GRILLING TIPS FOR THE KITCHEN KLUTZ

- Don't use a grill in high winds.
- Don't place lighter fluid on coals that are warm or hot—it's dangerous!
- Have everything you need for grilling ready before you begin, such as long-handled tongs, spatula, pot holder, and spray bottle filled with water for flame-ups. An easy way to remember which items you will need is to keep them in a basket. It's easy to carry, and easy to find what you need. Always repack your basket after everything has been washed so it will be ready the next time you grill.
- In order to minimize the risk of harmful bacteria, the platter or pan you take the raw meat to the grill on should be washed, or a new one used, when the meat has finished cooking and you remove it from the grill.
- Warm the sauces used in grilling to blend the flavors before adding them to the meat on the grill.
- If the charcoal becomes too hot, remove some of the coals or spread them farther apart. If not hot enough, move them closer together or add more.
- Grilled bananas are great with grilled meat. Place bananas, in their peels, on the grill and cook for 7 minutes, turning once.
- Onions placed in aluminum foil with a pat of butter are delicious cooked on the grill.
- To keep fish from sticking to the grill, rub mayonnaise on the fish before grilling. It will cook off during the grilling and not affect the flavor of the fish.
- Spray the grill with nonstick cooking spray before heating to provide an easier clean-up.
- Make sure the grill is clean! Flavors will linger from old foods stuck to the grill. Use a wire brush to clean the grill. It's easiest to clean the grill after cooking while it's still warm.

MICROWAVING

The microwave saves a lot of time when cooking and it's easy to use. You may defrost or cook food in less time by using the microwave. There is no difference in taste when cooking most foods in the microwave, although a few items such as bread taste better when cooked in the oven. Many tips in this chapter are for using the microwave successfully, as well as shortcuts that may be done to ease your time in the kitchen.

MICROWAVING BASICS

When microwaving, the energy turns to heat inside the food as soon as it penetrates it. Foods at room temperature will take less time to cook in the microwave than refrigerated or frozen foods. The arrangement of foods to be microwaved plays a key role in the process. Foods should be arranged in a circle so that all sides are exposed to the microwave. Round-shaped foods cook more evenly than foods with corners; since microwaves penetrate the food from all angles, corners have a tendency to overcook. In addition, thick pieces should be placed on the outside and thin places on the inside of your dish, because thin pieces cook faster than thick pieces, just as small amounts cook faster than large amounts. For even cooking when microwaving large amounts, reduce the power level and increase the cooking time.

The texture of the food also determines the amount of time and power setting in the microwave. Prick foods that are tightly covered with a skin or shell such as eggs, potatoes, and squash. This will help release the pressure caused from the build-up of steam. Dense foods (such as a potato) cook slower than porous foods (such as cakes and breads). Foods with a "delicate texture" such as custard or pudding need to be cooked at a low power setting to avoid "toughening."

Knowing when to cover food is important. Cover foods according to the moisture content desired. Paper towels absorb moisture, wax paper holds moisture in but allows any excess steam to escape, and plastic wrap holds the most moisture and steam in. You may also cut a few slits in plastic wrap to "vent" it for the same effect as wax paper. Microwaves are attracted to water so moist foods will cook more evenly. Cover food that is "uneven" in moisture to help the heat spread easily. The chart later in the chapter will help you determine what to cover.

Often, you will be asked to rotate your dish at a certain point in the microwaving time. Some microwaves have a rotating function. If not, you will need to rotate the food. To rotate a ½ turn, turn the dish so that the side facing the back is now facing the front. To rotate a ¼ turn, turn the dish so that the side facing the back is now facing the side.

When stirring, stir from the outside to the center. Remember, though, that foods which normally require constant stirring when using a stove (such as cheese or butter) only require occasional stirring in the microwave. If boiling a milk-based liquid in the microwave, watch the liquid carefully, since microwaves intensify the boiling in milk-based liquids.

Microwaved foods should stand for 2 to 10 minutes before eating. Wrap the microwave container in a dishcloth while it is standing so the container will not get cold.

MICROWAVE-SAFE DISHES

Microwave Safe
Wooden toothpicks
Plastic picks (you may leave the frills on if they are paper, not foil)
Paper plates
Glass
China plates (without any metallic decoration)
Plastic (be sure to check—not all plastic is microwave safe)

Non-Microwave Safe
Metal skewers
Aluminum foil or wrapping (like cream cheese package)
Metal pots, dishes
Glassware that has been broken and repaired

Remember: Watch for any metal on dishes, including handles, decorations, and glazes.

To test a dish to discover if it is microwave safe: microwave a cup of water in the dish on high for 1 minute. If the dish becomes very hot, it is not microwave safe.

REHEATING LEFTOVERS IN THE MICROWAVE

Arrange the plate of food so that the thick and dense foods are on the outside of the plate, and the easier-to-heat foods are on the inside. If possible, arrange the food in a circle for even heating and spread the food so that it has a low and even profile. The center is the last to heat, so the edges may bubble a little. For the fastest reheating, cover the food according to the amount of moisture desired. Remember to tuck the covering under the dish to ensure the food is adequately covered. Use the following helpful chart to determine what type of covering to use:

Food	*Covering*
Appetizers, dips	Wax paper, plastic
Bakery goods	Uncovered
Beverages	Uncovered
Main dishes	Plastic (if sauce-based), Wax paper
Meat	Uncovered if rare or medium

Food	Covering
Pancakes, waffles	Uncovered
Sandwiches	Paper towel
Sauces	Wax paper
Soups	Wax paper, plastic
Vegetables	Wax paper, plastic

In general, microwave on High (10) for 3 to 5 minutes or until the center of the bottom of the plate is hot. Rotate the plate a $1/2$ turn after 1 to 2 minutes have elapsed.

MICROWAVE SHORTCUTS

Bacon Place strips of bacon between paper towels, and cook on High (10) for 1 to 3 minutes per slice, depending on its thickness. Or use the new microwave bacon holder and follow the manufacturer's directions.

Brown sugar To soften, place brown sugar and a slice of apple in a microwave container, cover, microwave on High (10) for 15 to 20 seconds. You may also place the box of brown sugar in the microwave with a cup of hot water and microwave on High (10) for $1^{1}/2$ to 2 minutes.

Butter To melt, microwave for 1 minute on High (10). **To clarify butter**, microwave it for 2 minutes on High (10). Let it stand for a few minutes, and a clear, clarified layer will float to the top while the salt and milk curd will settle on the bottom. If your recipe calls for clarified butter, pour off the clarified layer and use it. Clarified butter is also called "drawn butter."

Cheese For easier slicing, warm cheese for $1/2$ to 1 minute on Medium (5). To melt processed cheese, microwave for 12 minutes on Low (3). If melting natural cheese, add liquid such as milk, to prevent stringiness.

Chocolate Melts easily in the microwave and is less likely to scorch than on the stove.

Coffee/Tea Microwave 1 cup on High (10) for $1^{1}/2$ to $3^{1}/2$ minutes, depending on how hot you like your coffee. If you do not want the water heated to boiling, microwave for only $1^{1}/2$ minutes.

Corn-on-the-Cob Leave the husk on and place the corn in a glass dish. Cover the dish with plastic wrap and cook on High (10). A single ear of corn will take 3 to 4 minutes. If you have 5 ears of corn, microwave them for 15 minutes.

Cream Cheese To soften, remove the foil and microwave for $1^{1}/2$ minutes on Medium (5).

Croûtons   Place bread crumbs in a dish, and microwave on High (10) for 5 to 6 minutes. Put butter and seasonings (garlic, onion salt, etc.) on the bread crumbs and toss them to coat. Microwave another 5 to 6 minutes on High (10).

Dried Fruit   Sprinkle fruit juice or water over the dried fruit, cover with plastic wrap, and microwave $1/2$ to 1 minute on High (10).

Ice Cream   To soften, microwave on High (10) for 15 seconds.

Milk   To scald milk, place 1 cup on High (10) power for 2 to $2^1/2$ minutes. Stir once after each minute.

Nuts   Shell nuts by microwaving 2 cups in 1 cup of water on High for 4 to 5 minutes. Shells will remove easily. To toast nuts, spread $1/4$ cup nuts and 1 Tbsp. butter in a dish and microwave on High for 5 to 6 minutes. Stir every 2 minutes until toasted. Stir in $1/2$ tsp. seasoned salt for flavoring.

Orange Juice   To thaw frozen orange juice, remove the metal lids and place the opened can in a bowl in the microwave on High (10) for 30 seconds for 6 ounces, and 45 seconds for 12 ounces.

Baked Potato   Stick a whole potato with a fork several times so the steam can escape while cooking. Microwave on High (10) for 9 to 10 minutes per potato.

Snacks (pretzels, chips)   To freshen, place snacks in the microwave and cook for 5 seconds. Allow snacks to stand for 1 minute to crisp.

Tortillas   To soften, wrap in a damp towel and microwave on High (10) for $1/2$ to 1 minute.

Vegetables   To sauté, place 1 cup chopped vegetables and 1 Tbsp. butter in a dish, cover, and microwave for 3 to 4 minutes until the vegetables are soft.

GARNISHES

Garnishes are a great way to enhance the food you are serving and are relatively simple to create. They are used to make the appearance and taste of a dish more appealing by adding color to the plate. Garnishes are like a frame to a painting; they should enhance without detracting from the food.

Add the garnish to the plate right before you are ready to serve it so that the garnish looks fresh. Garnishes should be edible and should "echo" the food they are garnishing. Choose fresh herbs, fruits, and vegetables that are in close to perfect shape. Always leave some of the plate showing, so the frame is complete.

Be imaginative and create your own or use some of the many listed in this chapter. Just remember that to present a beautiful plate of food, you will need to garnish it, whether it's simply a sprig of fresh parsley or one of the fancier garnishes, such as a turnip flower.

QUICK READY-MADE GARNISHES

Grated cheese
Cherry tomatoes
Lemon slices
Orange slices
Lime slices
Nuts
Bread crumbs

Olives
Julienned vegetables
Chopped chives
Parsley sprigs
Minced basil
Dollop of yogurt or sour cream
Paprika

SPECIAL GARNISHES TO SPRUCE UP ANY PLATE

Artichoke Cup for Dips

Cut off the stem of the artichoke so that the artichoke will sit on a flat surface. With kitchen scissors, snip the tips off the leaves. Steam the artichoke about 45 minutes, or until it's tender (see pp.120–21). With a knife, hollow out the inside of the artichoke. You may then place a bowl in the cavity and fill it with dip. Put on a plate or tray and place crackers around it.

Bacon Curl

Fry bacon until it's crisp, making sure to press the bacon flat as it cooks. As soon as you remove the bacon from the skillet, roll it into a coil (be careful—it might be very hot). The bacon will remain in the curl shape as it cools. This is a great garnish for egg dishes.

Butter Balls

Dip a melon ball scooper in hot water for 2 minutes. Next, scoop butter, and drop scooped ball into ice water. Refrigerate until ready to use.

Butter Curls

Place a butter peeler in hot water for 2 minutes. Then lightly pull the peeler across the top of a firm but not too cold stick of butter. Place the curl into ice water and refrigerate until ready to use.

Cabbage Cup

Buy a cabbage with large outer leaves. Cut the bottom of the cabbage so that it will sit on a flat surface. Fold back the outer leaves very carefully. With a knife, cut a large hole in the center and place a small glass or bowl in the hole. You may then fill the glass or bowl with dip and surround it with boiled shrimp or fresh vegetables.

Carrot Curls

With a vegetable peeler cut long strips off a carrot. Roll the strips up and hold them in place with toothpicks. Drop toothpick rolls in ice water and chill for 2 to 3 hours. When ready to use the carrot curls, remove the toothpicks.

Stuffed Celery

Take two ribs of celery, approximately the same size, cut the leaves off as well as the large ends. Fill each rib with a cheese spread and place one celery rib on top of the other. Tie the ribs together at each end and refrigerate for 1 hour. When ready to use, remove the celery ribs, cut the string off, and cut stacked celery crosswise into layered slices.

Cherry Tomato Flowers

Slice a cherry tomato, starting on one end, slicing from the top to almost the bottom (but not slicing all the way through). Remove the seeds and pulp and spread the tomato out so it looks like a flower. Spoon a seasoned cream cheese into the center of the tomato and lay a slice of olive on top, if you like.

Chocolate Curls

Pull a dry, warmed vegetable peeler across a chocolate bar to make curls. Place the curls on top of dessert.

Chocolate Cutouts

Melt 6 to 8 ounces of semisweet chocolate over low heat in a small saucepan. (Watch the chocolate because it burns easily.) Cover a cookie sheet with aluminum foil. Let the melted chocolate cool slightly and then pour it on the cookie sheet. Spread the chocolate out until it's smooth—about 1/8 to 1/4 inch thick. Wait until the chocolate is almost set and then cut it with cookie cutters. When chocolate shapes are firm, lift them with a spatula and place them on a plate. Cover the plate with foil or plastic and refrigerate until ready to use.

Cranberry Garland

String fresh cranberries with a needle and thread and then tie around the turkey tray.

Frosted Grapes

After washing and drying grapes, dip them in slightly beaten egg whites and then in granulated sugar. Place on a rack to "set" and then refrigerate until ready to use. Add to cheese trays, dessert trays, or cakes. You may frost other small fruits in the same manner such as raspberries, blackberries, and strawberries.

Lemon, Lime, or Orange Bows

With a knife, cut a continuous thin strip around the fruit at least 8 inches long. Use strip as a curlicue or tie it in a bow.

Lemon Rose

Use a firm lemon. Beginning at the bottom of the lemon, peel a continuous strip, about 1 inch wide, as long as you can. Once peeled, coil the strip with the outer skin facing out so that it forms a rose. Use a toothpick to hold the bottom together if necessary. You may then place the "rose" on a leaf of lettuce.

Onion Blossom

Buy a medium-sized white onion with a nice round shape. Peel the onion and cut off the top of the non-root end. With a sharp knife, begin slicing the onion in 1/8-inch to 1/4-inch slices starting at the non-root end and slicing down to within 1/2 inch of the root end. Once you have sliced all around the onion, place it in hot water for 5 minutes. Chill in ice water until ready to use. It will look like a chrysanthemum. You may add food coloring to the ice water if you want to color your blossom.

Peach or Pear Halves

Peach or pear halves filled with cranberry sauce, currant jelly, chutney, or mint jelly make a great garnish for lamb or ham.

Green, Red, and Yellow Pepper Cups

Buy green, red, or yellow peppers that will sit on a flat surface. Cut the stem end off and remove the seeds and inner parts. Fill the hollowed inside with mayonnaise, mustard, or any other dip or condiment you may want to use.

Pineapple Boat

Slice a pineapple in half lengthwise. Scoop out the fruit with a knife and spoon. You may fill the "boat" with cut-up fruit, chicken salad, or tuna salad.

Pineapple Cubes

Place a maraschino cherry on top of a pineapple cube and anchor together with a toothpick. You may also anchor a maraschino cherry in the center of a pineapple slice.

Pumpkin Bowl

Cut the top (stem end) off of a small pumpkin and clean out the inside. You may then place a bowl inside the pumpkin and use it to serve dips, fresh fruit, or vegetables.

Radish Fan

Cut the stem off a radish, preferably a long, oval-shaped radish. With a knife, make diagonal cuts around the radish (but not cutting slices completely off), keeping the slices as close together as possible. After cutting, chill the radishes in ice water and they will open into a fan shape.

Strawberry Fan

Slice a strawberry lengthwise from right below the green cap to the tip. Spread slices out into a fan shape.

Tomato Rose

Use a firm tomato, if possible. Beginning at the bottom of the tomato, peel a continuous strip, about 1 inch wide, as long as you can. Once peeled, coil the strip with the outer skin facing out so that it forms a rose. Use a toothpick to hold the bottom together if necessary. You may then place the "rose" on a leaf of lettuce.

Turnip Flowers

Slice a turnip into thin pieces. Cut flower shapes out of the slices with flower-shaped canapé cutters. You may tint the "flowers" by soaking in food color. For a center in the flower, cut smaller circles out of the turnips or use carrots. Use a toothpick to hold the center and flower together and cover the toothpick with a green onion to look like the stem.

Vegetable Wreath

Buy a small green florist's wreath. Using wire florist picks as fasteners, cover the wreath with fresh parsley sprigs. You may then "decorate" the wreath with fluted mushrooms, carrot curls, radish roses, etc. and secure the decorations with toothpicks. In the center of the wreath you may place a bowl of dip.

GARNISHES FOR BEVERAGES

- Place a strawberry in a glass of champagne or white wine.
- Make a fruit kebab for fruit drinks. On a toothpick, place a pineapple chunk, a cherry, or an orange wedge.
- Place a cinnamon stick or peppermint stick in hot chocolate or coffee.
- Place a sprig of mint in iced or fruit tea.
- Cut slices of lemon, orange, or limes. Cut a slit in each slice and place on the rim of a glass.
- Drop an olive or pickled tomato into a martini.

□ □ □ □ □ □

LEAN AND LIGHT COOKING TIPS

It's amazing what substitutions can be made in the kitchen when you want to cook lean and light! In this chapter there are lots of tips on helping you cook with fewer calories and less fat. Watch out for extra sodium, though, because many of the light or nonfat foods contain more sodium. Always read the labels of the products you purchase to check the fat, sugar, and sodium content. Learning to cook light and lean is sometimes challenging but still rewarding for the health-conscious cook. In this chapter you wil find tips for cooking light and lean while still serving delicious food.

LEAN AND LIGHT COOKING TIPS

- When the recipe calls for **vegetable oil**, use corn, canola, safflower, or sunflower oil.
- Use olive oil, canola oil, or liquid margarine in place of **butter**. In recipes, use ³/₄ Tbsp. unsaturated oil or 1 Tbsp. margarine for 1 Tbsp. butter. Olive oil contains the same amount of calories as butter (about 120 calories per Tbsp.) but does not contain cholesterol.
- Substitute skim milk for **whole milk**. In recipes that use 1 cup whole milk, you will need to substitute 1 cup of skim milk + 1 Tbsp. of unsaturated oil (corn, olive, sunflower, safflower, canola) in order to make the skim milk comparable to whole milk so you can prepare the recipe correctly. This is especially true when baking cakes and pies.
- For **eggs**, use cholesterol-free egg substitutes or 1 egg white + 2 Tsp. of unsaturated oil (corn, olive, sunflower, safflower, canola). In baking, use 2 egg whites for 1 whole large egg or 3 egg whites per 2 whole large eggs.
- Instead of **sour cream** or **mayonnaise** in a recipe, use buttermilk, plain lowfat yogurt, nonfat yogurt, or lite or nonfat sour cream. Also 1 cup of sour cream may be substituted by 1 Tbsp. lemon juice + 2 Tbsp. skim milk + 1 cup lowfat cottage cheese (or 1 Tbsp. lemon juice + enough evaporated milk to make 1 cup).
- Instead of using **cream** for whipped toppings, use *chilled* canned evaporated lowfat or skim milk that has been beaten with an electric mixer.
- Add lemon juice or olive oil to **pasta** water instead of salt.

- For 1 cup of **cream cheese**, use 4 Tbsp. margarine + 1 cup dry low-fat cottage cheese.
- For 1 ounce unsweetened **baking chocolate** use 3 Tbsp. cocoa/carob + 1 Tbsp. margarine or corn, canola, safflower, or sunflower oil.
- Avoid butter, lard, coconut oil, and palm oil.
- Use herbs and spices instead of **salt**.
- When **cooking meat** (such as sausage) for a casserole, drain the cooked meat on paper towels that are placed on top of brown paper bags to absorb the fat and grease before you add it to the casserole. In addition, place the cooked meat in a colander and run hot water over it to wash off more grease.
- Use onion or garlic *powder* instead of **onion** or **garlic salt**.
- Reduce the amount of **salt** called for in a recipe or eliminate it. **Note:** Do not eliminate or reduce the amount of salt in bread baking recipes; it is necessary to interact with the yeast.
- When using **processed meats** such as hot dogs, sausage, and bologna, try to buy those with reduced fat and salt.
- Remove the skin and fat (light yellow or white in color) from **poultry** before cooking.
- Buy **lean cuts of meat**.
- Trim all visible **fat** from meat before cooking (**Note:** This will make the meat drier).
- Serve meat in **smaller portions:** 4 ounces instead of 6 to 8 ounces; add more vegetables and grains to your diet.
- **Organ meats** are high in cholesterol, so limit these in your diet.
- Rinse with water **fish** that is canned in oil.
- Use **less caloric methods of cooking:** simmering, steaming, baking, poaching, and wokking.
- To remove fat from **sauces** and **soups**, lay a paper towel or piece of lettuce on top. (If you have time, make the sauce or soup, place it in the refrigerator, and remove the fat layer from the top after it is chilled.)

□ □ □ □ □ □

HIGH-ALTITUDE COOKING

Don't allow high altitudes to keep you out of the kitchen. There are, however, adjustments that will need to be made when cooking at high altitudes. Cake mixes usually have directions on the box, but other recipes will need to be adjusted. Make notes of what adjustments work so you'll have them the next time you prepare the recipe. Remember that yeast bread rises faster at high altitudes, so allow it to rise for a shorter amount of time. Cakes, cookies, and water also cook differently, so learn the adjustments needed.

ADJUSTMENTS TO MAKE WHEN COOKING
AT HIGH ALTITUDES

"Higher Altitude" refers to any place that is 3,500 feet or more above sea level.

At high altitudes:

• The boiling point is lower so it takes longer to boil food
• Water evaporates faster because the air pressure is lower
• Cooking takes longer

Following are the adjustments you will need to make when cooking at altitudes of 3,500 to 7,000 feet above sea level. If you are cooking at an altitude higher than 7,000 feet above sea level, also follow the guidelines below but increase the adjustments slightly.

When Baking and Using Ingredients and Equipment

Ingredient or Cooking Direction Involved	*Action to Take*
Baking powder	Reduce each teaspoon by 1/8 to 1/4
Baking soda	Reduce each teaspoon by 1/4 unless fruit juices or sour milk are also ingredients

213

Ingredient or Cooking Direction Involved	Action to Take
Fats	No adjustments are necessary (**Note:** If substituting, then 1 cup shortening = $3/4$ cup oil or butter)
Liquids	Increase each cup of liquid by 4 Tbsp.
Sugar	Decrease each cup of sugar by 2 to 3 Tbsp.
Pan size	Use smaller pans
Temperature	Increase the oven temperature by 25°F.
Cooking time	Lengthen the cooking time a little

Remember to grease and flour all baking pans or line them with wax paper, unless the recipe specifically says not to (such as an angel food cake recipe). When you bake at high altitudes, food tends to stick to the pan.

When Baking Cookies

Often when baking cookies, you do not need to make any adjustments. It is a good idea, however, to bake a sample cookie first to determine if you will need to decrease the sugar and baking powder.

When Cooking Vegetables, Soups, Pasta

Remember that the boiling point is lower but water evaporates faster. You will need to increase the cooking time by 10 to 15 minutes. For each cup of water used, increase it by $1/4$ cup.

When Baking Desserts

Pound cakes will need less fat than called for in the recipe. Watch when cooking frostings and candy because they can burn quickly since the water evaporates so fast at high altitudes.

When Baking Yeast Bread

When mixing the dough, use slightly less flour per cup of liquid. Remember that flour dries out at high altitudes. The first rise will not fully double in size, and the second rise will take approximately 25 to 30 minutes to conclude. Using less yeast will also give you a finer texture. Increase the baking temperature by 25°F. and decrease the baking time by 10 to 15 minutes. Watch the bread carefully since bread rises faster at higher altitudes.

When Cooking Meats

Meats may take almost twice as long to cook. Use a meat thermometer to make sure the meat is thoroughly cooked. When frying food, it is easy to brown the outside and have uncooked food in the inside, so be careful. Reducing temperature and cooking longer will help.

□ □ □ □ □ □

HELPFUL SUBSTITUTIONS

You will find this chapter invaluable! There is nothing worse than being in the middle of preparing a recipe and not having an ingredient. These substitutions will help you tremendously and will prevent an unnecessary trip to the grocery store. Remember that it is always best to use the ingredients called for in the recipe, but the substitutions in this chapter are acceptable. You may even decide that you prefer the substitution to the ingredients listed in the recipe.

SIMPLE SUBSTITUTIONS

Ingredient	*Helpful Substitution*
1 tsp. allspice	1 tsp., equal parts, of cinnamon, clove, nutmeg
1 Tbsp. arrowroot	1 1/2 Tbsp. all-purpose flour or 2 1/4 tsp. cornstarch
1 tsp. baking powder	1/2 tsp. cream of tartar + 1/4 tsp. baking soda
1 tsp. basil	1 tsp. oregano
1 cup barbecue sauce	1 cup ketchup + 2 tsp. Worcestershire sauce
1 cup biscuit mix	1 cup flour + 1 1/2 tsp. Baking Powder + 2 Tbsp. shortening
1 cup bread crumbs	3/4 cup cracker crumbs
1 cup broth (beef or chicken)	1 bouillon cube dissolved in 1 cup boiling water
1 cup brown sugar	1 cup granulated sugar + 2 Tbsp. molasses
1/3 cup butter	1/3 cup vegetable shortening + 2 tsp. water
1 cup butter	1 cup vegetable shortening + 2 Tbsp. water
1 cup buttermilk or sour milk	1 Tbsp. vinegar or lemon juice + milk to fill up to 1 cup—wait 5 minutes before using
1 tsp. dried herbs	1 Tbsp. fresh herbs
1 tsp. caraway	1 tsp. anise
1 tsp. cayenne	1 tsp. chili pepper
1 tsp. chervil	1 tsp. tarragon or parsley
1 cup chili sauce	1 cup tomato sauce + 1/2 cup sugar + 2 Tbsp. vinegar
1 ounce chocolate	3 Tbsp. cocoa + 1/2 Tbsp. margarine
1 ounce chocolate, unsweetened	3 Tbsp. cocoa + 1 Tbsp. vegetable shortening, butter, or margarine
1 ounce chocolate, semisweet	1 ounce unsweetened chocolate + 1 Tbsp. sugar or 3–4 Tbsp. cocoa + 1/2 Tbsp. butter + 3 Tbsp. sugar

215

Ingredient	Helpful Substitution
1 cup grated coconut	1¹/₃ cups flaked coconut
1 Tbsp. cornstarch	2 Tbsp. all-purpose flour or 2 tsp. quick-cooking tapioca
1 cup corn syrup	³/₄ cup sugar + ¹/₄ cup water
1 cup heavy cream	³/₄ cup milk + ¹/₃ cup butter
1 cup light cream	⁷/₈ cup milk + 3 Tbsp. butter
2 large eggs	3 small eggs
1 cup cake flour	1 cup all-purpose flour less 2 Tbsp.
1 Tbsp. flour	¹/₂ Tbsp. cornstarch or ¹/₂ Tbsp. arrowroot or 1 Tbsp. granulated tapioca
1 cup self-rising flour	1 cup all-purpose flour + 1 tsp. baking powder + ¹/₂ tsp. salt
1 cup all-purpose flour	1 cup cake flour + 2 Tbsp. cake flour
1 tsp. dried herbs	1 Tbsp. fresh herbs
1 Tbsp. fresh herbs	1 tsp. dried herbs
1 cup honey	1¹/₄ cups sugar + ¹/₄ cup water or 1 cup molasses
¹/₈ tsp. garlic powder	1 tsp. garlic salt
1 garlic clove (fresh)	1 tsp. garlic salt or ¹/₈ tsp. garlic powder
¹/₂ cup ketchup	¹/₂ cup tomato sauce + 2 Tbsp. sugar + 1 Tbsp. vinegar + ¹/₈ ground cloves
1 tsp. lemon juice	1 tsp. vinegar
10 miniature marshmallows	1 large marshmallow
1 cup molasses	1 cup honey
1 cup whole milk	¹/₂ cup evaporated milk + ¹/₂ cup water or ¹/₂ cup of condensed milk + 1 cup water
1 cup whole milk	4 Tbsp. dry whole milk + 1 cup water
1 cup whole milk	1 cup buttermilk + ¹/₂ tsp. baking soda
1 cup skim milk	4 Tbsp. nonfat dry milk + 1 cup water
1 cup sour milk	1 Tbsp. lemon juice or vinegar + enough regular milk to make 1 cup—let stand for 5 minutes
1 pound of fresh mushrooms	6 ounces canned mushrooms or 3 cups of freeze-dried mushrooms
1 Tbsp. mustard	1 tsp. dry mustard + 1 Tbsp. white wine or vinegar
1 cup minced onion	1 tsp. onion powder
1 tsp. oregano	1 tsp. marjoram or basil
A few drops of hot pepper sauce	A dash of cayenne or red pepper
¹/₂ cup raisins	¹/₂ cup pitted and cut prunes or dates
1 tsp. sage	1 tsp. thyme
1 Tbsp. dry sherry	1 Tbsp. dry vermouth
1 cup sour cream	3 Tbsp. butter + ³/₄ cup milk or 1 Tbsp. lemon juice + evaporated milk to make 1 cup
1 cup granulated sugar	1¹/₂ cups maple syrup or 2 cups corn syrup or 1 cup light brown sugar, well-packed
2 tsp. tapioca	1 Tbsp. flour
1 cup canned tomatoes	1¹/₃ cups cut-up fresh tomatoes, simmered for 10 minutes

Ingredient	Helpful Substitution
1 cup tomato juice	$1/2$ cup tomato sauce + $1/2$ cup water
1 Tbsp. tomato paste	1 Tbsp. tomato catsup
1 cup tomato purée	One 6-ounce can tomato paste + 1 can water
1 Tbsp. Worcestershire sauce	1 Tbsp. soy sauce + dash hot sauce
1 cup wine	1 cup apple juice, apple cider, chicken broth or beef broth
$1/2$ cup wine for marinade	$1/4$ cup vinegar + 1 Tbsp. sugar + $1/4$ cup water
Whipped cream	beat together a mashed banana and egg white until stiff
1 cake compressed yeast	5 tsp. active dry yeast or 1 strip yeast
1 cup yogurt	1 cup buttermilk or sour cream or sour milk

❏ ❏ ❏ ❏ ❏ ❏

FIRST AID IN THE KITCHEN

Accidents occur in the home, and the kitchen is no exception, especially since cooking often involves using boiling water, knives, electrical appliances, and the like. Here are a few guidelines to help you when an accident happens. Most importantly, remember to stay calm and call 911 or your doctor if you are in doubt about what you should do. It's always better to be safe than sorry.

TO KEEP ON HAND FOR EMERGENCIES
IN THE KITCHEN

Fire extinguisher
Antibiotic ointment
Bandages-various sizes

Aloe plant (on your windowsill)
Emergency telephone numbers: 911, your doctor
Aspirin, Ibuprofen, over-the-counter pain
medication

WHAT TO DO WITH A . . .

Burn: Immediately run the burn under cold water to reduce blistering. Soak the burn in cold water for 15 minutes, apply an antibiotic ointment, and cover with a bandage. Change the dressing periodically. You may also leave the burn open to the air; however, by keeping a bandage and ointment on the burn until the healing process has begun, you will reduce the risk of a scar. If you have an aloe plant, cut part of it off, and squeeze the gooey juice onto the burn as

> **If the burn is severe, see a doctor. You have a severe burn if the burn:**
>
> - **is on your face**
> - **is over a joint**
> - **there is no feeling in the burned area**
> - **the burn is several skin layers deep**

□ □ □ □ □ □

HELPFUL COOKING AND FOOD TERMS

This list of cooking and food terms will help you become knowledgeable about the kitchen and keep you from feeling like a klutz. Refer to it often, especially when you are unsure about a cooking or food term.

À la king—Method of preparing cut-up food such as fish, poultry, or meat in a cream sauce

À la mode—Meat braised in marinade, or pie served with ice cream

Al dente—Cooked pasta that is slightly firm but still tender

Amandine—Served or prepared with almonds

Angostura bitters—A powerful liquid spice used sparingly in beverages; good for digestive purposes

Antipasto—Usually an assortment of cold meats, fish, and vegetables served by Italian cooks before the pasta dish; can be served as an appetizer or as a main course

Appetizer—Food and beverage served before a meal to whet the appetite

Arrowroot—Thickening powder that is mixed with cold liquid and stirred into mixtures for thickening

Aspic—A jelly that is made from seasoned vegetable or meat stock and may contain vegetables, fish, or chicken.

Aubergine—Another term for eggplant

Au gratin—Food with a browned covering of bread crumbs, often mixed with cheese or butter and is baked or broiled

Au jus—Refers to meat that is served with the meat juices that are result of the cooking process

Bake—Cooking by dry heat covered or uncovered in an oven; when meats are cooked uncovered, it's called roasting

Barbecue—To cook meat by roasting or broiling and basting frequently in a highly seasoned vinegar-based sauce, usually on a grill, rack, or spit

Barding—The method of covering meat with a layer of fat during roasting to keep meat moist while it cooks

Baste—To moisten meat by pouring/brushing on melted fat, meat drippings, or sauce while cooking to add flavor and to prevent drying

Batter—A mixture of liquid, flour, and other ingredients that is somewhat thick but still thin enough to pour or spread

Béarnaise sauce—A sauce made with egg yolks, vinegar, Tarragon, butter, chives, and sometimes parsley or cayenne; good with meat, vegetables, and fish.

Beat—To mix ingredients with brisk and vigorous stirring in order to add air and make the mixture lighter and smoother

Béchamel—A white sauce of butter, flour, milk, and seasonings

Beignet—A fritter (French); *see* Fritters

Bisque—A rich, creamy soup that usually consists of vegetables or meat or shellfish

Blanch—To immerse food into boiling water briefly (or pour boiling water over the food in a colander) and then into cold water and drain immediately so as to seal in the juices, remove any strong flavors, set colors, and destroy any bacteria before canning or freezing

Blanc mange—A French term that means "white food," usually a thick cornstarch pudding

Blend—To mix two or more ingredients thoroughly by hand or with an electric mixer so neither ingredient is identifiable

Boil—To heat liquid until it bubbles (about 212°F.); **Note:** slow boiling (gentle bubbles) is as good as rapid boiling (large, fast bubbles)

Borscht—A Russian term for beet soup made with beets, cabbage, onion, bouillon, and seasonings; may be served hot or cold

Bouillabaisse—A French stew containing many varieties of fish in combination with vegetables and other seasonings

Bouillon—A soup made from beef stock that has been clarified until it is clear; may also be made from chicken stock

Bouquet garni—A blend of herbs and spices added to stews and soups for flavoring; to make, tie together 1 sprig each of thyme, bay leaf, basil, rosemary, and celery with a slice of carrot

Braise—To cook slowly in a covered pot over low heat (300–325°F.) in the oven, or low to medium heat on the stove), and with a small amount of liquid or fat; this method is often used with tougher cuts of meat

Brazed—Meats that are flame-cooked, such as a shish kebab

Bread—To coat food with finely chopped cracker or bread crumbs or flour and eggs

Breathe—Refers to opening a bottle of wine an hour or more before serving in order to maximize the flavor before drinking

Brioche—A rich, light roll made with flour, eggs, yeast, and butter that is shaped like a muffin

Broil—To cook closely under strong direct heat; the top burner in the oven is the broiler

Broth—The liquid in which vegetables, fish, or meat has been cooked

Brown—To cook quickly the outside of food until the exterior is "brown"; it is usually done to seal in flavor and juices and can be done in a pan on the stove or in the oven

Brown sauce—A French gravy containing onions, butter, beef broth, flour, salt, pepper, and sometimes carrots and tomatoes

Brûlée—Food that has been glazed with carmelized sugar

Canapé—A small piece of toasted bread or cracker that is topped with cheese, meat, or seafood spread

Candy—To boil with sugar in order to preserve

Caramel—Candy; also may refer to burnt sugar syrup that can be used for flavor or coloring in food

Caramelize—To melt granulated sugar or food containing sugar over low to medium heat until a golden-brown syrup is formed

Casserole—A combination of sauce and meat and vegetables or pasta and vegetables or rice and meat

Caviar—The processed salted eggs of the sturgeon or other large fish

Charlotte Russe—A gelatin dessert made of cake or lady fingers and whipped cream

Chateaubriand—The center cut of beef tenderloin that is very tender and wonderful

Cheesecloth—A lightweight cotton cloth used for wrapping certain foods (such as fish) while cooking to contain them; it does not fall apart when heated or is wet and does not interfere with the food's flavor; may be purchased at a hardware or kitchenware store

Chicory—The root of the chicory plant used in preparing coffee or salad

Chill—To refrigerate or place in ice until cold

Chitterlings—The intestines of a young pig

Chop—To cut into pieces by using a knife, scissors, or a food processor; you may chop into small-, medium-, or large-size pieces—unless a recipe specifies what size, usually chop into medium-size pieces

Choux—Pastry made from eggs; examples are éclairs and cream puffs

Chowder—Soup that is made with fish, shellfish and/or vegetables, milk, and chopped or diced potatoes

Cider—Apple juice that has been pressed from apples for drinking; also used to flavor vinegar

Chutney—A spicy and sweet relish that contains vegetables and fruits; often served with curry

Citron—The French term for "lemon"; the small round fruit is placed in syrup and used in fruitcakes and cookies

Clarify—To remove the solids from a liquid by heating a substance in a pan until a clear, clarified layer floats to the top while the sediment settles on the bottom; butter is the most common item to be clarified.

Coat a spoon—Refers to the stage in cooking food when a thin and even film forms on the back of a metal spoon when placed in the mixture

Cobbler—A deep-dish fruit pie with a pastry crust

Cocktail—Alcoholic drink mixture; may also refer to an appetizer such as fruit cocktail or shrimp cocktail

Coddle—To barely simmer just below the boiling point for a short amount of time

Combine—To mix ingredients

Compote—A stew of fruits that has been cooked in a syrup, or a mixture of different fresh fruits

Condensed milk—Canned whole milk made by evaporation that is sweetened with sugar

Condiment—A seasoning added to food for more flavor, such as mustard, ketchup, mayonnaise, relish, chutney, spice, herbs, salt, pepper, etc.

Confectioners' Sugar—Also called powdered sugar; may be labeled XXX or XXXX, which is more fine—they may be used interchangeably

Consommé—A clear, highly seasoned broth made from boiling meat and bones (usually chicken, beef, or veal)

Cool—To allow to stand at room temperature until food is no longer hot but is at room temperature

Coq au vin—Refers to chicken prepared and served in red wine sauce with mushrooms, bacon, and onions

Coquille—A small dish made in the shape of a shell used for serving fish or meat

Court-bouillion—Used as a sauce; broth that is flavored with meat, fish, and vegetables

Cracklings—The crisp pieces remaining after cooking the fat of meat or poultry

Cream—To beat foods until fluffy, light, and soft (such as sugar and butter and shortening)

Crème fraîche—A thick sauce made from cream and buttermilk often used as a topping for pastries and fruit

Créole—Food prepared with peppers, onions, tomatoes, and sometimes okra and filé powder and usually served over rice (Louisiana's famous food)

Crêpes—Very thin, crisp pancakes made of flour and egg batter

Crisp—To rinse leafy vegetables in water and chill to make crisp, or to heat dry foods to make crisp

Croissant—Crescent-shaped flaky roll

Croquette—Made with finely chopped meat or poultry and cream sauce that is shaped and coated with egg and crumbs, fried in oil until crisp, and served with a white sauce

Croûte—Crust or pastry (French); "en croûte" refers to food wrapped in crust

Croûtons—Cubes of bread that have been toasted or baked, and used in salads or soups

Crûdités—An assortment of raw vegetables usually served with a sauce or dip

Crumb—To break into small pieces; to dip food into cracker or bread crumbs

Crumble—To break or crush into small pieces

Crush—To break into very fine pieces

Cube—To cut into small pieces

Curdle (separate)—To heat milk until lumps form; some sauces, such as hollandaise, will curdle or separate when too much heat occurs too fast

Curry—A dish composed of fish, meat, vegetables, or eggs that is seasoned with curry powder

Custard—A mixture of milk and eggs that is flavored and cooked over hot water or in an oven

Cut (as to cut in shortening)—To incorporate shortening with dry ingredients, such as flour, with chopping motions until the mixture resembles coarse cracker meal; if you do not have a pastry cutter, use two knives, one in each hand, and use a cutting motion where they come together (be sure to chill your shortening before doing this)

Dash—$1/16$ teaspoon

Deep-fry—To cook in a skillet containing hot oil

Degrease—To remove the fat from the surface of foods

Demitasse—A small coffee cup and/or spoon used to serve after-dinner coffee

Devil—To spice up food or make it "hot" by adding condiments (such as deviled eggs or sauces)

Dice—To cut food into small cubes

Dissolve—To mix food thoroughly with a liquid to form a solution (such as sugar in water)

Dollop—A small mound dropped by a spoon; term is often used with placing sour cream or whipped cream on food

Dough—A mixture of flour, a liquid and other ingredients to form a thick substance that can be rolled out, patted, kneaded, or molded; dough is thicker than batter

Drain—To place food in a colander to remove as much liquid as possible from the foods

Drippings—The fat and liquid that cook out of meat into the pan

Dredge—To cover thickly by dipping in bread crumbs, flour, sugar, or any other dry mixture; this may be done be placing the food in a paper bag with the dry mixture, closing the bag, and then shaking the bag

Dust—To sprinkle lightly with flour, sugar, etc.; often used in dessert recipes that call for dusting a cake with confectioners' or powdered sugar; a salt shaker containing the ingredient you wish to sprinkle works well for dusting

Dutch oven—A very heavy pot with a very tight fitting lid; it often has a rack in the bottom of the pot

Duxelles—Mushrooms that have been minced and sautéed in butter until no liquid is left; use for seasoning

Éclair—An oblong-shaped cream puff filled with custard or whipped cream; often iced on top

En brochette—Meat cooked on a skewer

Entrails—Intestines or insides of fish, poultry, and other animals

Entrée—The French term for the main dish of a meal

En papillote—To cook and serve food in foil or oiled paper

Escargot—The French term for snail

Evaporated milk—Whole milk that is concentrated through evaporation

Eviscerate—To remove the guts or entrails (organs) of fish or fowl or any other animal before cooking

Fillet/Filet—Boneless piece of meat or fish; as a verb—to remove all of the bones from any piece of meat or fish

Filet mignon—Thick end of beef tenderloin used for small tender steaks and kebabs

Flambé—To light a match to food covered with warm alcohol (such as cognac, rum, brandy, vodka, or whiskey), which causes a flame on the food

Flan—An open tart containing a filling of fruit or cream that is usually baked in a metal flan ring

Flute—To take pie crust and make scallops around the edges by pinching dough with your fingers

Fold—To mix food with a rubber spatula or spoon in an up-and-over motion to keep air bubbles.

Fondant—Sugar syrup that has been cooked to the soft-ball stage and kneaded until creamy

Frappé—Frozen fruit juice, often mixed with liqueur and sometimes sweetened, that is crushed fine and poured over crushed ice

Fricassee—To braise meat or stew chicken in fat and then simmer in a seasoned liquid with vegetables

Frost—To spread icing or a topping

Fritters—Foods such as fruits, meats, vegetables that are first coated in batter and then usually fried in deep fat (like a beignet); they are very crisp on the outside and moist inside

Frosting—Also called icing; either a cooked or uncooked sweetened mixture that is used to cover cakes, cookies, etc.

Fry—To cook food in hot fat or oil; pan-fry involves a small amount of fat; deep-fry involves enough fat so the food is completely covered while being fried; French-fry means to use just enough hot oil or fat to cover the food

Garnish—To decorate food with items such as fresh parsley, mint, vegetables, etc.

Gash—To make cuts using scissors or a knife

Gelatin—A jelly-like substance that is used as a thickening agent and is made from the bones and connective tissue in animals

Giblets—The liver, heart, neck, and gizzard of poultry

Glacé—To coat food with a sugar syrup that has been cooked to the "crack" stage

Glaze—To cover with syrup, sauce, butter, egg, milk, jelly, or icing, causing a shiny appearance

Goulash—A thick, meaty Hungarian stew

Grate—To rub food on something rough such as a grater to produce small slivers, chunks, or curls

Grease—To spread fat, oil, or grease in a baking pan in order to prevent food from sticking during the cooking process

Grill—To cook with indirect or direct heat on an open grating

Grind—To cut food very finely or coarsely

Gristle—The cartilage from an animal that is smooth and elastic

Gumbo—Créole dish made with okra and usually seafood

Haute cuisine—Term referring to very fancy French cuisine

Hibachi—A Japanese barbecue grill

Hollandaise—A sauce of egg yolks, butter, and lemon juice; usually served warm with fish or vegetables

Hor d'oeuvres—French term referring to appetizers, canapés, or tidbits served before the main meal in order to whet the appetite

Hydrogenated fats—Soft fats or oils that have been changed to a solid by using hydrogen

Ice—Refers to frozen water or a mixture of frozen juice, sugar, and water

Infuse—To steep flavoring in a boiling liquid; usually herbs or spices; **Tip:** The herbs or spices can be put in a fine-textured cheesecloth, tied up, and then dropped into the liquid

Jigger—A small container used to measure liquor for drinks that is equivalent to 1½ ounces of liquid

Julienne—To cut food into matchlike strips

Kidneys—Delicacy organ meat from beef, lamb, or veal

Knead—To manipulate, usually bread dough, with a combination motion of pressing, folding, and stretching

Lard—Fat from pork that is oilier and fattier than either butter or margarine

Larding—To insert strips of fat or bacon on top of or in lean meat or fish to keep it moist during cooking; may also be done with a larding needle

Leaven—To cause dough to rise by adding a leavening agent such as yeast; the leavening agent forms and releases gas during baking and thus makes the dough light

Legumes—Vegetables which bear their fruit or seeds in a pod, such as beans

Lemon zest—The colored part of a lemon rind minus the white pith (which is bitter); use a grater or knife to pare the lemon zest from the lemon

Lyonnaise—A dish seasoned with onions and parsley

Macédoine—A mixture of fruits or vegetables

Macerate—To place fruit in sugar, wine, liqueur, or lemon juice and steep for a while

Madrilene—A clear soup that is flavored with tomato and generally served chilled

Marinate—To soak food in a seasoned oil-acid mixture (called a marinade) to tenderize and flavor

Marmite—A clay cooking pot used in Europe

Marzipan—A paste of sugar, almonds, and egg whites that is molded into shapes and decorated; prepared marzipan bars may be purchased at the grocery store or in a confectionary shop

Mash—To beat food with an electric mixer, fork, or spoon to obtain a smooth consistency

Mask—To cover completely with a thick sauce, salad dressing, or jelly

Melt—To liquefy solid foods with low heat

Meringue—A mix of stiffly beaten egg whites, sugar, and flavoring used on pies and desserts or folded into other ingredients

Mince—To chop, grind, or cut food into very small pieces

Minestrone—A thick Italian vegetable soup

Mirepoix—A French seasoning consisting of diced carrots, celery, parsley, thyme, and bay leaf

Mix—To combine two or more ingredients by stirring in order to distribute them evenly; may also mean a commercially packaged food such as a cake mix

Mocha—A mix of coffee and chocolate flavors or just coffee flavor

Moisten—To pour, brush, or spoon liquid over food

Mold—To shape food, usually by pouring liquefied food into a form/mold; when cool, it will keep its shape

Monosodium glutamate—A chemical made from glutanic acids in wheat, corn, or sugar beets that is used to enhance the flavor of foods; often referred to as MSG

Mornay—A delicious French white sauce made with eggs and cheese

Mousse—An airy dish usually containing whipped cream or egg whites and served chilled; can also be a mixture of cream, fruit, vegetables, or meat that has been steamed or poached and set in gelatin

Muffin—A quick bread baked by placing the batter in individual cups

Nesselrode—A mixture of candied fruits and nuts used as a sauce or in puddings and pie fillings

Oven-poach—To place a pan with food in a larger dish of water and bake in the oven

Oxtail—The tail of a beef animal; a very tasty and sweet meat

Paella—A Spanish dish of seafood, sausage, vegetables, chicken, and rice

Pan-broil—To cook meat or vegetables uncovered on top of the stove or open fire in a pan using only enough oil to keep food from sticking; food should be turned frequently in the beginning to seal in the juices, and the fat should be poured off during cooking

Parboil—To partially cook food in boiling water or juices and then to finish cooking using another method

Pare—To cut off the outer layer by finely shaving away (such as potatoes, carrots, etc.)

Parfait—A frozen dessert made with beaten egg yolks or whites that are cooked with syrup and sometimes whipped cream; usually served in tall glasses because it may be alternately layered with sauces, ice cream, and custard, and then topped with whipped cream, nuts, or fruit bits

Paste—Made of dry ingredients and liquid that can be meat, tomatoes, etc.

Pastry board—A board used to roll out or knead dough on

Pasteurize—To preserve food by heating to a temperature that destroys all micro-organisms and stops fermentation; used for milk and fruit juice

Pastry cutter—A utensil used to trim pastry

Pastry wheel—A utensil used to cut straight or decorative edges on pastry.

Pat—To use fingertips to make flat

Pâté—A seasoned dish of ground meats (usually including pork, liver—pâté de foie gras: goose liver—or fish) with a touch of brandy, served cold and used for hors d'oeuvres or sandwiches

Pâté en croûte—Pâté that is baked in a crust or pastry

Patty—Meat that is shaped into round, flat pieces

Patty shells—Puff pastry filled with creamed mixture of chicken, fish, etc.

Pectin—A substance in fruits that causes fruit to gel when sugar is added and heated; may also be purchased at the grocery store; used to help jellies set

Peel—To strip off the outer layer of fruits, vegetables, and shellfish

Pepper sauce—A red sauce made from hot peppers and aged before bottling; use sparingly

Persillade—A French seasoning mixture of parsley and garlic often used with grilled beef

Petits four—Small fancy iced cakes on which frosting is poured and decorations are added; often a sheet cake cut into shapes is used to make petits four

Pilaf—An entrée consisting of meat, fish, or poultry and rice, vegetables, and spices; also rice that is first browned in oil and then cooked in consommé

Pinch—A measurement referring to the amount "pinched" between the thumb and forefinger; usually 1/16 of a teaspoon

Pipe—To use a pastry tube to place icing, etc., on food

Pit—To remove the seed or pit from fruit

Pith—The white skin between the outer skin and eatable part of various fruits

Poach—To cook food slowly in a small amount of simmering liquid—just enough liquid to cover the food

Pot-roast—To cook meat slowly in a covered pot with moist heat; often used for less tender cuts of meat

Pots de crème—Chilled dessert puddings served in individual cups

Pound—To crush food by beating it constantly

Precook—To cook food only partially at first and then at a later time finish the cooking process

Preheat—To heat your oven, pan, or stove to the desired temperature before placing your food in

Preserve—To keep food from spoiling through dehydrating, smoking, salting, pickling, or boiling in syrup

Press—To flatten with a spoon or the heel of your hand

Prick—To pierce with a fork

Proof—To test yeast for potency before using when making bread

Purée—To strain or blend the pulp of cooked vegetables and fruit to produce a smooth, thick liquid; may be done in a blender

Quiche—A custard-like mix poured and baked in a pie shell until puffy and lightly brown; may contain cheese, meat, fish, vegetables in combination

Rack—A utensil made of wire and containing holes or slits

Ragoût—A highly seasoned French stew made with meat, fowl, or fish

Ramekin or ramequin—An individual baking dish; often made of earthenware or glass

Ratatouille—A stew made with eggplant, green pepper, squash, tomatoes, garlic, and onion

Reconstitute—To take food such as frozen fruit juice back to its original strength

Render—To heat food until the fat melts (and can be poured off); to take solid fat and heat it slowly to turn the solid fat into a liquid

Rissole—A seasoned meat mixture wrapped in pastry and fried in deep fat

Roast—To cook in an oven or on hot coals by dry heat

Roe—Fish eggs; sturgeon roe is called caviar

Roux—A cooked mixture of butter or oil and flour that is browned and used to thicken and flavor sauces, soups, etc.

Sauté—To cook in a small amount of oil in a skillet over direct heat, turning frequently until food is soft or brown

Scald—To heat liquid to almost boiling and then pour over food, let food stand in water for a few minutes, and drain; **Note:** To scald milk, place milk in the top of a double boiler with water in the bottom and cover, and heat until the milk looks like little beads around the edge; if you want to scald food, just drop it in boiling water for a couple of seconds

Scallop—Used to describe a casserole baked with sauce, such as a potato scallop (or scalloped potatoes); also a thin slice of boneless meat, usually veal; also the shellfish scallop.

Score—To cut diagonally and lightly to mark with lines or slits in the outer layer of food; this tenderizes and causes the food to keep its shape

Scramble—To stir and cook simultaneously (like scrambled eggs)

Sear—To brown the surface of food over high heat (turn frequently) in order to seal in the juices; usually the food is then cooked slowly, such as pot roast

Season—To use herbs and spices to add various flavorings, or to coat an iron skillet or pot with oil and bake so food cooks better and does not stick

Shell—To remove the hard exterior covering on foods.

Sherbet—A frozen mixture consisting of fruit juice, egg whites, sugar, and water or milk

Shirr—To break an egg into a dish, adding cream or crumbs, and bake/broil until the whites have set

Shish kebabs—Meat placed on a skewer and cooked; sometimes marinated first; kebabs can also be made of vegetables, fruits, with or without meat, poultry, or fish

Shred—To cut food into slivers

Shuck—To remove the outer layer from food such as the husks from corn or the shells from clams or oysters

Sieve—A utensil with wire netting or small holes used to separate small particles from larger ones

Sift—To shake dry ingredients, such as flour or powdered sugar, through a sifter, strainer, or sieve to remove any lumps

Sifter—A utensil used for removing lumps from flour, sugar, etc.; a strainer for dry ingredients

Simmer—To cook food in a liquid at a temperature just below or at boiling point on top of the stove (the liquid should barely bubble)

Skewer—To thread food with sharpened rods of metal or wood (example: shish kebabs)

Skim—To spoon off excess fat from the surface of a liquid

Slice—To cut food into pieces

Sliver—To slice food into thin and long strips

Smoke—To cook through continuous exposure to wood smoke

Sofrito—A Spanish seasoning mixture of chopped onion, tomatoes, peppers, and garlic and sometimes sausage and ham; available at the grocery store

Soft peaks—To beat whipping cream or egg whites until peaks with tips that curl over form as the beaters are lifted from the mixture

Soy sauce—A liquid made from fermented soy beans that is used in Chinese cooking, often instead of salt

Sparkling—Refers to wine that has been carbonated by natural fermentation

Spice—Seasoning from the bark, bud, root, leaves, stems, or seeds of a plant

Spirits—Term used for liquor such as whiskey, Scotch, and bourbon

Sponge—Term used for a light cake containing eggs and/or baking powder or soda; also used to describe a batter containing yeast

Spread—To take a spatula or knife and smooth a soft substance such as butter or icing on top of food

Sprinkle—To lightly scatter a dry ingredient over the top or sides of food

Steam—To cook or heat food with water vapor from a pan of boiling water; the food never touches the water

Steam-bake—To cook in the oven by placing a baking dish or pan in a larger pan filled with water

Steep—To pour boiling water over an item (usually tea) and let it stand to absorb the flavor

Sterilize—To purify food (destroy germs and bacteria) through exposure to intense heat by using water, dry heat, or steam

Stew—To cook food in a small amount of boiling or simmering liquid in a covered pan for a long, slow time in order to make food tender

Still—Refers to wine that is not sparkling

Stir—To mix ingredients with a spoon using a circular motion for uniform consistency and to keep it from sticking or burning

Stir-fry—To cook quickly by stirring constantly over direct heat foods such as vegetables, fish, or meat in a small amount of oil or sauce

Stiff peaks—To beat whipping cream or egg whites until peaks with tips stand up straight as the beaters are lifted from the mixture

Stock—The liquid in which fish, vegetables, poultry, or meat has been cooked; broth; used in soups and gravy

Strain—To break down solids by passing through a strainer

Strainer—A utensil usually with wire netting or small holes used to separate large items from the liquid surrounding them

Stuff—To fill cavities

Succotash—An equal amount of cooked lima beans mixed with an equal amount of cooked corn, then seasoned with butter, salt, and pepper

Suet—The white fat of beef or mutton

Sukiyaki—A Japanese dish prepared with thin slices of beef, soy sauce, bean curd, and vegetables

Sweetbreads—The thymus gland of a calf, cow, or lamb; very delicate and tender

Swirl—To spread an ingredient such as icing with a broad circular motion

Tear—To break into bite-size pieces

Tempura—A method of cooking raw meat, poultry, fish, or vegetables by coating them with a cold, thin batter and then quickly deep-frying them in hot oil

Thicken—To make food or liquid less thin by adding egg yolks, cornstarch, or flour

Thin—To make food or liquid less thick by adding any liquid such as milk, stock, or water

Timbale—An unsweetened white sauce or custard mixed with meat, poultry, vegetables, or fish and baked in ramekins (individual molds)

Toast—To brown food lightly by direct heat such as broiling or grilling

Top—To garnish; to spread on the highest part

Torte—A rich cake usually containing eggs, nuts, and crumbs; also a cake made from meringue

Toss—To blend ingredients loosely with an upward motion, being careful not to crush them

Tournedos—Filet cut of beef from the beef tenderloin

Trim—To take the edges off by using a knife or scissors (such as trimming the fat from meat)

Tripe—The muscular inner linings of the stomach of beef

Truss—To fasten meat together with skewers or strings (such as turkey after you stuff it) so it will hold its shape while cooking

Vegetable marrow—An egg-shaped gourd that is about 8–10" long

Velouté—A French white sauce made from veal or chicken stock, butter or margarine, and flour that is used as a base for other sauces

Vinaigrette—A sauce made from vinegar, oil, and seasonings; used in salads and as a marinade

Well—To make a hole in the middle of dry ingredients and place a liquid in the hole. Then mix the dry and liquid ingredients together

Welsh rarebit—Melted cheese that is combined with milk or beer and seasonings and served over toast or crackers

Whip—To beat mixture rapidly to incorporate air to produce a light texture and cause the mixture to expand; may be done with a wire whisk, electric beater, or mixer

Whisk—To whip or beat with a wire whisk (a utensil with metal wires looped at the end) often until the mixture is frothy; great way to blend sauces

Wiener Schnitzel—A cutlet of veal that is coated with bread crumbs and egg and cooked in fat

Zest—The colored part of the rind of citrus fruit used for flavoring (not the bitter white part); 1 Tsp. of freshly grated zest = 1 teaspoon of dried zest = 1/2 teaspoon extract or 2 Tablespoons fresh juice

Zwieback—A type of toasted bread

INDEX

Recipes appear in bold type

238